AN INTRODUCTION TO
ISRAEL'S WISDOM TRADITIONS

AN INTRODUCTION TO

Israel's Wisdom Traditions

John L. McLaughlin

WILLIAM B. EERDMANS PUBLISHING COMPANY

GRAND RAPIDS, MICHIGAN

Wm. B. Eerdmans Publishing Co.
2140 Oak Industrial Drive NE, Grand Rapids, Michigan 49505
www.eerdmans.com

27 26 25 24 23 22 21 20 19 18   1 2 3 4 5 6 7 8 9 10

ISBN 978-0-8028-7454-2

Library of Congress Cataloging-in-Publication Data

Names: McLaughlin, John L., author.
Title: An introduction to Israel's wisdom traditions / John L. McLaughlin.
Description: Grand Rapids : Eerdmans Publishing Co., 2018. |
    Includes bibliographical references and index.
Identifiers: LCCN 2018001814 | ISBN 9780802874542 (pbk. : alk. paper)
Subjects: LCSH: Wisdom literature—Criticism, interpretation, etc.
Classification: LCC BS1455.M43 2018 | DDC 223/.061—dc23
    LC record available at https://lccn.loc.gov/2018001814

Translations follow NRSV.
All biblical citations use English-language versification.
Abbreviations follow *The SBL Handbook of Style* (2nd ed.).

Contents

Preface

This volume is the product of twenty-five years of teaching Israel's wisdom literature at the undergraduate and graduate levels, in both survey courses and those dealing with individual books. I have benefited greatly from interactions with my students over the years, and especially from those enrolled in my "Israel's Wisdom Traditions" course in the fall of 2016 who served as guinea pigs for the penultimate version of this book. I have also learned much from other scholars of Israel's wisdom literature. Ultimately, the discussion of the individual wisdom books represents my own reading of the material, but those familiar with the field will recognize my debt to others along the way. However, rather than encumber those chapters with footnotes for every point of interpretation, I have limited references to specific insights and discussions of parallel material outside the wisdom books themselves.

Many others have contributed to my efforts in this book. An earlier version of portions of chapter 3 was presented during the Old Testament Colloquium at St. John's University in Collegeville, Minnesota, held February 12–14, 2016. I am deeply grateful for the insightful response by Kathleen O'Connor as well as the helpful contributions by the other members of the colloquium, all of which helped me clarify my thinking about the pedagogical process in the book of Proverbs. John Kloppenborg and Colleen Shantz provided bibliographical references concerning wisdom in the Second Testament. My research assistants helped with different stages of the book. David Alcorn reviewed the manuscript prior to submission, double-checking references and citations, and Aleksander Krogevoll reviewed the page proofs and helped compile the indexes. My editor at Eerdmans, Andrew Knapp, provided invaluable guidance throughout; not only did he save me from a number of infelicities, his helpful suggestions on many aspects of the content and format have resulted in a much better volume. As indebted as I am to all of them, I alone am responsible for the content of this publication.

The staff of St. Michael's John M. Kelly Library InfoExpress service provided invaluable support during my research and writing of this volume. The team of Manda Vrkljan, Sarah Stiller, Carmen Cachia, Bridget Collings, and Eunice Choi tracked down and delivered articles and books from across the widely dispersed University of Toronto library system, as well as by Inter-library Loan from other institutions, often on very short notice. Their constantly cheerful efforts over many months allowed me to focus on writing, greatly facilitating the completion of this work.

Toronto, December 5, 2017

Abbreviations

AB	Anchor Bible
ABD	*Anchor Bible Dictionary*. Edited by David Noel Freedman. 6 vols. New York: Doubleday, 1992
AIL	Ancient Israel and Its Literature
AJEC	Ancient Judaism and Early Christianity
AnBib	Analecta Biblica
ANETS	Ancient Near Eastern Texts and Studies
AnGreg	Analecta Gregoriana
AnOr	Analecta Orientalia
AOAT	Alter Orient und Altes Testament
AOTC	Abingdon Old Testament Commentaries
BBRSup	Bulletin for Biblical Research Supplement Series
BCOTWP	Baker Commentary on the Old Testament Wisdom and Psalms
BETL	Bibliotheca Ephemeridum Theologicarum Lovaniensium
Bib	*Biblica*
BibOr	Biblica et Orientalia
BibSem	The Biblical Seminar
BibInt	Biblical Interpretation Series
BJS	Brown Judaic Studies
BLS	Bible and Literature Series
BTB	*Biblical Theology Bulletin*
BWANT	Beiträge zur Wissenschaft von Alten und Neuen Testament
BZAW	Beihefte zur Zeitschrift für die alttestamentliche Wissenschaft
CAT	*The Cuneiform Alphabetic Texts from Ugarit, Ras Ibn Hani and Other Places (KTU3)*. Third, enlarged edition. Edited by Manfried Dietrich, Oswald Loretz, and Joaquín Sanmartín. AOAT 360/1. Münster: Ugarit-Verlag, 2013
CBC	Cambridge Bible Commentary

CBET	Contributions to Biblical Exegesis and Theology
CBQ	*Catholic Biblical Quarterly*
CBQMS	Catholic Biblical Quarterly Monograph Series
ConBOT	Coniectanea Biblica: Old Testament Series
DCLS	Deuterocanonical and Cognate Literature Studies
EBC	Earth Bible Commentary
EBib	Études bibliques
FAT	Forschungen zum Alten Testament
FCB	Feminist Companion to the Bible
FOTL	Forms of the Old Testament Literature
FRLANT	Forschungen zur Religion und Literatur des Alten und Neuen Testaments
GBS	Guides to Biblical Scholarship
HAR	*Hebrew Annual Review*
HBIS	History of Biblical Interpretation Series
HCOT	Historical Commentary on the Old Testament
HTR	*Harvard Theological Review*
HTS	Harvard Theological Studies
HUCA	*Hebrew Union College Annual*
IBT	Interpreting Biblical Texts
ICC	International Critical Commentary
ITC	International Theological Commentary
JAAR	*Journal of the American Academy of Religion*
JAL	Jewish Apocryphal Literature Series
JBL	*Journal of Biblical Literature*
JBQ	*Jewish Bible Quarterly*
JJS	*Journal of Jewish Studies*
JNSL	*Journal of Northwest Semitic Languages*
JSJSup	Journal for the Study of Judaism Supplement Series
JSOT	*Journal for the Study of the Old Testament*
JSOTSup	Journal for the Study of the Old Testament Supplement Series
JTISup	Journal of Theological Interpretation, Supplements
JTS	*Journal of Theological Studies*
LHBOTS	Library of Hebrew Bible/Old Testament Studies
LXX	Septuagint
MBS	Message of Biblical Spirituality
MT	Masoretic Text
NABRE	New American Bible Revised Edition
NCBC	New Century Bible Commentary

NICOT	New International Commentary on the Old Testament
NRSV	New Revised Standard Bible
OBO	Orbis Biblicus et Orientalis
OBT	Overtures to Biblical Theology
OLA	Orientalia Lovaniensia Analecta
OTE	*Old Testament Essays*
OTL	Old Testament Library
OTM	Oxford Theological Monographs
OTS	Old Testament Studies
PIBA	*Proceedings of the Irish Biblical Association*
PRSt	*Perspectives in Religious Studies*
PTMS	Pittsburgh Theological Monograph Series
RB	*Revue biblique*
SAC	Studies in Antiquity and Christianity
SAOC	Studies in Ancient Oriental Civilizations
SBLAB	Society of Biblical Literature Academia Biblia
SBLDS	Society of Biblical Literature Dissertation Series
SBLMS	Society of Biblical Literature Monograph Series
SBT	Studies in Biblical Theology
SBT	*Studia Biblica et Theologica*
SCS	Septuagint and Cognate Studies
SHBC	Smyth & Helwys Bible Commentary
SJT	*Scottish Journal of Theology*
SNTSMS	Society for New Testament Studies Monograph Series
SOTSMS	Society for Old Testament Studies Monograph Series
SPOT	Studies on Personalities of the Old Testament
SSN	Studia Semitica Neerlandica
STDJ	Studies on the Texts of the Desert of Judah
SubBi	Subsidia Biblica
SWBA	Social World of Biblical Antiquity
SymS	Symposium Series
TD	*Theology Digest*
THOTC	Two Horizons Old Testament Commentary
VT	*Vetus Testamentum*
VTSup	Supplements to Vetus Testamentum
WAW	Writings from the Ancient World
WBC	Word Biblical Commentary
WUNT	Wissenschaftliche Untersuchungen zum Neuen Testament
ZAW	*Zeitschrift für die alttestamentliche Wissenschaft*

The Nature of Wisdom

Israel's biblical wisdom literature consists of five books, with traces of wisdom influence in other books within the First Testament.[1] The books of Proverbs, Job, and Qoheleth (or Ecclesiastes) are all part of the canon common to Jews, Protestants, Roman Catholics, and Eastern Christians, while Ben Sira (Ecclesiasticus) and the Wisdom of Solomon (or simply Wisdom) are also considered canonical by Roman Catholics and Eastern Christians. These five books share common themes and emphasize reflection on human experience, while at the same time they differ from much else in the First Testament. Proverbs, Job, and Qoheleth do not mention any of the great figures from Israel's history, such as Sarah and Abraham, Moses, Deborah, David, any of the prophets, etc., nor do they refer to central events from Israel's history, such as the flood, the exodus, the covenant at Sinai, etc. Ben Sira and Wisdom do deal with such material to a fair extent, but that is a later development within the wisdom tradition that confirms the distinctive nature of the earlier wisdom books.

---

1. Traditional terminology for the two main divisions of the Bible is problematic and has implications for how one interprets both sections. For some, "Old Testament" connotes "antiquated," "outdated," and even "replaced." "Hebrew Bible" is popular in many circles but does not encompass the Aramaic portions of Daniel and Ezra or scholars' extensive use of ancient versions in other languages. Nor does "Hebrew Bible" incorporate the deuterocanonical books, some written exclusively in Greek, that Roman Catholics and Eastern Orthodox Christians consider scriptural but Protestants and Jews do not. Moreover, the second part of the Bible is still usually called the "New Testament," which implies that there is an "old" one as well. As an uneasy compromise, the terms First and Second Testament are used in this book for the two main divisions of the biblical literature.

Defining Wisdom

What is "wisdom"? What does it mean to be "wise" or "to act wisely"? Modern dictionaries provide various but similar present-day definitions of each of these terms. However, the meaning of words may change over time, so in order to understand what the wise, i.e., the sages, in ancient Israel meant by the equivalent Hebrew terms, it is necessary to examine how they were used within the biblical material while also taking note of related words that were used in association with them. The Hebrew word translated as "wisdom" is ḥokmâ, the adjective "wise" is ḥākām, and the verb "to be or become wise" is ḥākam. They are regularly used in poetic parallelism (see chapter 2 below) with terms such as "knowledge," "skill," "instruction," "insight," and "aptitude." An examination of the actual use of the Hebrew words for "wise," "wisdom," etc., shows that the words have all of these connotations and more.

One place to look for the biblical understanding of "wise," "wisdom," etc., is with the person who is most associated with Israel's wisdom traditions, King Solomon. Solomon was legendary in Israel for his wisdom, although the historical connections between the king and wisdom are debated, and usually doubted. The most that can be said, and even then only conditionally, is that he may have fostered the development of wisdom at his court in Jerusalem, and this might be why much wisdom, then and later, is linked to him. Both Proverbs and Qoheleth are attributed to him, even though the latter was written six hundred years later. Even the Wisdom of Solomon is associated with Solomon, although it was written in Greek some nine hundred years after Solomon died.

This traditional connection between Solomon and wisdom is reflected in the stories about him that are preserved in the Bible, and those stories nicely illustrate some of the various senses of "wisdom." The identification of Solomon with wisdom begins with his ascent to the throne: 1 Kings 3 tells how he went to the shrine at Gibeah, where the Lord appeared to him in a dream and offered to grant whatever Solomon might request.

> The Hebrew word translated as "wisdom" has a number of nuances in the First Testament, including:
>
> - politics (kingship and international relationships)
> - science
> - pragmatism
> - cunning
> - technical skill

He asked, "Give your servant therefore an understanding mind to govern your people, able to discern between good and evil; for who can govern this your great people?" (1 Kings 3:9). The phrase "an understanding mind" is literally "a listening heart," which in Egypt was synonymous with wisdom. In 1 Kings 3:12 God explicitly grants Solomon great wisdom: "I now do according to your word. Indeed, I give you a wise and discerning mind; no one like you has been before you and no one like you shall arise after you." Solomon's words in 1 Kings 3:9 characterize wisdom ("an understanding mind / a listening heart") as the ability to rule or govern. This nuance of what is necessary for kingship is also present in a narrative about Solomon's international dealings. As Solomon negotiates with Hiram, king of Tyre (Phoenicia), for workers and material to build the temple, Hiram says, "Blessed be the LORD this day, who has given to David a wise son to be over this great people" (1 Kings 5:7). "Wisdom" is also associated with competent diplomacy in the summary statement of 1 Kings 5:12: "So the LORD gave Solomon wisdom, as he promised him. There was peace between Hiram and Solomon; and the two of them made a treaty."

This is not the only connotation for wisdom in connection with Solomon. In 1 Kings 4:29–34 Solomon's wisdom is illustrated by an itemization of his encyclopedic knowledge, but what the passage calls wisdom we today call science, specifically zoology and botany. Another perspective is found in the famous story of Solomon's legal decision concerning two prostitutes who both claimed a child as their own. The biblical author presents Solomon's strategy for determining the true mother as an indication of the discernment proper to courtroom proceedings (1 Kings 3:28—"All Israel heard of the judgment which the king had rendered; and they stood in awe of the king, because they perceived that the wisdom of God was in him, to execute justice"). However, this is more a case of Solomon skillfully manipulating human nature, specifically the parental tendency to protect and nurture one's child, in order to trick the real mother into revealing herself and the false one to give herself away.

A similar sense of the term "wisdom" is illustrated by David's death-bed instruction to his son Solomon. David wishes to be avenged against Joab, whose own act of vengeance against Abner for killing Joab's brother Asahel (2 Sam. 2:23; 3:27–30) had serious repercussions for the peace of the kingdom under David, and against Shimei, who cursed David when David's son Absalom initiated a coup against him (2 Sam. 16:5–13). In 1 Kings 2:6 David says about Joab, "Act therefore according to your wisdom, but do not let his gray head go down to Sheol in peace." Similarly, concerning Shimei he says, "Therefore do not hold him guiltless, for you are a wise man; you will know what you ought to do to him, and you must bring his gray head down with blood to Sheol" (1 Kings 2:9). In these instances "wisdom" has the sense of craftiness or cunning, and the rest of the chapter details how Solomon accomplished this task.

The sense of wisdom as cunning or pragmatism is not restricted to Solomon. In Exodus 1:10 Pharaoh proposes that the Egyptians deal with the multiplying Israelites "shrewdly" (NRSV) but the verb at this point is *ḥākam*, meaning "to act wisely." Such expediency is also seen in 2 Samuel 20:16–22, where the wise woman of Abel negotiates to have a siege of her city lifted by cutting off the head of the individual whom the army seeks and throwing it over the city wall. She takes her "wise plan" (20:22) to the inhabitants and they agree. These examples show that a moral component was not an essential part of "wisdom" in ancient Israel. The starkest illustration of this comes in the story of the rape of Tamar in 2 Samuel 13. Amnon, one of David's sons, lusts after his half-sister Tamar, until his friend Jonadab advises him how to lure her to his bedroom, at which point he rapes her. The NRSV introduces Jonadab and the value of his ensuing plan with the statement that he was "a very crafty man" but the Hebrew has the adjective "wise." The common element in all these examples is the skill necessary to accomplish the task at hand, and in the last three examples that task could easily be morally reprehensible from our perspective, but not that of the biblical characters performing the deed.

In fact, "wisdom" is often used in this neutral sense of "skill." The best example is Exodus 35:31–36:1. Moses designates Bezalel to oversee the construction of the sanctuary with the statement that he has been filled "with divine spirit, with skill [*hokmâ*; "wisdom"], intelligence, and knowledge in every kind of craft, to devise artistic designs, to work in gold, silver and bronze, in cutting stones for setting, and in carving wood, in every kind of craft." So too, his assistants are described as "wise of heart" (NRSV "filled . . . with skill" / "skillful"). Elsewhere "wisdom" is used of the skill necessary for a number of other specific tasks, including warfare (Prov. 21:22; Isa. 10:13); commerce (Ezek. 28:4–5); sorcery (Isa. 47:9–13; cf. the Babylonian magicians in Dan. 2); and of occupations as diverse as tailors (Exod. 28:3), scribes (Jer. 8:8), professional mourners (Jer. 9:17), and shipbuilders (Ezek. 27:8–9). This is often lost in translation, with words like "skill" being used to convey the nuance involved, but it is important to be aware of the connotations. A good example is Psalm 107:27, which speaks of sailors caught in a storm at sea. The NRSV renders the verse as, "they reeled and staggered like drunkards, and were at their wits' end" but in Hebrew the final phrase is literally, "their wisdom was swallowed up."

One final thing to note: wisdom is not associated exclusively with human beings. Members of the animal kingdom are also said to be wise in Proverbs 30:24–28: "Four things on earth are small, / yet they are exceedingly wise." The nature of their wisdom consists of ordering their lives, often in a way that does not fit with one's immediate expectations. Thus we read,

the ants are a people without strength,
    yet they provide their food in the summer;
the badgers are a people without power,
    yet they make their homes in the rocks;
the locusts have no king,
    yet all of them march in rank;
the lizard can be grasped in the hand,
    yet it is found in kings' palaces.

Gaining Wisdom

How do all these nuances for "wisdom" relate to the wisdom literature itself? Why did the sages write and collect the material they did? Why seek wisdom? The prologue to Proverbs (Prov. 1:1–6) gives some insight into their motives; it combines the term "wisdom" with a number of parallel concepts to indicate the purpose of this wisdom book. The implication is that "wisdom," "instruction," "skill," "knowledge," etc., are all valuable in their own right, but at the same time there was an underlying purpose to wisdom in general and to the wisdom literature in particular. Each generation needs to be integrated into the society, to learn the traditions and customs of the local community and of the nation as a whole. As part of this process of socialization the sages presented the collective wisdom of the community, handing on what had been experienced as right, true, and valuable in society and in the world. In this way individuals came to know the ways of the world in which they lived, both in terms of the created world around them and the specific social organization in which they found themselves, namely the people of Israel and its tribal traditions and structures.

In other words, the acquisition of wisdom meant developing an awareness and recognition of how the world and what is in it works. In practice this means developing the necessary skills, insights, knowledge, etc., to relate to nature, inanimate things, other people, even God, properly and profitably. The one who can manage his or her interaction with all of these elements and factors is the truly wise person. Thus, wisdom is not a theoretical or abstract concept, entailing purely intellectual knowledge or inner insight. These play a role, since one often has to apply oneself to understand how and why things are the way they are, but true wisdom goes beyond them to encompass one's entire existence. The purpose of wisdom is nothing less than the mastery of life, in all its complexities, so that one may enjoy an existence characterized by order.

When one is able to do that, one experiences "shalom," which is more than just peace, the absence of conflict, but rather harmony and well-being in one's life.

The wisdom writers held out life, in all its fullness, as both the goal of wisdom and the motivation for enduring the discipline it requires. Wisdom can be elusive, difficult to acquire at times. The sages harshly criticize the lazy person who will not make the effort, denouncing such people as fools, but they also consider them responsible for their own foolishness. Yet if she is consistently sought after, Wisdom can be found, and when she is found she brings life. This point is made repeatedly in Proverbs: the teacher describes her in such terms in Proverbs 3:13–18 and Lady Wisdom does so herself in Proverbs 8:32–36.

But how is wisdom acquired? How do the wisdom writers communicate their insights? The first thing to note is that their approach is not primarily one of argumentation but rather appeals to universal experience. For instance, Qoheleth repeatedly says, "I saw X" or "I experienced Y," with the implication being that everyone else could as well if they wanted. The attitude of the wise, therefore, is that the truth of what they say is self-evident. There is no need to back up their words because it's obvious that this is the course of action to be followed.

Second, it is precisely human experience that constitutes the basic data upon which the wisdom tradition reflects. The premise behind most of the sayings in Proverbs, for instance, is that this is the way things are, and this is the way the world works. The wisdom teachers can make such assertions because they are transmitting the cumulative wisdom of the culture, built upon the collective experience of the larger society. Even when they use an admonition or prohibition, the motive clause is itself based on experience: "if you do X, Y will happen" or "Do this so that you will reap this reward." Thus Proverbs 20:13 says, "Do not love sleep, or else you will come to poverty; open your eyes, and you will have plenty of bread." But more often it is a simple statement of cause and effect, that this is the way the world works, and it is left to the reader to draw a conclusion as to the proper course of action, as in, for example, Proverbs 15:1—"A soft tongue turns away wrath, but a harsh word stirs up anger."

There is a secondary effect to this approach, in that it implicitly involves the reader or listener. It challenges one to reflect upon what has been said in order to decide whether or not it is correct. It draws us into the teaching process and transforms it into a learning process. In other words, it makes us examine individual sayings in order to determine whether or not they are consistent with our own experience. The flip side of this is that we also check our experience against the saying. Does our own experience of a particular situation match the experience reflected in the saying? If it does not, why not? Perhaps there is something in my personal experience that makes it incompatible with a particular saying. If we engage in this process of comparing the wisdom tradition with our own life experiences, we can either conclude that a specific saying is incorrect, at least in some cases such as my own, or else it may be that my experience is inadequate and needs to be supplemented by the wisdom presented in a given saying. In one sense it does not matter what conclusion I draw; what is far more important is that *I* have drawn it. I have entered into the process and in so doing I have integrated it into my own experience.

By leaving the conclusion to the addressee the wisdom writers are acknowledging the limitations of human wisdom. There may be another perspective that needs to be acknowledged. Since the basic principle of wisdom instruction is that insight can be drawn from human experience, one must always be open to new insights coming from that source, including insights that are directly opposite to the "conventional wisdom." The book of Job is a vehement protest against the standard wisdom doctrine of retribution, which holds that the good are blessed and the wicked punished. Qoheleth takes a rather cynical stance toward previous wisdom traditions. Even within the normally conservative book of Proverbs we find the opposite advice placed side by side. Proverbs 26:4 asserts, "Do not answer fools according to their folly, or you will be a fool yourself" but the very next verse commands, "Answer fools according to their folly, or they will be wise in their own eyes" (Prov. 26:5). Obviously the situation determines which is the appropriate wisdom, and being able to determine what the proper response to any situation should be is what characterizes an individual as wise. The key to making that determination is experience, both one's own and that of society, mutually interpreting each other, complementing and supplementing individual insights with collective experience and vice versa.

FURTHER READING

Barré, Michael L., ed. *Wisdom, You Are My Sister: Studies in Honor of Roland E. Murphy, O.Carm., on the Occasion of His Eightieth Birthday.* CBQMS 29. Washington, DC: Catholic Biblical Association of America, 1997.

Bartholomew, Craig G., and Ryan P. O'Dowd. *Old Testament Wisdom: A Theological Introduction.* Downers Grove, IL: InterVarsity Press, 2011.

Bergant, Dianne. *Israel's Wisdom Literature: A Liberation-Critical Reading.* A Liberation-Critical Reading of the Old Testament. Minneapolis: Fortress, 1997.

————. *What Are They Saying about Wisdom Literature?* New York: Paulist, 1984.

Brenner, Athalya, ed. *A Feminist Companion to the Wisdom Literature.* FCB 9. Sheffield: JSOT Press, 1995.

Brooke, George J., and Pierre Van Hecke, eds. *Goochem in Mokum, Wisdom in Amsterdam: Papers on Biblical and Related Wisdom Read at the Fifteenth Joint Meeting of the Society for Old Testament Study and the Oudtestamentisch Werkgezelschap, Amsterdam, July 2012.* Leiden: Brill, 2016.

Brown, William P. *Character in Crisis: A Fresh Approach to the Wisdom Literature of the Old Testament.* Grand Rapids: Eerdmans, 1996.

Ceresko, Anthony R. *Introduction to Old Testament Wisdom: A Spirituality for Liberation.* Maryknoll: Orbis Books, 1999.

Clifford, Richard J. *The Wisdom Literature.* IBT. Nashville: Abingdon, 1998.

Clifford, Richard J., ed. *Wisdom Literature in Mesopotamia and Israel.* SymS 36. Atlanta: Society of Biblical Literature, 2007.

Collins, John J. *Jewish Wisdom in the Hellenistic Age.* OTL. Louisville: Westminster John Knox, 1997.

Crenshaw, James L. *Old Testament Wisdom: An Introduction.* 3rd ed. Louisville: Westminster John Knox, 2010.

————. *Urgent Advice and Probing Questions: Collected Writings on Old Testament Wisdom.* Macon, GA: Mercer University Press, 1995.

Crenshaw, James L., ed. *Studies in Ancient Israelite Wisdom.* New York: Ktav, 1976.

Crossan, John Dominic, ed. *Gnomic Wisdom.* Semeia 17. Chico, CA: Scholars Press, 1980.

Day, John, Robert P. Gordon, and Hugh G. M. Williamson, eds. *Wisdom in Ancient Israel: Essays in Honour of J. A. Emerton.* Cambridge: Cambridge University Press, 1995.

Dell, Katharine J. *"Get Wisdom, Get Insight": An Introduction to Israel's Wisdom Literature.* London: Darton, Longman and Todd, 2000.

Gammie, John G., Walter A. Brueggemann, W. Lee Humphreys, and James M. Ward, eds. *Israelite Wisdom: Theological and Literary Essays in Honor of Samuel Terrien.* Missoula, MT: Scholars Press, 1978.

Gammie, John G., and Leo G. Perdue, eds. *The Sage in Israel and the Ancient Near East.* Winona Lake, IN: Eisenbrauns, 1990.

Gilbert, Maurice, ed. *La Sagesse de l'Ancien Testament.* BETL 51. Leuven: Leuven University Press, 1979.

Hill, R. Charles. *Wisdom's Many Faces.* Collegeville, MN: Liturgical Press, 1996.

Hoglund, Kenneth G., E. F. Huwiler, J. T. Glass, and R. W. Lee, eds. *The Listen-*

ing Heart: Essays in Wisdom and the Psalms in Honor of Roland E. Murphy, O. Carm. JSOTSup 58. Sheffield: JSOT Press, 1987.

Jarick, John, ed. *Perspectives on Israelite Wisdom: Proceedings of the Oxford Old Testament Seminar.* London: Bloomsbury T&T Clark, 2016.

Leclant, J., ed. *Les sagesses du proche-orient ancien.* Colloque de Strasbourg, 17–19 Mai 1962. Paris: Presses Universitaires de France, 1963.

Murphy, Roland E. *The Tree of Life: An Exploration of Biblical Wisdom Literature.* 3rd ed. Grand Rapids: Eerdmans, 2002.

Noth, Martin, and D. Winton Thomas, eds. *Wisdom in Israel and in the Ancient Near East: Essays Presented to Harold Henry Rowley.* VTSup 3. Leiden: Brill, 1955.

O'Connor, Kathleen M. *The Wisdom Literature.* MBS 6. Wilmington, DE: Glazier, 1988.

Penchansky, David. *Understanding Wisdom Literature: Conflict and Dissonance in the Hebrew Text.* Grand Rapids: Eerdmans, 2012.

Perdue, Leo G. *The Sword and the Stylus: An Introduction to Wisdom in the Age of Empire.* Grand Rapids: Eerdmans, 2008.

———. *Wisdom Literature: A Theological History.* Louisville: Westminster John Knox, 2007.

Perdue, Leo G., ed. *Scribes, Sages, and Seers: The Sage in the Eastern Mediterranean World.* FRLANT 219. Göttingen: Vandenhoeck & Ruprecht, 2008.

Perdue, Leo G., Bernard Brandon Scott, and William J. Wiseman, eds. *In Search of Wisdom: Essays in Memory of John G. Gammie.* Louisville: Westminster John Knox, 1993.

Perry, Theodore Anthony. *God's Twilight Zone: Wisdom in the Hebrew Bible.* Peabody, MA: Hendrickson, 2008.

Rad, Gerhard von. *Wisdom in Israel.* Translated by James D. Martin. London: SCM, 1971; reprinted Nashville: Abingdon, 1988.

Rankin, O. S. *Israel's Wisdom Literature: Its Bearing on Theology and the History of Religion.* Edinburgh: T&T Clark, 1964.

Schipper, Bernd U., and D. Andrew Teeter, eds. *Wisdom and Torah: The Reception of "Torah" in the Wisdom Literature of the Second Temple Period.* JSJSup 163. Leiden: Brill, 2013.

Scott, R. B. Y. *The Way of Wisdom in the Old Testament.* New York: Collier, 1971.

Sneed, Mark R. *The Social World of the Sages: An Introduction to Israelite and Jewish Wisdom Literature.* Minneapolis: Fortress, 2015.

Sneed, Mark R., ed. *Was There a Wisdom Tradition? New Prospects in Israelite Wisdom Studies.* AIL 23. Atlanta: Society of Biblical Literature, 2015.

Troxel, Ronald L., Kelvin G. Friebel, and Dennis Magary, eds. *Seeking Out the*

Wisdom of the Ancients: Essays Offered to Honor Michael Fox on the Occasion of His Sixty-Fifth Birthday. Winona Lake, IN: Eisenbrauns, 2005.

Weeks, Stuart. *Early Israelite Wisdom.* Oxford Theological Monographs. Oxford: Oxford University Press, 1994.

————. *An Introduction to the Study of Wisdom Literature.* T&T Clark Approaches to Biblical Studies. London: T&T Clark, 2010.

CHAPTER 1

The International Context for Israel's Wisdom

Wisdom was not and is not unique to Israel. Most nations and peoples have their own wisdom traditions that are preserved and passed on. This ranges from Confucianism and Buddhism to African tribal traditions, Native American lore, and more. Western society preserves a number of popular proverbs that pass on the collected wisdom and insights of the culture, such as "a stitch in time saves nine" or "an apple a day keeps the doctor away." Even when the content is not the same, the method and general stance toward reality often are.

The same situation pertained in ancient Israel, which did not exist in historical or geographical isolation. Situated at the crossroads of the ancient Near East, Israel existed between the two power centers of Egypt and Mesopotamia. Most often, one or the other was dominant in the area, and Israel survived as a vassal. Only rarely was ancient Israel a free nation. Goods flowed through the land between the two centers during times of peace and armies followed the same routes during times of conflict. Thus Israel interacted with other countries and other peoples, sometimes willingly through trade and commerce, at other times under force of arms because of conquest or political subservience.

Israel's wisdom must be seen within this context. The nations and peoples that surrounded Israel had their own wisdom traditions, which were developed and passed on in dialogue with still other cultures and peoples. One cannot understand Israel's wisdom tradition, especially in its formal written form, apart from the international context of these surrounding ancient Near Eastern wisdom traditions. Israel's wisdom was firmly rooted in and operated from the perspective of experience, and in areas of common human experience we can expect to find a similarity and even an identity between the wisdom responses of Israel and its neighbors—even though, with a few exceptions, these

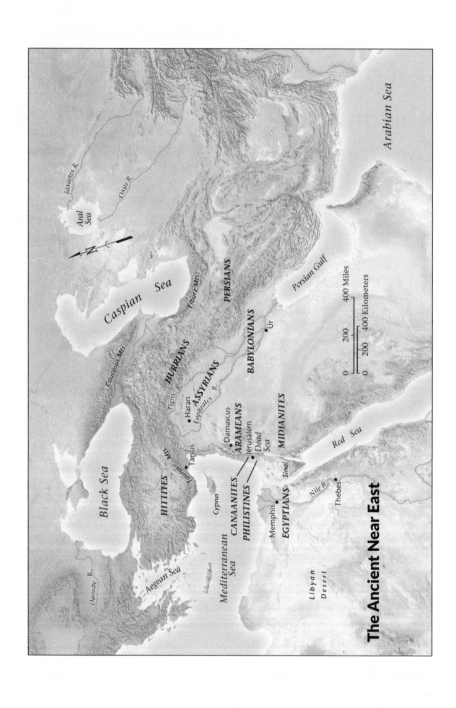

The Ancient Near East

similar responses developed independently rather than one nation borrowing directly from another. Nevertheless, in order to isolate what is particular to Israel's own wisdom tradition, it is necessary first to note what it has in common with others. Only then can we identify what is not shared with other peoples and seek what gave rise to such elements in Israel's experience.

The international scope of wisdom is recognized by the Bible itself. In 1 Kings 4:30 we read, "Solomon's wisdom surpassed the wisdom of all the people of the east, and all the wisdom of Egypt," while Edom's reputation for wisdom is noted in Jeremiah 49:7 and Obadiah 8. Apart from their historicity, some biblical narratives describe contact with the sages of Egypt in particular: Joseph interacts with members of Pharaoh's

> **Ancient Near Eastern Proverbs**
>
> To eat modestly does not kill a man, but coveting murders. (Sumer)
>
> Better is bread with a happy heart than wealth with vexation. (Egypt)
>
> Do not eat bread with an insulter. (Ugarit)
>
> Better is a dry morsel with quiet than a house full of feasting with strife. (Prov. 17:1)

court and Moses was not only raised in Pharaoh's house but also engaged with Egyptian magicians and wise men prior to the Exodus (Exod. 7:11). Solomon is said to have married Pharaoh's daughter, establishing social and political links that would have included an exchange of bureaucrats and scribes, who would have brought their wisdom traditions with them. In addition, Isaiah 19:11–15 mocks "the wise counselors of Pharaoh" (v. 11).

Egypt

Egyptian wisdom literature can be categorized according to each work's attitude concerning the tradition itself. The conservative strand preserves and passes on the traditional values of Egyptian life and society, while the other is more skeptical and pessimistic concerning established positions. The former approach consists of Instructions and related scribal material.

Certain characteristic features appear in several Egyptian texts, which are categorized with the genre label "Instruction." The genre had impressive staying power; Instructions appeared over the span of two millennia. The earliest preserved examples present a father's instruction to his son, and "father" and "son" eventually evolved into technical terms for a teacher and a pupil. They contain a call to listen, motivations for doing so that are often based on the speaker's own authority, and the teaching proper (see further in chapter 2 below concerning the structure). The teaching centers on how to behave in the royal court, including interactions with those above and below you in the class structure, dining etiquette, honesty, and especially avoiding temptation by women, who in this context would be related to powerful men.

The earliest extant Instructions date to the Old Kingdom period (ca. 2686–2160 BCE). The *Instruction of Ptahhotep* advises the reader to guard one's words in order to demonstrate wisdom: for instance, one should not dispute with an angry man nor berate someone who is weaker. One should always acknowledge one's social standing, and the Instruction provides advice for interacting with superiors, equals, and subordinates in a large number of different situations, including if one is a leader, a messenger, or invited to dine with a person of importance (for the latter cf. Prov. 25:6–7; Sir. 13:8–10; 29:26–27). As in most Instructions, Ptahhotep warns the reader to beware seductive women who will lead to death (cf. Prov. 5:3–6; 6:24–25; 7:13, 16–17; Qoh. 7:26–28). The lengthy epilogue expounds how Ptahhotep's teaching will lead to success but rejecting his words will result in failure.

> **Representative Instructions from Major Periods in Egypt's History**
>
> **Old Kingdom (ca. 2686–2160 BCE)**
> * *Instruction of Ptahhotep*
> * *Instruction of Prince Hardjedef*
> * *Instruction of Kagemni*
>
> **Middle Kingdom (ca. 2055–1650 BCE)**
> * *Instruction of King Merikare*
> * *Instruction of King Amenemhet*
> * *Instruction of Khety (The Satire of the Trades)*
>
> **New Kingdom (ca. 1550–1069 BCE)**
> * *Instruction of Any*
> * *Instruction of Amenemope*
>
> **Late Dynastic and Ptolemaic Periods (ca. 664–30 BCE)**
> * *Instruction of Ankhsheshonq*
> * *Papyrus Insinger*

The two other Instructions from this period are both fragmentary. Hardjedef is mentioned frequently in later texts, attesting to his importance, but all that remains of the *Instruction of Prince Hardjedef* (which is probably the earliest Instruction, even earlier than *Ptahhotep*) is less than twenty lines that encourage his son to find a wife, build a home, and bear a son, while at the same time preparing for death. Similarly, we only have the end of the *Instruction of Kagemni*, which opposes bragging and speaks at greater length against gluttony before describing the book's positive reception by the author's children.

The Instructions of *King Merikare* and *King Amenemhet* are from the Middle Kingdom period (ca. 2055–1650 BCE) and are more pessimistic, in response to the political discord of that time. *Merikare* begins with advice on dealing with rebellions by denouncing the instigator and dealing with the people's dissatisfaction. Counsel about how to interact with courtiers as well as commoners, similar to the advice in the *Instruction of Ptahhotep*, follows. The work includes reflections on maintaining a well-trained army for national defense, as well as the importance of observing one's religious duties in anticipation of a final judgment. *Amenemhet* consists of the king's posthumous advice that his son not trust anyone, because Amenemhet had been killed by members of his own household. Also from this period, the *Instruction of Khety* discusses the unpleasant nature of a number of occupations (sculptor, smith, carpenter, barber, potter, etc.), giving rise to its alternative title, *The Satire of the Trades*. Each occupation requires hard, often dirty, labor under the eye of an overseer, except for the scribe (cf. Sir. 38:24–39:11). Since the scribe is the only pleasant profession, it is more valuable than loving one's mother.

In the New Kingdom period (ca. 1550–1069 BCE) people began to question the idea that the Pharaoh was a direct means of communicating with God, and as a result the Instructions from that period began to emphasize personal piety instead. For instance, the Instructions of *Any* and *Amenemope* both present morality and love of God as the motives for right action. *Amenemope* is the source for Proverbs 22:17–24:22 and will be treated in more detail in chapter 3 below. Unlike most Instructions, which address the children of royalty or courtiers, *Any* is aimed at the general population. His advice includes the value of obtaining a wife when young, developing a positive relationship with her, and raising a family, which is accompanied by warnings against foreign women. The work's advice on social manners is comparable to that found in other Instructions, including silence in disputes, respect for superiors, and what to do when entering another's house: wait for an invitation, do not snoop while there, and do not gossip about what you have seen afterwards. There are frequent exhortations to observe religious propriety, such as "God is angry if [the feast] is neglected" and "Do not raise your voice in the house of god / he abhors shouting." One innovative element is that while most Instructions end by describing how the author's children received their father's advice, in the *Instruction of Any* the son rejects the counsel found in this work, after which the father rebuts his arguments.

The *Instruction of Ankhsheshonq* (fifth century BCE) and the *Papyrus Insinger* (fourth or third century BCE) both comprise collections of short sayings comparable to the biblical books of Proverbs and Ben Sira, and their content frequently parallels biblical proverbs. *Ankhsheshonq* addresses his son but the content indicates a more general audience. Unlike the more developed, thematically organized earlier Instructions, in the *Instruction of Ankhsheshonq* the sayings follow one another haphazardly, resembling the central portion of the book of Proverbs. In contrast, *Papyrus Insinger* does link its one-line sayings together, addressing such topics as people who are either wise or foolish, the importance of patience and controlling one's speech, warnings against gluttony, greed, worry, meanness, retaliation, and ignoring "small things," the value of balance in life, and divine punishment on those who disrupt that balance.

In addition to the Instructions, other works also reflect the conservative branch of Egyptian wisdom by promoting the work of the sages. Regularly updated lists of items grouped according to their resemblance or difference indicate the scribes' ever-expanding awareness of the nature of the world. Going further, some texts contrast the scribal profession with the drudgery of other occupations; the *Instruction of Khety* (or *The Satire of the Trades*) was noted above, while other works describe the preferential treatment of a scribe compared to a farmer (*Papyrus Sallier*) and contrast the scribe with a soldier (*Papyrus Anastasi I*). According to *In Praise of Learned Scribes*, the written output from scribes preserves their memory far better and longer than pyramids or inscriptions that will eventually crumble.

In contrast to the conservative approach of the preceding literature, other works are more skeptical of the established traditions, comparable to the biblical books of Job and Qoheleth. Two Egyptian books parallel Job's structure of prose material around speeches formulated in poetry. *The Tale of the Eloquent Peasant* contains increasingly eloquent speeches protesting a corrupt official's theft of his property, after which his property is restored. The peasant's pleas for justice are reminiscent of Job's complaints, although the former's problem is caused by a human whereas Job's is caused by God, and the peasant appeals to other humans while Job insists on being heard by God. *The Dispute over Suicide* (also known as *The Dialogue of a Man with His Soul*) proposes suicide in response to injustice, in order to replace the man's current distress with a changed reality in the afterlife (Job considers neither suicide nor an afterlife), but his soul insists that humans should just enjoy any pleasure that comes their way on earth. This view is also found in *The Song of the Harper*, as well as in Qoheleth 2:24; 3:12–13, 22; 5:17–18; 8:15; cf. 11:9. Finally, works like *The Admonitions of Ipuwer*, *The Lamentations of Khakheperre-sonbe*,

---

Some Skeptical Egyptian Wisdom Texts

- *The Tale of the Eloquent Peasant*
- *The Dispute over Suicide* (*The Dialogue of a Man with His Soul*)
- *The Song of the Harper*
- *The Admonitions of Ipuwer*
- *The Lamentations of Khakheperre-sonbe*
- *The Prophecies of Neferti*

and *The Prophecies of Neferti* complain that Egypt is in chaos and needs a strong ruler to restore order, with *The Lamentations of Khakheperre-sonbe* adding that traditional wisdom is inadequate. Qoheleth is similarly skeptical about social order and exploitation by the powerful, is uncertain how to act, and is dissatisfied with the wisdom traditions that he has inherited.

The general and thematic relationship between Egyptian and Israelite wisdom is relatively clear: both the conservative and skeptical Egyptian literature have similarities and parallels to various First Testament wisdom passages (e.g. Prov. 1–7; 22:17–24:22; Qoheleth; Sirach), as well as a shared underlying stance and approach to wisdom. Wisdom stems from a reflection on experience, of what does and does not work in ordering and stabilizing society. And whenever the distance between theory and practice, between the traditional wisdom and the concrete experience of individuals, becomes too great, voices of disagreement and protest arise within the wisdom tradition to offer a corrective.

Mesopotamia

Mesopotamia, the region covering modern Iraq and parts of surrounding nations ("Mesopotamia" literally means "between the rivers," i.e., the Tigris and Euphrates) may be even more significant than Egypt for Israel's wisdom traditions. Despite the greater geographical distance, Israel had more in common with the various Mesopotamian cultures than with Egypt. They shared similar languages and for most of Israel's history the Mesopotamian empires controlled the area and often intervened in Israel's politics. Therefore it is worthwhile to look at the Mesopotamian wisdom tradition as well.

In Mesopotamia the term "wisdom" itself primarily refers to skills in rituals and incantations, and this approach is integrated into some texts. For instance, *Advice to a Prince*, from the early first millennium BCE, warns the ruler that he will be held accountable for the leadership he provides and includes omens and divination techniques for determining the proper course of action. But despite the different nuances for "wisdom," Egyptian and Mesopotamian wisdom texts share many of the same approaches and principles. In Mesopotamia we also find word lists, proverb collections, moral exhortations, scholastic disputes in the form of fables, and a number of works dealing with the life of a schoolboy, which, like the Egyptian Instructions, also use "father" and "son" to refer to a teacher and student.

The Mesopotamian wisdom traditions differ most from Egypt in questions of theodicy. Two factors made the issue of divine justice less of a problem for

Egyptians than for Mesopotamians. First, Egyptian belief in an afterlife, where one could receive reward and punishment, mitigated apparent innocent suffering in Egypt. In contrast, Mesopotamians did not believe in life after death, and so the question of reward and punishment in this life was more urgent. Second, since Egypt lacked a codified set of laws, they were less likely to expect that the divine realm would agree with rules about human behavior. But there were legal codes in Mesopotamia (e.g., those of Eshnunna and Hammurabi), which provided a basis for questioning divine accountability. As a result, protests against undeserved suffering and the prosperity of the wicked arose early and often. While they are similar to Job, they do not go as far in questioning divine justice.

The Sumerian work *A Man and His God* describes a successful man who is scorned by his friends after he falls ill. But since all humans sin, he petitions his personal god, seeks forgiveness, and is restored to health. In the Babylonian *Ludlul bēl nēmeqi* ("I Will Praise the Lord of Wisdom"), when a devout man becomes sick his friends mock him and his family abandons him. Feeling rejected by both the gods in general and his personal deity in particular, he wonders if humans really know what the gods desire. Nevertheless, he assumes that he must have committed some inadvertent sin, so he repents and is then restored to health. *The Babylonian Theodicy* contains a man's discussion with his friend about human suffering and divine justice. In response to each instance of injustice the friend offers traditional explanations but eventually claims that the gods have made humans sinful.

Mesopotamia saw a succession of civilizations over three millennia. The following lists the most important, along with significant individuals and events associated with each:

Sumer (ca. 3500–2400 BCE)
- the invention of writing

Akkad (ca. 2350–2154 BCE)
- Sargon the Great (ca. 2334–2279 BCE)

Old Babylonian Empire (ca. 1894–1550 BCE)
- Hammurabi (ca. 1792–1750 BCE)

Middle Assyrian Empire (ca. 1365–1056 BCE)

Neo-Assyrian Empire (ca. 911–609 BCE)
- conquered northern Israel, ca. 722 BCE
- Judah was a vassal

Neo-Babylonian Empire (609–539 BCE)
- Nebuchadnezzar (ca. 605–562 BCE)
- destroyed Jerusalem and the Temple ca. 586 BCE
- deported leading citizens to Babylon (the Babylonian exile)
- fell to the Persians in 539 BCE

Persian Empire (539–333 BCE)
- Darius the Great (ca. 522–486 BCE)

Although the sufferer repeatedly asserts his innocence, he eventually prays for divine assistance. Job also endures physical suffering and his so-called friends attempt to explain his situation, but he never abandons his claim that he is innocent.

Two Mesopotamian works have similarities to Qoheleth. On a general level, *The Dialogue between a Master and His Slave* reflects a growing sense of futility attached to any course of action. The slave offers arguments in support of whatever the master proposes, as well as its opposite when the master wavers; humorously, when the slave takes the initiative and proposes that they kill themselves, the master demurs. This combines the series of opposites in Qoheleth 3:1–9 (both works share an interest in embracing/making love) with Qoheleth's ongoing uncertainty about God's plan for humans. More specifically, two segments of *The Epic of Gilgamesh* offer advice comparable to Qoheleth.[1] First, Gilgamesh reinforces the advantage of two working together with an assertion that a three-ply cord cannot be cut, which is paralleled in Qoheleth 4:9–12, including the same motif of a three-ply cord:

> **Significant Mesopotamian Wisdom Texts**
>
> - *A Man and His God*
> - *Ludlul bēl nēmeqi* ("I Will Praise the Lord of Wisdom")
> - *The Babylonian Theodicy*
> - *The Dialogue between a Master and His Slave*
> - *The Epic of Gilgamesh*
> - *The Story of Ahiqar*

> [9] Two are better than one, because they have a good reward for their toil. [10] For if they fall, one will lift up the other; but woe to one who is alone and falls and does not have another to help. [11] Again, if two lie together, they keep warm; but how can one keep warm alone? [12] And though one might prevail against another, two will withstand one. A threefold cord is not quickly broken.

In another passage, an alewife encourages Gilgamesh to enjoy what humans are destined to experience, namely food, clean clothes and hair, and a wife, all of which are also mentioned in the same order in Qoheleth 9:7–9:

> [7] Go, eat your bread with enjoyment, and drink your wine with a merry heart; for God has long ago approved what you do. [8] Let your garments always be white; do not let oil be lacking on your head.

1. Nili Samet, "The Gilgamesh Epic and the Book of Qohelet: A New Look," *Bib* 96 (2015): 375–90.

⁹ Enjoy life with the wife whom you love, all the days of your vain life that are given you under the sun, because that is your portion in life and in your toil at which you toil under the sun.

The wording in both cases is sufficiently different that they do not constitute direct dependence, but they do indicate a shared reflection on human experience.

The earliest version of *The Story of Ahiqar*, an Aramaic text from ca. 500 BCE, was found at the Jewish military colony at Elephantine in southern Egypt. The protagonist was a vizier under Sennacherib and Esarhaddon, rulers of Assyria in the seventh century BCE. Ahiqar was betrayed by his adopted nephew Nadin, escaped execution, and was eventually restored to his position. A king list from Uruk mentions a high official of Esarhaddon named Ahiqar, suggesting that the story is based on a real figure even if it is not entirely historical. The combination of the popular Babylonian motifs of a disgraced official and an ungrateful nephew point to a Mesopotamian origin for the tale. In addition to the general parallel with Job of a just individual who experiences undeserved suffering, the story includes many proverbs that he teaches to his nephew. These express the usual concerns for correct speech, behavior at court, honoring parents, etc., that are found in biblical and extrabiblical wisdom literature. Sometimes the formulation of these ideas is similar to biblical proverbs, as in the use of physical discipline to educate children (Ahiqar 6:81 and Prov. 13:24; compare also Ahiqar 7:105 and Prov. 25:15; Ahiqar 9:138 and Prov. 20:20). Ahiqar also refers to personified Wisdom, although the actual description is quite different than Proverbs 8; Sirach 24; etc.[2]

> **Parallels between Ahiqar and Proverbs**
>
> Spare not your son from the rod, otherwise, can you save him from wickedness? (Ahiqar 6:81)
> He who spares the rod hates his son,
> but he who loves him is diligent to discipline him. (Prov. 13:24)
>
> The king's tongue is gentle,
> but it breaks a dragon's rib (Ahiqar 7:105)
> With patience a ruler may be persuaded,
> and a soft tongue will break a bone. (Prov. 25:15)
>
> Whoever takes no pride in his father's and mother's name,
> may Šamaš not shine on him; for he is an evil man. (Ahiqar 9:138)
> If one curses his father or his mother,
> his lamp will be put out in utter darkness. (Prov. 20:20)

2. But see the dissenting view of Seth A. Bledsoe, "Can *Ahiqar* Tell Us Anything about

Canaan[3]

Older treatments of Israelite wisdom suggested that there was no significant wisdom tradition in the area prior to its development in Israel under the influence of the two great cultures of Egypt and Mesopotamia. This was often an argument from silence, since no literary remains had been found, combined with a bias for Mesopotamia as the cradle of civilization from which all else spread. However, this situation has changed.[4]

The oldest Canaanite discoveries are from Tell Mardikh in northern Syria, which covers the ancient city of Ebla. This was the site of a thriving culture ca. 2400 BCE that rivaled the Akkadian empire of Sargon and conquered Mari. Archaeologists have unearthed dictionaries, bilingual lists coordinating Akkadian and Eblaite, and some proverb collections comparable to those found elsewhere.

Ancient Emar occupied the site of contemporary Tell Meskene, on the banks of the Euphrates river about 100 km southeast of Aleppo, and a few wisdom texts dating to ca. 1400–1200 BCE have been found there. *Šimâ milka* ("Hear the Advice") is a debate between a father and son (or teacher and student). The father offers a series of admonitions concerning everyday life, after which the son presents his view that there is nothing of value in life because of the finality of death (cf. the Egyptian *Instruction of Any* above). Other Emar texts build upon Mesopotamian ones, indicating both continuity and development between the two regions. *The Ballad of Early Rulers*, which expands upon Sumerian and Akkadian predecessors, and *Enlil and Namzitarra*, known from Babylonia, both argue that since the length of one's life is determined by the gods one should enjoy life now before death occurs. This carpe diem theme recurs in Qoheleth. *The Date Palm and*

> **Important Canaanite Wisdom Texts**
>
> - *Šimâ milka* ("Hear the Advice")
> - *The Ballad of Early Rulers*
> - *Enlil and Namzitarra*
> - *The Date Palm and the Tamarisk*
> - *The Righteous Sufferer*
> - *The Epic of Kirta*
> - *The Epic of Aqhat*

Personified Wisdom?" *JBL* 132 (2013): 119–37. The quotations of Ahiqar are taken from James M. Lindenberger, *The Aramaic Proverbs of Ahiqar* (Baltimore: Johns Hopkins University Press, 1983).

3. The following employs the ancient view that Canaan's boundaries encompassed Israel and the surrounding nations, including Aram (modern Syria).

4. See especially Yoram Cohen, *Wisdom from the Late Bronze Age*, WAW 34 (Atlanta: Society of Biblical Literature, 2013).

the Tamarisk, also known from Mesopotamia, is an example of disputation literature in which the title plants debate which of the two is more beneficial for humans.

A third significant discovery was Ras Shamra, in northwest Syria, where the ancient city of Ugarit was excavated beginning in 1929. Ugarit, destroyed ca. 1200 BCE, provides a glimpse into Canaanite civilization of the Late Bronze Age. The site eventually yielded a large stock of literary, economic, and mythological texts.[5] Many texts from Ugarit also fall in the wisdom tradition, including portions of *Šimâ milka* and *The Ballad of Early Rulers*, as well as *The Righteous Sufferer*, a hymn to Marduk with similarities to the much longer Mesopotamian work *Ludlul bēl nēmeqi*. One such similarity is the theme of the righteous sufferer, also shared with the book of Job. The story of King Kirta also has affinities with Job: he loses his children, his wife, and his health, and is in danger of death when El heals him and gets him a new wife, with whom Kirta fathers a new family. In addition, the common wisdom contrast between the wise and foolish is central to the Aqhat story in the figures of Danel and Aqhat as well as Pughat and Anat.[6] The righteous judge Danel is a legendary wisdom figure in the ancient Near East. He is reflected in the biblical book of Daniel, but the connection between the First Testament and the Danel of Ugarit is clearest in Ezekiel 14:14, 20, where the prophet asserts that not even the presence of Noah, Job, and Danel in Jerusalem would protect the city from God's chastisement, and in Ezekiel 28:3, where Danel is an exemplar of wisdom. The spelling of Danel in all three verses in Ezekiel (*dn'l*, versus *dny'l* in the book of Daniel) reflects the Ugaritic usage. Ugarit also contained school exercises, encyclopedic lists, bilingual language helps, a treatise on the art of writing, and even an example of the numerical x / x+1 saying listing the three kinds of feasts that Baʻal hates (*CAT* 1.4.3.17–21; see the next chapter for further discussion of this). The location where the texts were found is also significant, namely the libraries of a priest and a private citizen, which indicates that they valued the composition and preservation

---

5. On the wisdom texts at Ugarit, in addition to Cohen in the previous note, see John Khanjian, "Wisdom in Ugarit and in the Ancient Near East with Particular Emphasis on Old Testament Wisdom Literature," PhD diss. (Claremont: Claremont Graduate School, 1974); John Khanjian, "Wisdom," in *Ras Shamra Parallels: The Texts from Ugarit and the Hebrew Bible*, vol. 2, ed. Loren R. Fisher, AnOr 50 (Rome: Biblical Institute Press, 1975), 371–400; Edward L. Greenstein, "Wisdom in Ugaritic," in *Language and Nature: Papers Presented to John Huehnergard on the Occasion of His 60th Birthday*, ed. Rebecca Hasselbach and Naʻama Pat-El, SAOC 67 (Chicago: The Oriental Institute of the University of Chicago, 2012), 69–89.

6. Greenstein, "Wisdom in Ugaritic," 77.

of such wisdom material and suggests that the texts found to date are part of a larger wisdom tradition at Ugarit.

Finally, we can note the citation of proverbs to reinforce the points made in a number of eighteenth-century BCE letters from Mari (located in the Syrian side of the Euphrates Valley, 50 km north of the current Iraq border), in some fourteenth-century BCE letters from Canaanite vassals (but never from the rulers of the greater powers) to el-Amarna in Egypt, and in three Hittite letters. These suggest that proverbs from which the writers could draw circulated in those regions, either orally or in written collections, and they point to a widespread wisdom tradition.

The preceding suggests that the biblical allusions to wisdom among other neighboring nations should not be dismissed. Thus, the association of wisdom with Edom (Jer. 49:7; Obad. 8), for example, probably reflects an historical reality. Although he is a fictional character, Job is from the land of Uz, which most scholars connect with Edom, although a few locate it farther north in the Transjordan. However, his three friends definitely come from Edom (Eliphaz the Temanite) and northern Arabia (Bildad the Shuhite and Zophar the Namaathite). These locations call to mind Agur (Prov. 30) and Lemuel (Prov. 31), who are from Massa, a kingdom in northwest Arabia mentioned in Genesis 25:14 and in recently discovered inscriptions. At the same time, Ezekiel's attribution of wisdom to the Phoenicians (Ezek. 27–28) and their mythological connections with wisdom in Ezekiel 28 probably reflect earlier Canaanite traditions (cf. Hiram's Phoenician artisans used in the construction of the Jerusalem temple).

Wisdom was quite at home in Canaan. It is not necessary to appeal to Egypt and Mesopotamia to explain the presence of wisdom elements in Israel, since Canaanite wisdom traditions were still nearer at hand, and many biblical texts reflect her neighbors' influence on Israel's wisdom traditions. This is in keeping with many of the religious and mythological traditions reflected in the Bible, which are derived from Canaan rather than Egypt or Mesopotamia. Canaan itself was a vibrant center of culture and wisdom reflection, and even after major centers such as Ebla or Ugarit ceased to exist, the traditions associated with them would have continued. The chronological proximity of Ugarit and Israel is especially significant in this regard. This doesn't mean that Israel's wisdom was not related to Egypt's and Mesopotamia's, but this was not necessarily always a matter of direct dependence. The common characteristics and concerns reflect the universal nature of the issues. Thus, although it is important to recognize points of contact between and among the various wisdom centers, we should not denigrate the value and importance of wisdom origins within Israel and neighboring regions.

FURTHER READING

Alster, Bendt. *Proverbs of Ancient Sumer: The World's Earliest Proverb Collection.* Bethesda, MD: CDL, 1997.

Bryce, G. E. *A Legacy of Wisdom: The Egyptian Contribution to the Wisdom of Israel.* London: Associated University Presses, 1979.

Clifford, Richard J., ed. *Wisdom Literature in Mesopotamia and Israel.* SymS 36. Atlanta: Society of Biblical Literature, 2007.

Cohen, Yoram. *Wisdom from the Late Bronze Age.* WAW 34. Atlanta: Society of Biblical Literature, 2013.

Denning-Bolle, Sara. *Wisdom in Akkadian Literature: Expression, Instruction, Dialogue.* Mededelingen en verhandelingen van het Vooraziatisch-Egyptisch Genootschap "Ex Oriente Lux," vol. 28. Leiden: Ex Oriente Lux, 1992.

Gordon, E. I. *Sumerian Proverbs: Glimpses of Everyday Life in Ancient Mesopotamia.* Philadelphia: Fortress Press, 1959.

Hallo, William W., ed. *The Context of Scripture.* I. *Canonical Compositions from the Biblical World.* Leiden: Brill, 1997.

Khanjian, John. "Wisdom in Ugarit and in the Ancient Near East with Particular Emphasis on Old Testament Wisdom Literature." PhD diss. Claremont: Claremont Graduate School, 1974.

Lambert, W. G. *Babylonian Wisdom Literature.* Oxford: Clarendon, 1960. Reprinted Winona Lake, IN: Eisenbrauns, 1996.

Lichtheim, Miriam. *Ancient Egyptian Literature.* 3 vols. Berkeley: University of California Press, 2006.

Lindenberger, James M. *The Aramaic Proverbs of Ahiqar.* Baltimore: Johns Hopkins University Press, 1983.

Marzal, Angel. *Gleanings from the Wisdom of Mari.* Studia Pohl 11. Rome: Biblical Institute Press, 1976.

Pritchard, James B., ed. *The Ancient Near East: An Anthology of Texts and Pictures.* Princeton: Princeton University Press, 2011.

Römheld, Diethard. *Wege der Weisheit: Die Lehren Amenemopes und Proverbien 22,17–24,22.* BZAW 184. Berlin: de Gruyter, 1989.

Shupak, Nili. *Where Can Wisdom Be Found? The Sage's Language in the Bible and in Ancient Egyptian Literature.* OBO 130. Fribourg: Editions Universitaires/Göttingen: Vandenhoeck & Ruprecht, 1993.

CHAPTER 2

The Expression of Wisdom

Most of Israel's wisdom literature is written in poetry. But Hebrew poetry differs from English poetry in significant ways. Therefore, to understand Israelite wisdom literature one must understand how Hebrew poetry works. The sages also expressed themselves through established literary forms with regular features. Identifying these different forms aids in understanding the text and will also enable the reader to recognize when an author departs from the conventions of a given form.

Hebrew Poetry[1]

For many English-speaking readers, what distinguishes poetry from prose is a pattern of rhymed sounds at the end of lines, whether it is an ABBA pattern, or ABAB, or ABCABC, etc. In reality, not all English poetry rhymes, but even when it does not, it still usually flows with a certain rhythm of

---

1. Treatments of Hebrew poetry include James L. Kugel, *The Idea of Biblical Poetry: Parallelism and Its History* (New Haven: Yale University Press, 1981); Wilfred G. E. Watson, *Classical Hebrew Poetry: A Guide to Its Techniques*, JSOTSup 26 (Sheffield: JSOT Press, 1984); Robert Alter, *The Art of Biblical Poetry* (New York: Basic Books, 1985); Adele Berlin, *The Dynamics of Biblical Parallelism* (Bloomington: Indiana University Press, 1985); L. Alonso Schökel, *A Manual of Hebrew Poetics*, trans. Adrian Graffy, SubBi 11 (Rome: Biblical Institute Press, 1988); David L. Petersen and Kent Harold Richards, *Interpreting Hebrew Poetry*, GBS, OT Series (Minneapolis: Fortress, 1992); Wilfred G. E. Watson, *Traditional Techniques in Classical Hebrew Poetry*, JSOTSup 170 (Sheffield: Sheffield Academic, 1994); Jan Fokkelman, *Reading Biblical Poetry: An Introductory Guide*, trans. Ineke Smith (Louisville: Westminster John Knox, 2001); F. W. Dobbs-Allsopp, *On Biblical Poetry* (Oxford: Oxford University Press, 2015).

speech (meter) that is missing from a straightforward narration of an event. For instance, Shakespeare wrote primarily in iambic pentameter, which is five combinations of an unstressed then a stressed syllable in each line. In contrast to English poetry, however, rhyme does not play a significant role in Hebrew verse, and any end rhyme is accidental. This is good news for those who cannot read Hebrew, since they would not be able to detect rhymes unless the English version they are reading paid extra attention to make the translation rhyme, which could be very difficult if the priority is to render the Hebrew meaning as closely as possible. In addition, scholars debate the role that meter plays in Hebrew poetry, but once again this would not be noticeable in translation. In the absence of rhyme and readily identifiable meter, several other features characterize Hebrew poetry and distinguish it from prose.

Parallelism

Fortunately, the most characteristic feature of Hebrew poetry is easily detectable even in translation, namely a correspondence in the content of successive lines that is sometimes labelled "thought rhyme." This attribute, called parallelism, is the dominant distinguishing feature of Hebrew poetry, though it does not appear in every instance. Parallelism has traditionally been classified into three main kinds:[2]

- synonymous
- antithetical
- synthetic

In *synonymous* parallelism the lines seem to say the same thing in different words. Consider the following examples:

I will bless the LORD at all times;
    his praise shall continually be in my mouth. (Ps. 34:1)

---

2. The classic formulation of parallelism is Robert Lowth, *De sacra poesi Hebraeorum (Lectures on the Sacred Poetry of the Hebrews)*, 1753; also Robert Lowth, *Isaiah: A New Translation with a Preliminary Dissertation and Notes Critical, Philological, and Explanatory*, 1778. A critique of his taxonomy is found in Kugel, *The Idea of Biblical Poetry*.

I passed by the field of one who was lazy,
>   by the vineyard of a stupid person. (Prov. 24:30)

In the first example, "I will bless the LORD" in the opening line corresponds to "his praise" in the second line, while "at all times" is echoed by "continually be in my mouth." Similarly, in Proverbs 24:30 the initial "by the field" is paralleled with "by the vineyard" and "one who was lazy" is partnered by "a stupid person," with "I passed" doing double duty for both lines.

In contrast, in *antithetical* parallelism the second line seems to say the opposite of what was said in the first, although this usually amounts to two different aspects of one thing. For instance,

The young lions suffer want and hunger,
>   but those who seek the LORD lack no good thing. (Ps. 34:10)
The mind of one who has understanding seeks knowledge,
>   but the mouths of fools feed on folly. (Prov. 15:14)

The first example articulates God's provision for those who seek him, contrary to the young lions who go hungry, while the second contrasts what either those with understanding or fools try to obtain, in order to indicate the value of the former.

Synthetic parallelism is a catch-all category, used for anything that does not clearly fit into either of the other two, such as,

Many are the afflictions of the righteous,
>   but the LORD rescues them from them all. (Ps. 34:19)
Listen to advice and accept instruction,
>   that you may gain wisdom for the future. (Prov. 19:20)

Here the second line does not directly correspond to the first line, but rather expresses God's salvation of the righteous (Ps. 34:19) or the result of accepting instruction (Prov. 19:20).

More recently, scholars have recognized that the terms "synonymous" and "antithetical" are as inappropriate as the term "synthetic."[3] The second line doesn't just repeat the first line in different words or echo its meaning by saying the opposite; the second line goes beyond the first to add an additional element of meaning to it. As a result, it is more appropriate to say

---

3. Kugel, *The Idea of Biblical Poetry*, 1–58; Alter, *Biblical Poetry*, 3–84.

that the second line intensifies, specifies, focuses, heightens, sharpens, etc., the first line. It may move from the general to the particular, from the part to the whole, from a large geographical region to a specific city, etc. What is important is that there is a development between the two parts, and so the categories synonymous and antithetical, while helpful in describing the superficial appearance of a verse, should not be taken literally or accepted uncritically.

This makes a difference for how we understand and interpret Hebrew poetry. If we think that the second line simply duplicates or contrasts with the first, we will miss the nuances and deeper meanings that are present. Let us return to the examples above from the book of Proverbs, beginning with the "synonymous" parallelism of Proverbs 24:30:

> I passed by the field of one who was lazy,
> by the vineyard of a stupid person.

Keeping in mind the same points of correspondence described earlier but being attentive to how the second line might provide new information not contained in the first, the first thing to note is that this verse does not describe the property of two different people but rather a single individual about whom the second line provides additional information. Therefore, the lazy person is subsequently revealed to be "stupid." This is consistent with the wisdom tradition, which held that wisdom could be attained by anyone willing to make the effort to gain it. Therefore, some people were not wise simply because they failed to engage in the hard work of study and reflection through which they could have become wise. In other words, a stupid person is stupid because that person is lazy. In addition, the second line clarifies that this person does not own just any field, but rather a vineyard, with the implication that this person deals in wine, which is also critiqued in the wisdom literature (see especially Prov. 23:31–35).

Similarly, a development in meaning can be seen between the two halves of the "antithetical" saying in Proverbs 15:14:

> The mind of one who has understanding seeks knowledge,
> but the mouths of fools feed on folly.

The first line mentions a "mind" whereas the second concerns "mouths." This too reflects a bias of the sages, who thought that fools cared more about physical appetites than intellectual endeavors. This point is further reinforced by the different verbs used for each type of individual: one with understanding "seeks" whereas fools "feed." Finally, the results of their different efforts are not just opposites; fools do not feed on a lack of knowledge, but rather their lack of knowledge is itself "folly," and continuously feeding on it reinforces their foolishness.

Finally, there is the so-called "synthetic" parallelism in Proverbs 19:20:

> Listen to advice and accept instruction,
>> that you may gain wisdom for the future.

Here, too, the second line adds new information not contained in the first line. In this case the new information is the result of what is encouraged in the first line: the reason you should "listen to advice and accept instruction" is so "that you may gain wisdom for the future."

Because the majority of the Israelite wisdom books are written in poetry, one should always be conscious of how the parallel lines of a verse function together to develop the meaning. Scholars continue to use the adjectives "synonymous," "antithetical," and "synthetic" to describe the types of parallelism, but rather than assuming that they are simply saying the same thing in similar words or making the same point through opposite words, be attentive to what new information the second line provides. James Kugel's formula is helpful: "A, and what's more, B."[4]

Major Structural Elements

Hebrew poetry uses a number of formal elements to structure poems:

- Acrostic
- Inclusio
- Key Words
- Mirror Pattern

An *acrostic* is based on the twenty-two letters of the Hebrew alphabet, with a different letter used to start each line or verse (e.g., Pss. 111, 112) or every second line (e.g., Ps. 37): some poems add a twenty-third line starting with *peh* (*p*), so that the first letter of the initial, middle, and final lines spell *aleph*

---

4. Kugel, *The Idea of Biblical Poetry*, 58.

('*lp*), the first letter of the alphabet (e.g., Pss. 25, 34). Sometimes, the acrostic is not complete, as in Psalms 9 and 10. Since wisdom literature does not have many long compositions (e.g., much of the book of Proverbs consists of two-line sayings), acrostics are rare, but there are clear examples in Proverbs 31:10–31 and Sirach 51:13–30. Even when the feature itself is not present, the number of letters in the Hebrew alphabet can serve as the basis for the length of a poem, namely eleven-, twenty-two-, and twenty-three-line poems. For instance, Proverbs 2, Sirach 1:11–30, and Sirach 24:3–22 all comprise discrete units of twenty-two lines, while Proverbs 5 and Sirach 51:13–30 each have twenty-three lines.

Another major structural element is the *inclusio*, the repetition of a word, phrase, or concept at both the beginning and the end of a unified work. For instance, Psalm 1 repeats "wicked" in vv. 1 and 6, Psalm 8 is bracketed by "O LORD, our Sovereign, / how majestic is your name in all the earth," Psalm 82 repeats *'ĕlōhîm* with a singular nuance ("God") in vv. 1 and 8, Psalm 103 repeats "Bless the LORD, O my soul," and Psalms 146–50 all begin and end with "Praise the LORD." Similarly, the phrase *hăbēl hăbālîm* (NRSV "vanity of vanities") forms an inclusio in Qoheleth 1:2 and 12:8, as do the poems about Lady Wisdom in Sirach 1 and 51. On a smaller scale, Proverbs 25:2 has the words *kbd* ("glory") and *ḥqr* ("search"), which are repeated in the reverse order in v. 27, rendered in the NRSV as "seek" (*ḥqr*) and "honor" (*kbd*).

Key words involve the repetition of words throughout a poetic section, helping to unify it. For instance Psalm 63 repeats the word *nepeš* ("soul/life") in vv. 1, 5, 8, 9; the verb *špṭ* ("to judge") appears in Psalm 82 in vv. 1, 2, 3, 8; Psalm 121 has variations of the verb *šmr* ("to keep") in vv. 3, 4, 5, 7, 8; and Psalm 119 has various words for law throughout: "command," "decree," "precept," "ordinance," "word," "promise," etc. In the same way, "fool" is repeated in Proverbs 26:1, 3–12 and "lazy person" in Proverbs 26:13–16.

A *mirror pattern* is the repetition of two or more words or concepts across subsequent lines or sections of a work, followed by their repetition in the reverse order, thereby turning the lines back on themselves like a mirror in order to establish a self-contained unit. Both the number of repeated elements and the amount of material they can encompass is theoretically unlimited, and scholars have proposed such patterns at the level of entire books and more. Here it is enough to note that Qoheleth 5:10–6:9 has the following thematic mirror pattern:[5]

---

5. Daniel C. Fredericks, "Chiasm and Parallel Structure in Qoheleth 5:6–6:9," *JBL* 108 (1989): 17–35. See further in chapter 5 below.

    A Limits to Satisfaction (Qoh. 5:10–12)
       B Coming and Going in Darkness (Qoh. 5:13–17)
          C God's Blessing or Curse (Qoh. 5:18–20)
          C' God's Blessing or Curse (Qoh. 6:1–2)
       B' Coming and Going in Darkness (Qoh. 6:3–6)
    A' Limits to Satisfaction (Qoh. 6:[5], 7–9)

The central element is usually the focal point, especially if it does not have a balancing component.

Minor Structural Elements

Many of these major structural elements can also mark the beginning and end of smaller units. For instance, *acrostics* can also organize sections: Psalm 119 consists of 22 sets of 8 lines, with every line within each set beginning with the same letter, and subsequent sets using subsequent letters. On the other hand, Psalm 82 is marked off by the repetition of "God" in vv. 1 and 8, but is also sub-divided by the inclusio of "wicked" in vv. 2 and 4 plus "earth" in vv. 5–8. In the same way, Proverbs 25:2–27 is delineated by the repetition of *kbd* and *ḥqr* (see above) but is also subdivided by the semantic inclusio of "kings" (*mĕlākîm*) and "ruler" (*qāṣîn*) in vv. 2 and 15 as well as the repetition of "honey" and "eat" (in mirrored order) in vv. 16 and 27. Similarly, Psalm 84:8–12 is encompassed by "O Lord (God) of Hosts," Psalm 85 has "our/your salvation" in vv. 4 and 7, and Qoheleth 9:1–12 begins and ends with a reference to "not knowing," while "love" and "hate" are repeated in vv. 1 and 6.

Key words function on the level of units within a larger poem as well. I have already noted above the repetition of the verb "to judge" across Psalm 82, but "wicked" occurs only in vv. 2 and 4, along with "evil" in v. 2, and the word *dal* is found in vv. 3 and 4 (translated by the NRSV as "weak" and "lowly" respectively). At the same time, vv. 5–8 are unified by the repetition of "all" in vv. 5, 6, 8, "earth" in vv. 5, 8, and "like" twice in v. 7. Similarly, in addition to being the start of an inclusio in Proverbs 25:2, the word "king" is repeated in vv. 3, 5, 6 (note also "the great" in v. 6b and "noble" in v. 7).

A *mirror pattern* can also structure a smaller portion of Hebrew poetry. The pattern is evident in Psalm 105:1–6 ("peoples," "wonderful works," "seek the Lord" // "seek the Lord," "wonderful works," "offspring"/"children") and vv. 7–11 ("earth" [*'ereṣ*], "covenant forever" // "eternal covenant," "land" [*'ereṣ*]), as well as Psalm 136:10–15 ("Egyptians," "Israel," God's action // God's action,

"Israel," "Pharaoh and his army"). A brief mirror pattern is also found in Proverbs 31:20–21:

> She puts her hands (*yādêhā*) to the distaff
> and her palms (*kappêhā*) hold the spindle
> She opens her palm (*kappâ*) to the poor,
> and reaches out her hands (*yādêhā*) to the needy. (author's translation)

By turning the two verses back on each other, this mirror pattern reinforces the fact that it is the labor of her hands and palms that enables her to aid the poor and needy with her palms and hands.

Hebrew poetry uses other minor structural elements as well:

- Refrain
- Chorus
- Chiasm(us)

In addition to the major elements discussed above, a *refrain* repeats phrases at regular intervals. The lines "Why are you cast down, O my soul, / and why are you disquieted within me? / Hope in God; for I shall again praise God, / my help and my God" (slight variation from the NRSV) recur in Psalms 42:5, 11; 43:5, while Psalm 67:3, 5 repeat "Let the peoples praise you, O God; / let all the peoples praise you!" The refrain can vary within a psalm, as the following verses from Psalm 80 illustrate:

> Restore us, O God;
> let your face shine, that we may be saved. (v. 3)
> Restore us, O God of hosts;
> let your face shine, that we may be saved. (v. 7)
> Restore us, O LORD God of Hosts;
> let your face shine, that we may be saved. (v. 19)

Two refrains can alternate in a single poem, as in Psalm 107:

> Then they cried to the LORD in their trouble,
> and he delivered/saved (2×)/brought them (out) from their distress.
> (vv. 6, 13, 19, 28)
> Let them thank the LORD for his steadfast love,
> for his wonderful works to humankind. (vv. 8, 15, 21, 31)

A *chorus* is more frequent than a refrain: Psalm 136 repeats "for his steadfast love endures forever" as the second line of every verse (cf. the same feature and phrase in the poem inserted between Sirach 51:12 and 13).

A *chiasmus*, or *chiasm*, gets its name from the Greek letter *chi* (χ), and refers to the reversal of two elements from one line in the next line. For instance, Psalm 7:16 reads

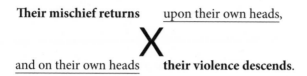

Drawing a line from the bold material in each line plus another between the underlined material would produce an X, which looks like the Greek letter *chi*. The same effect is produced antithetically in Proverbs 13:24:

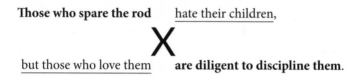

A chiasmus can also occur with two lines that are distant from each other, as in the reversal of *kbd* and *ḥqr* in Proverbs 25:2 and 27 noted above.

Poetic Devices

Important poetic devices in Hebrew include:

- Merism(us)
- Abstract for concrete
- Breakup of composite phrases

Hebrew poetry uses many of the same poetic devices as English poetry, such as metaphors and similes, but there are some poetic devices that are used more frequently than in contemporary English poetry. A *merismus*, or *merism*, is the use of two extremes to indicate totality. For instance, Psalm 139:7–12 describes the psalmist's efforts to escape God's presence. Verse 8 mentions heaven and Sheol (the underworld) not as two locations but to encompass the totality of the divine and earthly realms. Verse 9 then alludes to the east ("the wings of the morning") and the west ("the [Mediterranean] sea") while "right hand" (v. 10b) is a common idiom for the south, suggesting that "hand" alone (v. 10a) is the left hand, or the north; thus vv. 9–10 include the four cardinal directions to indicate that there is nowhere on earth that the psalmist can flee to elude God. The same device is used in Psalm 148:12 to refer to both sexes ("young men and women alike") and all ages ("old and young together"). Awareness of this poetic device yields additional meaning in Proverbs 6:22, which describes the value of paying attention to a parent's teaching. According to the first two lines, "When you walk, they will lead you; / when you lie down, they will watch over you," which could indicate two separate events but as a merismus covers when one is both active and inactive, i.e., as long as one is awake. But a third line adds that, "when you awake, they will talk with you," which taken with the second line develops the idea further to convey the impact that the teaching will have both when asleep (line 2) and when awake (line 3).

The use of the *abstract for concrete* pairs an abstract concept such as justice or satiety with a concrete instance of the concept, such as right judgment or wine; the abstract term is meant to be understood concretely in light of the concrete term. Thus, Psalm 36:11 literally reads, "Do not let the foot of pride [NRSV has 'the arrogant'] tread on me, / or the hand of the wicked drive me away." Similarly, when Proverbs 11:14a says, "Where there is no guidance, a nation falls," the noun "guidance" is to be read in light of the concrete reference to "counselors" in v. 14b: "but in an abundance of counselors there is safety."

Sometimes a poet will *break up a composite phrase* by distributing the parts of a stereotyped phrase over one or more verses. Job 38:6 asks, "On what were its [the earth's] bases sunk, / or who laid the stone of its corner?" (NRSV "its cornerstone"). That concluding phrase is distributed across two lines in Psalm 118:22: "The stone that the builders rejected / has become the head of the corner" (NRSV "chief cornerstone"). Job's rejection of the idea that "my heart has been enticed by a woman [or wife], / and I have lain in wait at my neighbor's door" (Job 31:9) takes on added significance in light of the commandment, "You shall not covet your neighbor's wife" (Exod. 20:17); Job is not just denying that he was seduced by a neighboring woman but rather that he has not committed adultery with his neighbor's wife. Similarly, since shedding "innocent blood" is widely prohibited in most types of biblical literature,[6] when sinners say, "Come with us, let us lie in wait for blood; / let us wantonly

---

6. Deut. 19:10, 13; 21:8, 9; 27:25; 1 Sam. 19:5; 2 Kings 21:16; 24:4; Pss. 94:21; 106:38; Prov. 6:17; Isa. 59:7; Jer. 7:6; 19:4; 22:3, 17; 26:15; Joel 3:19; Jon. 1:14.

ambush the innocent" (Prov. 1:11), they are not proposing an ordinary crime but rather are enticing the individual to violate an established taboo.

Wisdom Forms[7]

Characteristic wisdom forms include:

- Proverb: sentence plus command or prohibition
- Instruction
- Numerical saying
- List
- Challenge to a rival
- Disputation/dialogue/diatribe
- Autobiographical narrative
- Didactic/example story
- Appeal to tradition
- Allegory
- Fable
- Riddle

The Hebrew word used to designate the most common wisdom form is *māšāl*, which is generally translated into English as *proverb*, as in the headings found in Proverbs 1:1; 10:1; 25:1. This may not be the best rendering, since the word is also used of parables (Ezek. 17:2), prophetic utterances (Num. 23:7), taunts (Isa. 14:4), speeches (Job 27:1; 29:1), bywords (Jer. 24:9), etc. Moreover, properly speaking a proverb is a pithy, succinct, and memorable saying that has currency among the general population. English examples include "curiosity killed the cat" and "better late than never." There are some proverbs embedded in biblical narrative contexts outside wisdom literature that function in this way. In 1 Samuel 24:13 Saul has been pursuing David seeking to kill him and

---

7. General form-critical discussions of wisdom literature can be found in James L. Crenshaw, "Wisdom," in *Old Testament Form Criticism*, ed. John Haralson Hayes, Trinity University Monograph Series in Religion 2 (San Antonio: Trinity University Press, 1974), 225–64; Roland E. Murphy, *Wisdom Literature: Job, Proverbs, Ruth, Canticles, Ecclesiastes, Esther*, FOTL 13 (Grand Rapids: Eerdmans, 1981); Philip Johannes Nel, "The Genres of Biblical Wisdom Literature," *JNSL* 9 (1981): 129–42; W. Dennis Tucker Jr., "Literary Forms in the Wisdom Literature," in *An Introduction to Wisdom Literature and the Psalms: Festschrift Marvin E. Tate*, ed. H. Wayne Ballard Jr. and W. Dennis Tucker Jr. (Macon: Mercer University Press, 2000), 155–66.

David asserts his innocence by stating, "Out of the wicked comes forth wickedness." In 1 Kings 20:11 the king of Israel responds to Ben-hadad's military boast with, "One who puts on armor should not brag like one who takes it off." And both Jeremiah and Ezekiel quote the people using the same proverb: "The parents have eaten sour grapes, and the children's teeth are set on edge" (Jer. 31:29; Ezek. 18:2).[8] However, Proverbs is a collection of sayings with no narrative context to indicate how they were used. As a result it is difficult to determine whether any of the sayings in Proverbs is a true proverb. It is likely that many of the sayings in this collection are there by virtue of their common usage, but some may have been coined by the sages and subsequently became popular as a direct result of their collection into the book. Ultimately, however, there is insufficient evidence to be certain on the matter.

The majority of Proverbs 10–31 consists of two-line sayings, most of which can be categorized as a *sentence*, a simple statement in the indicative that makes a comparative observation about human affairs or human nature, or draws an analogy with the natural world. A smaller number are either a *command* or a *prohibition*: the former demands an action through an imperative, while the latter bans an action with "do not," and the second line of each provides a motivation. At times, this goes beyond two lines: in Proverbs 25:6–7 and 27:23–24 the first verse contains a prohibition (27:23) or admonition (25:6) and the second verse constitutes the motivation. Proverbs 23:6–8 consists of a one-verse prohibition and a two-verse motivation, in Proverbs 23:22–25 the admonition and motivation span two verses each, and Proverbs 23:31 warns against consuming wine followed by four verses describing its negative effects. In each of these cases, however, the basic form of admonition or prohibition plus motivation remains intact.

Another major wisdom form is the *instruction*, which as noted in chapter 1 above has extensive parallels in the Egyptian wisdom literature. Its structure is very straightforward:

1. A direct address to "my son" (traditional terminology for a student) followed by a command to "hear," "listen," etc.
2. Motive clause(s) giving the reasons for listening and obeying; these motives are typically the benefits that derive from the teaching.

---

8. On these and other examples of "proverb performance" see Carole R. Fontaine, *Traditional Sayings in the Old Testament: A Contextual Study*, BLS 5 (Sheffield: Almond, 1982), 72–170; Carole R. Fontaine, *Smooth Words: Women, Proverbs and Performance in Biblical Wisdom*, JSOTSup 356 (Sheffield: Sheffield Academic, 2002), 150–241.

3. The teaching itself, usually in the form of conditional and result clauses ("if . . . then"), although straightforward commands are also used. The teaching consists of exhortations and supporting arguments.

This form predominates in Proverbs 1–7, beginning with Proverbs 1:8–19. A "child" is called to "hear"/"not reject" its parents' teachings in Proverbs 1:8, after which v. 9 provides the motive for doing so. Verses 10–19 contain the teaching, namely, do not be led astray by robbers.

The *numerical saying* occurs primarily in the book of Proverbs (Prov. 6:16–19; 30:5–16, 18–19, 21–23, 24–28, 29–31) and Ben Sira (Sir. 25:7–11; 26:5–6, 28–29; 50:25–26), plus one example in Job 5:19–22. It consists of a numerical progression, beginning with an x / x+1 formula followed by an enumeration of items up to and including the higher number.[9] An x / x+1 sequence is not restricted to the wisdom literature or even the biblical literature, but the instances outside the wisdom tradition usually just have two incremental numbers in separate lines without using the formula (e.g., Hos. 6:2; Mic. 5:5). Amos 1–2 does denounce different nations "for three transgressions . . . and for four," but unlike the wisdom texts that list things up to the higher number, Amos names just one transgression by each of the foreign nations and Judah—Amos lists more than one transgression only in the case of Israel, and even then it is not clear that he has exactly four sins in mind. In contrast, the wisdom usage does not just list x+1 things, but emphasizes the final one, often with a divergent element that forces the reader to determine the connection with the preceding. This is evident in Proverbs 30:18–19:

> Three things are too wonderful for me;
>> four I do not understand:
> the way of an eagle in the sky,
>> the way of a snake on a rock,
> the way of a ship on the high seas,
>> and the way of a man with a girl.

The correlation among the ways of a bird, a serpent, and a ship is not immediately obvious, but how the way of a man and a woman fits with those three

9. On the form in general see Wolfgang M. W. Roth, "The Numerical Sequence x / x+1 in the Old Testament," *VT* 12 (1962): 300–11; Wolfgang M. W. Roth, *Numerical Sayings in the Old Testament*, VTSup 13 (Leiden: Brill, 1965); Georg Sauer, *Die Sprüche Agurs: Untersuchungen zur Herkunft, Verbreitung und Bedeutung einer biblischen Stilform unter besonderer Berücksichtigung von Proverbia c. 30*, BWANT 5.4 (Stuttgart: Kohlhammer, 1963).

is even less clear. The form is didactic, requiring that the reader not only link the disparate items but also determine the connections among them.

Lists that arranged things in terms of similarity or difference were a common feature in ancient international wisdom, and they are reflected in the biblical material as well. The numerical sayings reflect this approach to an extent but it is more clearly seen in texts like the list of opposites in Qoheleth 3:1–9; the nature of Wisdom's spirit in Wisdom 6:22–23; the categorization of fields of knowledge in 1 Kings 4:33 and Wisdom 7:17–20; the various trades in Sirach 38:24–39:11, and the catalogue of wisdom in Job 38–39.[10] Rowold sees a different form in Job 38–39, the *challenge to a rival*, in which an individual is challenged in a scholarly debate to demonstrate the extent of his knowledge through a series of questions aimed at professed areas of expertise.[11] The *disputation/dialogue* is related to this, and is exemplified by Job 3–27, although it is also reflected in Qoheleth's frequent challenges to the established wisdom traditions and in the *diatribe* in Wisdom 2:1–20; 5:3–13, where the author quotes the views of others in order to dispute them (cf. Prov. 1:11–14, 22–33).

In keeping with wisdom's reflection on human experience, the central feature of an *autobiographical narrative* is an appeal to one's own situation or experience as a motivation for the reader to accept one's words of instruction. In Qoheleth 1:12–2:26 the author assumes the guise of King Solomon in order to affirm the extent of his investigation of wisdom and pleasure and to support the credibility of his subsequent words. However, once he has presented his "credentials," so to speak, this Solomonic persona is not mentioned again after chapter 2. Proverbs 4:3–9 is another autobiographical narrative: the speaker appeals to the teaching he received when he was young as a motivation for his own children to accept his instruction (see also Sir. 33:16–18; 51:13–22). In contrast, a *didactic/example story* does not appeal to the speaker's own experience but rather is a story, perhaps directly observed, that provides the basis for a moral or lesson. Examples include the seduction of a youth (Prov. 7:6–23), a lazy person's dilapidated vineyard (Prov. 24:30–34), and the poor but wise man who saved a besieged city, only to be forgotten (Qoh. 9:14–16).

The *appeal to tradition* has three elements: the appeal itself, a citation of the tradition, and its application; examples include Job 8:8–13; 12:7–12; 15:17–35;

10. On the last see Gerhard von Rad, "Job 38 and Ancient Egyptian Wisdom," in *The Problem of the Hexateuch and Other Essays*, trans. E. W. T. Dicken (Edinburgh: Oliver & Boyd, 1966), 281–91.

11. Henry Rowold, "Yahweh's Challenge to Rival: The Form and Function of the Yahweh-Speech in Job 38–39," *CBQ* 47 (1985): 199–211.

20:4–29.[12] The application section corresponds to the "summary-appraisal" form that Childs identified in Isaiah 14:26–27; 17:14; 28:29.[13] The didactic aspect of the wisdom form's application may have been adapted by Isaiah to interpret his own oracles. Another clearly didactic but less frequent wisdom form is the *allegory*, which posits a one-to-one correspondence between elements in the text and things outside it. The clearest example in the wisdom books is Proverbs 5:15–23, in which a cistern is used as a cipher for one's wife (cf. Song 4:12, 15) and its water stands for sexual activity. Qoheleth 12:1–7 is often interpreted as an allegory for old age, but some correspondences are forced and the analogies break down before the end of the poem.

Curiously, two final wisdom forms are not found in the wisdom literature. A *fable* is a didactic story with talking animals, trees, etc. One can find fables in the First Testament in Judges 9:8–15 and 2 Kings 14:9; cf. Numbers 22:21–35. The absence of *riddles* is more significant, since Proverbs 1:6 indicates that the book will enable one to understand them and Sirach 39:3 lists riddles as one of the sage's characteristic concerns. However, the only clear riddle in the First Testament is Judges 14:14 ("Out of the eater came something to eat. / Out of the strong came something sweet"), although Crenshaw suggests that the Philistines' answer and Samson's retort in v. 18 also reflect the form.[14] Elsewhere Crenshaw proposes that the numerical sayings were originally riddles, with the x number corresponding to a riddle about what is like those items and the x+1 item giving the answer.[15] Thus Proverbs 30:18–19 would have asked "What is like the way of a bird . . . a serpent . . . a ship?" and the answer was "a man with a woman." Earlier, Torcszyner formulated the initial line as a question ("What are three or four things that move but leave no trace?") and the next four lines as the answer.[16] Another approach finds riddles behind some comparative sayings that contain an element of absurdity, reformulating the first half of the verse as a riddle question, with the second half as the answer:[17]

12. Norman C. Habel, "Appeal to Ancient Tradition as a Literary Form," *ZAW* 88 (1976): 253–72.

13. Brevard S. Childs, *Isaiah and the Assyrian Crisis*, SBT Second Series 3 (Naperville: Allenson, 1967), 128–36.

14. James L. Crenshaw, *Samson: A Secret Betrayed, A Vow Ignored* (Macon, GA: Mercer University Press, 1978), 111–20; James L. Crenshaw, "Riddles," in *ABD* 5.722.

15. Crenshaw, "Riddles," 5.722. Contrast Hans-Peter Müller, "Der Begriff 'Rätsel' im Alten Testament," *VT* 20 (1970): 465–69.

16. Harry Torcszyner, "The Riddle in the Bible," *HUCA* 1 (1924): 135–36.

17. See Alter, *Biblical Poetry*, 175–79. Contrast the straightforward sentence and a less explicit comparison of measurements in Prov. 11:1; 20:10.

[What is like] a gold ring in a pig's snout[?]
A beautiful woman without good sense. (Prov. 11:22)
[What is like] clouds and wind without rain[?]
One who boasts of a gift never given. (Prov. 25:14)

But however suggestive it is, recasting numerical sayings or comparative proverbs as riddles must remain speculative, even if they do challenge the reader to puzzle out the answer to the questions.

FURTHER READING

Hebrew Poetry

Alonso Schökel, Luis. *A Manual of Hebrew Poetics.* Translated by Adrian Graffy. SubBi 11. Rome: Biblical Institute Press, 1988.

Alter, Robert. *The Art of Biblical Poetry.* New York: Basic Books, 1985.

Berlin, Adele. *The Dynamics of Biblical Parallelism.* Bloomington: Indiana University Press, 1985.

Collins, Terence. *Line-Forms in Hebrew Poetry: A Grammatical Approach to the Stylistic Study of the Hebrew Prophets.* Rome: Biblical Institute Press, 1978.

Dobbs-Allsopp, F. W. *On Biblical Poetry.* Oxford: Oxford University Press, 2015.

Fokkelman, Jan. *Reading Biblical Poetry: An Introductory Guide.* Translated by Ineke Smith. Louisville: Westminster John Knox, 2001.

Follis, Elaine R., ed. *Directions in Biblical Hebrew Poetry.* JSOTSup 40. Sheffield: JSOT Press, 1987.

Gerstenberger, Erhard S. *Psalms: Part 1 with an Introduction to Cultic Poetry.* FOTL 14. Grand Rapids: Eerdmans, 1988.

Kugel, James L. *The Idea of Biblical Poetry: Parallelism and Its History.* New Haven: Yale University Press, 1981.

O'Connor, Michael. *Hebrew Verse Structure.* Winona Lake, IN: Eisenbrauns, 1980.

Pardee, Dennis. *Ugaritic and Hebrew Poetic Parallelism: A Trial Cut ('nt I and Proverbs 2).* VTSup 39. Leiden: Brill, 1988.

Petersen, David L., and Kent Harold Richards. *Interpreting Hebrew Poetry.* GBS OT Series. Minneapolis: Fortress, 1992.

Watson, Wilfred G. E. *Classical Hebrew Poetry: A Guide to Its Techniques.* JSOTSup 26. Sheffield: JSOT Press, 1984.

———. *Traditional Techniques in Classical Hebrew Poetry.* JSOTSup 170. Sheffield: Sheffield Academic Press, 1994.

Wisdom Forms

Crenshaw, James L. "Wisdom." Pages 225–64 in *Old Testament Form Criticism.* Edited by John Haralson Hayes. Trinity University Monograph Series in Religion 2. San Antonio: Trinity University Press, 1974.

Murphy, Roland E. *Wisdom Literature: Job, Proverbs, Ruth, Canticles, Ecclesiastes, Esther.* FOTL 13. Grand Rapids: Eerdmans, 1981.

Nel, Philip Johannes. "The Genres of Biblical Wisdom Literature." *JNSL* 9 (1981): 129–42.

——. *The Structure and Ethos of the Wisdom Admonitions in Proverbs.* BZAW 158. Berlin: de Gruyter, 1982.

Perry, T. A. *Wisdom Literature and the Structure of Proverbs.* University Park: Pennsylvania State University Press, 1993.

Thompson, John M. *The Form and Function of Proverbs in Ancient Israel.* SJ 1. Paris: Mouton, 1974.

Tucker, W. Dennis, Jr. "Literary Forms in the Wisdom Literature." Pages 155–66 in *An Introduction to Wisdom Literature and the Psalms: Festschrift Marvin E. Tate.* Edited by H. Wayne Ballard Jr. and W. Dennis Tucker Jr. Macon, GA: Mercer University Press, 2000.

CHAPTER 3

Proverbs

The book of Proverbs is not a single literary work but a compilation that combines a variety of forms and concerns. Most of Proverbs 1–7 uses the Instruction genre known from Egyptian wisdom literature, Proverbs 8 is a lengthy poem spoken by Lady Wisdom, and Proverbs 9 parallels her with personified Folly. In contrast, the rest of the book consists primarily of two-line sayings, although there are some slightly longer sections. Proverbs 30 includes a cluster of numerical x / x+1 sayings, and the book ends with an acrostic poem about the noble woman. Some individual sayings repeat within and across sections, while the point varies widely in many others. This diversity in form, content, and theme suggests that the book of Proverbs as we have it is the result of a lengthy and cumulative editing process during which sayings were gathered into collections, which were gradually linked with one another.

Structure

The clearest indication that Proverbs is a compilation of smaller collections is the presence of titles or headings for several of these component parts. Many biblical books have a title or introduction, and Proverbs 1:1 reads "The proverbs of Solomon, son of David, king of Israel." However, similar headings are found later in the book. These were probably the titles to smaller works that have been brought together to form a larger whole. The subsequent headings are:

The proverbs of Solomon (10:1)
The words of the wise (22:17)[1]
These also are sayings of the wise (24:23)
These are other proverbs of Solomon that the officials of King Hezekiah
    of Judah copied (25:1)
The words of Agur son of Jakeh (30:1)
The words of King Lemuel (31:1)

Although there have been attempts to demonstrate an editorial unity to the book, none have been widely accepted. Two very different and creative proposals illustrate how such attempts can have both positive and negative aspects. Patrick Skehan focused on the numerical value of the Hebrew consonants in the names and a noun from some of the headings.[2] For instance, Proverbs 1:1 refers to Solomon (*šlmh*), David (*dwd*), and Israel (*yśr'l*), which add up to 930, the number of lines in the book. Proverbs 10:1 names only Solomon, which has a value of 375, matching the number of sayings in Proverbs 10:1–22:16. Proverbs 22:17 and 24:23 both mention "the wise" (*ḥkmym*); this has a numerical value of 118, which is precisely how many lines are not governed by other titles (i.e., Prov. 22:17–24:32 plus 30:7–33). Finally, Hezekiah (*yḥzqyh*) in Proverbs 25:1 has a value of 140, the number of sayings in 25:1–29:27. This is open to critique on at least four points. First, we do not know when the numerical values were given to the Hebrew alphabet, although acrostics and twenty-two-line poems indicate that the sages did use the alphabet for structural purposes. Second, Skehan's proposal requires omitting 1:16; 8:11; 24:33–34 as later additions, although there may be some justification for the deletions. Proverbs 1:16 is missing from two ancient Greek manuscripts and duplicates Isaiah 59:7, Proverbs 8:11 is a third-person statement in the middle of a first-person speech and echoes Proverbs 3:15, and 24:33–34 is a second-person address in a first-person reflection and may have been copied from 6:10–11.[3] Third, Skehan reads *yḥzqyh* at 25:1 instead of *ḥzqyh* in the Hebrew text; either is a valid biblical spelling, and Skehan finds

---

1. The LXX, followed by the NRSV and NABRE, have this phrase at the beginning of the verse, whereas it is in the middle of the first line as the object of the verb "hear" in the MT.

2. Patrick W. Skehan, *Studies in Israelite Poetry and Wisdom*, CBQMS 1 (Washington: Catholic Biblical Association, 1971), 43–45. In Hebrew, each letter has a numerical value, so one can assign values to different words. For example, the name Solomon adds up to 375 because the four letters used to spell it have values of 300 (*š*), 30 (*l*), 40 (*m*), and 5 (*h*). This numerical worth of words lies behind the famous "number of the beast" passage in Revelation 13:18.

3. Roland E. Murphy, *The Tree of Life: An Exploration of Biblical Wisdom Literature*, 3rd ed. (Grand Rapids: Eerdmans, 2002), 32n35.

support for the initial *y* because the previous word ends in *y*—when adjacent words end and begin with the same letter, occasionally scribes omitted one through a phenomenon known as haplography. Fourth, Skehan does not deal with the numerical value of Agur (30:1) and Lemuel (31:1), which one would expect in light of the names in the other headings. Nevertheless, despite some weaknesses, at the very least Skehan's proposal provides some indication of a conscious editorial organization to the book and its subsections rather than a haphazard compilation.

Seenam Kim, on the other hand, argues for editorial unity within and between the sections of Proverbs on the basis of "exclusive" terminology, namely words that occur infrequently in the book, and identifies words that are either unique to one collection or appear in a few of them.[4] On this basis Kim isolates characteristic features for the individual collections as well as links among them. While the extensive lists of words and the correlations among them are intriguing, Kim does not address such things as the very different lengths of the collections and the divergent forms in Proverbs 1–9 versus the rest of the book. While few would dispute that the parts of the book have a degree of internal coherence as well as some connections among them, this coherence does not amount to the major editorial unity that Kim proposes.

Orientation to Proverbs	
Structure:	1:1–9:18
	10:1–22:16
	22:17–24:22
	24:23–34
	25:1–29:27
	30:1–33
	31:1–31
Date:	portions range from the preexilic to the exilic periods
Major Themes:	the "fear of the Lord"
	"strange"/"adulterous" women
	Lady Wisdom
	the two ways: good and evil/righteous and wicked
	gaining wisdom
	proper relationships
	analogies with nature

Author and Date

It is not possible to identify either the author or date of composition of Proverbs, or even of its subsections. The individual proverbs are too general to provide

---

4. Seenam Kim, *The Coherence of the Collections in the Book of Proverbs* (Eugene, OR: Pickwick, 2007).

any clues in this regard, and the longer material in Proverbs 1–9 lacks concrete historical information to indicate a date. One can try to determine when the subsections were finalized based on information in the headings, but that too is mostly elusive. The references to "the wise" in 22:17 and 24:23 are too broad to be of any help, and both Agur son of Jakeh (30:1) and King Lemuel (31:1) are unknown outside of those references. Two sections are attributed to Solomon (1:1; 10:1), but the tradition associating Solomon with wisdom is probably not historically correct. He may have supported and encouraged the development of the wisdom tradition in Israel during his reign, but it is not clear that he himself was one of "the wise." Moreover, the contents of these two sections do not fit the famous description of Solomon's wisdom in 1 Kings 4:29–34. Although the text states that he "composed three thousand proverbs" (1 Kings 4:32), the explication of this focuses on nature wisdom: "He would speak of trees, from the cedar that is in Lebanon to the hyssop that grows in the wall; he would speak of animals, and birds, and reptiles, and fish" (4:33). The sections of Proverbs that bear Solomon's name, on the other hand, concern human affairs, and any mention of animals or plants only illustrates a saying about human beings. Finally, Proverbs 25:1 refers to Solomon's proverbs collected by "the officials of King Hezekiah." These would have been scribes, teachers, or sages associated with the royal court. There may be some historical value to this verse, since there is less reason to associate King Hezekiah (ca. 715–687 BCE) with wisdom literature than there is with the legendary figure of Solomon. Hezekiah did emulate Solomon, and may have fostered the compilation of this section, but that cannot be proven.

With one exception, the contents of the individual sections do not help in dating them either. Some suggest that Proverbs 10:1–22:16 was used to instruct bureaucrats and royal courtiers, thus requiring a date during the monarchy and a location in Jerusalem. However, there is little in this unit specifically concerned with life in the royal court, and what sayings do refer to the king may have circulated among the common people just as easily. At the same time, there are a number of sayings that deal with rural and agricultural concerns that would not have been central to life in Jerusalem, especially at the palace. But this only illustrates the danger of arguing solely from content, because urban sages could have easily compiled, and perhaps even formulated, such sayings. The content of Proverbs 22:17–24:22 is more helpful. As will be shown below, this section is dependent on the Egyptian *Instruction of Amenemope* and so must postdate it. However, while *Amenemope* was written during the Ramesside period (ca. thirteenth-eleventh century BCE), the existing copies of the text date to 1000–600 BCE, so this section could have been written any time between the early monarchical period and the exile, or even later.

In sum, the authors and editors of the various sections of Proverbs are unknown, and the most that can be said about the date of composition is that the shorter sayings in most of the book may be preexilic while the more developed speeches in Proverbs 1–9 develop the concise views found in the proverbs in the subsequent sections and so probably date to the postexilic period.

Content

Proverbs 1–9

After the heading in Proverbs 1:1, vv. 2–6 form one sentence establishing the book's purpose, namely that the young and simple as well as the wise might learn, understand, and gain instruction concerning the various types of material to follow. Proverbs 1:7 then provides a motto for the book: "The fear of the LORD is the beginning of knowledge." The theme of "the fear of the LORD" recurs throughout the entire book but it only occurs in this phrase elsewhere at 9:10, using the parallel term *ḥokmâ* ("wisdom") and bracketing most of Proverbs 1–9. A variation is found at 4:7—"The beginning of wisdom is this: Get wisdom"—which highlights the first formula's uniqueness: it is only used elsewhere in the First Testament at Psalm 111:10 plus Sirach 1:14. "Fear of the LORD" does not mean "terror" or anything similar but rather "reverence," or "awe," what today might be called piety or religion, and the phrase "the beginning" here does not mean the starting point or initial lesson, but instead has the nuance of the "basis" or "first principle."

Proverbs 1:8–19 is the first of ten instructions in this section, but we will begin with the second instruction in Proverbs 2 because it is programmatic for the others. Proverbs 2:1–22 is the longest of the instructions, comprising a single sentence of twenty-two lines that contains all the elements of the Instruction genre. After the opening address to "my child," 2:1–4 exhorts him to attend to the father's/teacher's words, 2:5–19 provides motives for doing so, and the teaching itself is found in 2:20–22, a description of the two paths that the good and the wicked walk, which is a repeated motif in Israelite wisdom literature. This instruction is not an acrostic but the number of lines corresponds to the length of the Hebrew alphabet, suggesting that it is a complete composition conveying everything one needs to know. This is supported by its developmental structure: the poem is organized into two halves of eleven verses each, with the key word "wisdom" or a synonym occurring nine times in the first half and *derek* ("path" or "way") repeated nine times in the second half.[5] Each half is further subdivided on the basis of repeated letters and phrases.[6] Leaving aside the formulaic address to "my child," the next word is *'im* ("if"), starting with an *aleph*, the first letter of the Hebrew alphabet. The aleph is repeated at the beginning of verses 5 and 9 in the phrase *'āz tābîn* ("then you will understand"). Verse 12 begins with a *lamed*, the twelfth letter of the alphabet, in the word *lĕhaṣṣîlkâ* ("to deliver you"), which is repeated in 2:16, while a third *lamed* appears in 2:20 in the word *lĕmaʿan* ("therefore"). The result is that each half has three sections consisting of four + four + three verses, with a single word at the beginning of sections one and six surrounding repeated phrases in sections two and three plus four and five.

Each section deals with distinct but related subjects. Section 1 (2:1-4) is an extended conditional clause introducing wisdom as the object of the reader's desire, while the other five sections describe the consequences of achieving that goal. Section 2 (2:5-8) deals with religious understanding, referred to as "the fear of the Lord," which in turn leads to ethical understanding, distinguishing "righteousness and justice" (Section 3: 2:9-11). The effect of this will be to "deliver" the reader from both evil men (Section 4: 2:12-15) and "adulterous women" (Section 5: 2:16-19). All of this is then summarized in Section 6 (2:20-22) in terms of the "two paths" of the good and the wicked.

These six topics are developed individually and at greater length by the other nine instructions in Proverbs 1-7, as illustrated in the following chart:[7]

PROVERBS 2		TOPIC	ELSEWHERE IN PROVERBS 1-7
Part A	1) vv. 1-4	wisdom	4:1-9
	2) vv. 5-8	religious understanding	3:1-12
	3) vv. 9-11	ethical understanding	4:20-27
Part B	4) vv. 12-15	evil men	1:8-19; 4:10-19
	5) vv. 16-19	adulterous women	5:1-23; 6:20-35; 7:1-27
	6) vv. 20-22	the "two paths" (the good vs. the wicked)	3:21-35

5. Whybray takes these repetitions as evidence of secondary additions: R. N. Whybray, *Wisdom in Proverbs: The Concept of Wisdom in Proverbs 1-9*, SBT 45 (Naperville: Allenson, 1965), 40-41. But it is unlikely that the detailed structure of the poem is the result of inserted lines, since additions tend to disrupt clear structures, not create them. Moreover, if an editor could create this complex structure, so too could a single author.

6. Skehan, *Studies*, 9.

7. The following is based on, but goes beyond, the analysis of Skehan, *Studies*, 9-10.

Each of the other nine instructions has the same format as Proverbs 2, exhorting a "child" to following the teaching based on its intrinsic value rather than some external authority. In addition, the passages concerning adulterous women incorporate other forms into the Instruction genre to strengthen their point: Proverbs 5:15–18 uses water that is not shared as an allegory for marital fidelity, in 6:27–29 fire is a metaphor for adultery, and 7:6–23 is an example story about a young man's seduction. It is tempting to move 1:8–19 after Proverbs 2, in which case Lady Wisdom's direct speech in 1:20–33 and Proverbs 8 would form an inclusio around the teacher's instructions, suggesting that his teaching operates within the context and framework of hers.[8]

Lady Wisdom is the subject of much of the rest of Proverbs 1–9.[9] She first appears in 1:20–33 as a street preacher, proclaiming not Yahweh but herself, attacking the audience's stubbornness and their refusal to listen to the message. She assumes the persona and address of a prophet who would seek out crowds in order to deliver a message. Her "reproof" and threatening tone are characteristic of prophetic address, as is the question, "how long?" But most of the vocabulary is that of a teacher, characteristic of the wisdom traditions: "simple ones," "scoffers," "fools hate knowledge," "counsel," and "fear of the LORD." Unlike a prophet, Lady Wisdom demands attention rather than repentance and instead of announcing judgment after the indictment as a prophet would, she offers derision and laughter. Moreover, there is an implication that she herself has a hand in initiating the calamity that will come upon them.

Proverbs 3:13–20 also deals with Lady Wisdom, although vv. 19–20 may be a distinct fragment; by themselves the latter verses do not require that wisdom have any personal qualities, whereas vv. 13–18 definitely envision an individual. The passage emphasizes Lady Wisdom's value by using images of precious metals and jewels. She holds "life" and "riches" in her hands (v. 16) and is called "a tree of life" (v. 18). Yahweh created the world by wisdom and understanding, and Lady Wisdom's links with creation in 8:22–31 suggest that she is meant here as well, although 3:20 does state that Yahweh irrigated the world "by his knowledge."

The longest Lady Wisdom passage is Proverbs 8. Echoing 1:20–21, the chapter opens with another description of Lady Wisdom calling out in the

---

8. Skehan, *Studies*, 12n7 raises but rejects the idea of transposing Prov. 1:8–19 next to the comparable material in Prov. 4:10–19.

9. See also Bálint Károly Zabán, *The Pillar Function of the Speeches of Wisdom: Proverbs 1:20–33, 8:1–36, and 9:1–6 in the Structural Framework of Proverbs 1–9*, BZAW 429 (Berlin: de Gruyter, 2012).

public forum, followed by a lengthy speech divided into four sections. In 8:3–11 she functions as a teacher, describing the value of her words and the benefits that will come from following her teaching, which as in Proverbs 3:14–15 is better than silver, gold, and jewels (8:10–11). The second section, 8:12–21, outlines how rulers use her to govern and reiterates the financial benefits that she brings, once again comparing her favorably to silver and gold.

The high point of the chapter is 8:22–31, with its description of Lady Wisdom's presence with God "at the beginning of his work." A proper understanding of her nature in this poem is contingent on the meaning of *qānānî* in v. 22. The underlying verb *qānâ* usually means "acquire, possess," but it is sometimes rendered "create." Early translators of the Bible into Greek, Syriac, and Latin were split in how they rendered this verb, a division still seen today among the various modern English versions. For example, two widely used translations give the verse as follows:

> The LORD created me at the beginning of his work,
>   the first of his acts long ago. (NRSV)
> The LORD possessed me at the beginning of His way,
>   Before His works of old. (NKJV)

Some argue for the meaning "create" on the basis of Genesis 4:1; 14:19, 22; Deuteronomy 32:6; and Psalm 139:13, but strong counterarguments have been offered in each case.[10] Moreover, if *qānānî* does mean "create" in Proverbs 8:22, then in light of the birth imagery in the following verses it would have the nuance of "procreate" (thus "begot" in NABRE) as in Genesis 4:1, such that the text describes the birth of Wisdom, with Yahweh as her father. This would be supported if *'āmôn* ("master worker") in v. 30 is revocalized as *'ĕmûn* ("little child, infant") with some ancient versions of Proverbs. But rather than emend one word to support an unlikely meaning for another word, it is preferable to assume that the verb *qānâ* has the same meaning in 8:22 as it has in its twelve other occurrences in Proverbs, i.e., "acquire." Moreover, retaining *'āmôn* ("master worker") in v. 30 is consistent with taking "beginning" in v. 22 as the "basis" for the LORD's creative activity. At no point does Lady Wisdom herself create. She simply observes what Yahweh does, much as an architect would provide the blueprint for a project that she herself does not build. Therefore,

---

10. Bruce Vawter, "Proverbs 8:22: Wisdom and Creation," *JBL* 99 (1980): 208–14; Bruce Vawter, "Yahweh: Lord of the Heavens and Earth," *CBQ* 48 (1986): 461–67; see also Peter Katz, "The Meaning of the Root קנה," *JJS* 5 (1954): 126–31.

Lady Wisdom is a being who existed prior to and separate from Yahweh's creation, but also plays a mediating role between heaven and earth. Proverbs 8:30–31 is a mirror pattern with the words "delight" and "rejoicing" before God from 8:30 repeated in the reverse order in 8:31, where they refer to "his inhabited world" and "the human race."

Proverbs 8:32–36 concludes the chapter with Lady Wisdom's exhortation that her "children" attend to her message in order to gain wisdom. Those who do will find life and gain "favor from the LORD" (8:35), but those who reject her will experience death.

The final Lady Wisdom passage is 9:1–6. Proverbs 9:7–12, with the references to rebuking a scoffer, the fear of the LORD, and the contrast between the wise and the scoffer, interrupts the flow of the chapter and is probably an insertion. If those verses are removed, then Lady Wisdom appears side by side with Woman Folly. The repetition of "'You that are simple, turn in here!' / (And) to those without sense she says" in 9:4, 16 indicates that the two women are meant to be compared. However, what they offer to those they invite differs: Lady Wisdom provides bread and wine (9:5) resulting in life (9:6), while Folly offers "stolen water" and "bread eaten in secret" (9:17; both of these have sexual connotations, cf. 5:15–20), which result in death (9:18).

Scholars have interpreted the figure of Lady Wisdom in three ways. First, she may be a literary personification of either wisdom in general or Yahweh's wisdom in particular. Second, perhaps that characteristic eventually took on an independent status as a divine hypostasis, an autonomous entity representing an aspect of Yahweh, much like God's word (*Memra*) and presence (*Shekinah*) did in later Judaism. Third, Lady Wisdom might be a goddess. The final option is most consistent with her portrayal in Proverbs 1–9. In 8:22–31 in particular, Wisdom is definitely an entity distinct from Yahweh; whether he has "acquired" or "created" her, she is separate from him. She takes over a number of Yahweh's roles, as the one to be sought (1:28), the source of royal rule (8:15–16), one who loves and is loved (8:17), the giver of wealth (8:18–21), and the source of life and death (8:35–36). Thus, she acts like a goddess, either independent of Yahweh or born from him.

Scholars have proposed different goddesses as the source for Lady Wisdom's portrayal in Proverbs 1–9.[11] For instance, Maat was the principle of both truth and balance in Egyptian society as well as a goddess embodying

---

11. Compare the discussions in Claudia V. Camp, *Wisdom and the Feminine in the Book of Proverbs*, BLS 11 (Sheffield: Almond, 1985), 21–70 and Alice M. Sinnott, *The Personification of Wisdom*, SOTSMS (Aldershot: Ashgate, 2005), 10–52.

these characteristics. She was represented as an amulet giving protection and life, just as the sage's teaching was a garland worn for safety (1:8–9; 3:3; 6:21). Egyptian judges and the vizier wore her picture around their neck to express exemplary service to Maat, while Wisdom bestows a crown and a garland of honor (4:3–9). Both Maat and Wisdom existed before creation, are the effective agent in the king's rule, and they love and are loved by Yahweh or the gods. Maat holds the ankh, the symbol of life, in one hand and a scepter in another, which is comparable to Proverbs 3:16 ("Long life is in her right hand; in her left hand are riches and honor"). But one should not rush to identify the two deities as the same. Many other deities, such as Resheph, also hold life in their hand, and some of the other motifs connecting Maat and Wisdom may be attributable to a more general background. There is probably some influence from Maat to Wisdom, but there is an important difference between the two: the gods must live in accordance with Maat, but Wisdom is subordinate to Yahweh, serving as the medium through which he creates.

Another possible precursor closer to Israel's home is Asherah, the consort of the chief Canaanite deity El, who is the mother of the gods. Among other aspects, she is a fertility goddess frequently represented as a tree, which in one instance is nursing a king, and her cultic symbol, the *'ăšērâ*, was probably a stylized tree. Thus, she is a tree of life, as is Lady Wisdom in Proverbs 3:18 (but contrast 11:30; 15:4). Moreover, the word "happy" (*'ašrê*) is linked to Lady Wisdom in 3:13, 18, and the Hebrew *'ašrê* echoes the opening syllables of the name Asherah.

While these and other deities parallel the figure of Lady Wisdom, Bernhard Lang proposes that she was an Israelite goddess who served as the patron of the schools, held up as an exemplar for the schoolboys to seek.[12] Certainly her presence at creation and even prior to it, as well as her possible architectonic role, enhances her portrait and legitimizes her authority. But without denying this possibility, another aspect of Wisdom's function may lie precisely in the echoes of other goddesses, as a counter to their potential attraction. In Proverbs 9 she is explicitly paralleled with Folly, who offers sex to passersby but whose way or path, in contrast to that of Wisdom, leads to death. Woman Folly echoes the "strange woman" that the young men are warned against in the instructions of Proverbs 1–7. In at least one instance there is a cultic context for this strange woman's words (7:14–15), which implies that she is a participant in the fertility cult who is actively seeking to consummate her involvement

---

12. Bernhard Lang, *Wisdom and the Book of Proverbs: An Israelite Goddess Redefined* (New York: Pilgrim, 1986).

through sexual intercourse. However, she leads the young man astray through "seductive speech" (7:21), not through actions.

But wisdom also operates in the realm of speech, and Lady Wisdom serves as a counter to Woman Folly and the strange woman on two levels. First, Lady Wisdom assimilates Asherah's characteristics, as noted above, in order to weaken her attraction by taking over her fertility role. If Lady Wisdom provides fertility, then Asherah is unnecessary. This is a common feature of religious development, seen also in Yahweh's assimilation of certain features of the Canaanite deity El, Yahweh's assumption of many of Baal's functions and characteristics, setting the date of Christmas to compete with the Roman feast of Sol Invictus, or the timing of All Saints Day with ancient Druid festivals. Second, Lady Wisdom is an exemplar of marital fidelity. The reader is encouraged to find wisdom (3:13; 8:17, 35) just as one finds a good wife (18:22; 31:10). Proverbs 8:35 and 18:22 are especially striking, with their identical second lines:

> For whoever finds me finds life
>   and obtains favor from the LORD. (Prov. 8:35)
> He who finds a wife finds a good thing,
>   and obtains favor from the LORD. (Prov. 18:22)

Other marital language includes the admonition to "love and embrace" wisdom (4:6–8) and to call her "sister" (7:4; cf. Song 4:9–5:1). The exhortation to watch at her gates (8:34) may also have the same connotation as it has in Song of Songs 2:9. In other words, Lady Wisdom is presented as the ideal wife, and a spiritual or mystical marriage to her helps undermine any temptation to commit adultery.

Proverbs 6:1–19 contains additional material beyond the Instruction genre and the Lady Wisdom passages. Proverbs 6:1–5 offers advice against surety in loans; while it is addressed to "my child," it is distinguished from the Instruction form by the lack of reference to the speaker's words or motives for listening. Proverbs 6:6–11 uses the example of the industrious ant as a counterpoint to the sluggard who stays in bed, resulting in poverty. Proverbs 6:12–15 describes a person of "crooked speech" who uses different parts of the body to deceive others but also meets a negative fate. Finally, Proverbs 6:16–19 is a numerical saying that utilizes the x / x+1 formula (cf. Prov. 30) to itemize "six things that the LORD hates, / seven that are an abomination to him."

Proverbs 10:1–22:16

The beginning and end of this section are established by the titles in Proverbs 10:1 and 22:17. It is distinguished from the preceding section by the difference in form, which changes from the Instruction genre and Lady Wisdom passages to two-line sayings, although there are editorial links with the previous section. "Child" occurs in 10:1, but there it is a third-person reference rather than the direct address found in the instructions of Proverbs 1–7. Similarly, the two ways of the wicked and righteous are reflected in 10:2, 3, 6, 7, surrounding two sayings about laziness in vv. 4–5.

This is a diverse collection of self-contained individual sayings, which often have little thematic connection to each other. Knut Heim divides the entire section into a series of "proverbial clusters," but this is often a matter of catchword repetitions, or shared syntax or structural features rather than shared content.[13] For instance, 10:14 and 15 repeat the word "ruin" while 10:16 and 17 share the phrase "to life," but the content of both pairs is quite different. Similarly, 15:29–32 has different but related words for "hearing," with the last two verses repeating "heed admonition," while vv. 29 and 32 are antithetical lines surrounding synonymous and synthetic sayings in vv. 30–31. However, Heim's clusters often divide verses that others might link. He treats 10:6–11, 12–18, and 19–22 as separate units, although the verb *ksh* occurs in both vv. 11 and 12, and vv. 18–21 all deal with speech. He also divides 16:1–9, 10–11, and 12–15, but vv. 1–7, 9, 11 are about the LORD and vv. 10, 12–15 about kings; this overlap indicates that the two topics should be interpreted in light of each other.

Despite the absence of a clear structure for the entire section, it is still possible to identify common features within Proverbs 10:1–22:16. One example is the predominance of antithetical parallelism in Proverbs 10–15, with non-antithetical parallelism being more frequent from Proverbs 16 on, which might indicate earlier collections that have been combined. R. B. Y. Scott grouped the proverbs into seven types that structure human experience: (1) "identity, equivalence, or invariable association"; (2) "non-identity, contrast, or paradox"; (3) "similarity, analogy, or type"; (4) "what is contrary to right order, and so is futile or absurd"; (5) what "classifies and characterizes persons, actions,

---

13. Knut Martin Heim, *Like Grapes of Gold Set in Silver: An Interpretation of Proverbial Clusters in Proverbs 10:1–22:16*, BZAW 273 (Berlin: de Gruyter, 2001). Compare the earlier, less ambitious identification of "proverbial pairs" on similar grounds in Ted Hildebrandt, "Proverbial Pairs: Compositional Units in Proverbs 10–29," *JBL* 107 (1988): 207–24.

or situations"; (6) "value, relative value or priority, proportion or degree"; and (7) "the consequences of human character and behavior."[14]

In addition, the simple sentence form vastly outnumbers the admonition and prohibition combined.[15] While the latter contain specific advice with reasons for doing so, the sentences make simple observations that leave any decision up to the reader. Sometimes these provide insight into human nature and affairs, as in the following examples:

> Some pretend to be rich, yet have nothing;
>> others pretend to be poor, yet have great wealth. (Prov. 13:7)
> The poor are disliked even by their neighbors,
>> but the rich have many friends. (Prov. 14:20)
> A soft tongue turns away wrath
>> but a harsh word stirs up anger. (Prov. 15:1)
> "Bad, bad," says the buyer,
>> then goes away and boasts. (Prov. 20:14)

Note that these sayings do not specify what to do. The first two present contrasting financial situations, and while most people prefer to be wealthy than poor, instead of explicitly endorsing that option both sayings require that the reader make the decision. Proverbs 15:1 implies that a "soft tongue" is better than a "harsh tongue," but once again leaves it up to the reader to make the determination. Finally, 20:14 simply describes a haggler's attempt to negotiate a lower price through a negative evaluation of the item followed by his true perspective after the purchase.

Some proverbs make analogies between nature and humankind. At times this is explicitly conveyed by a simile using a comparative particle ("like," translating the Hebrew *kî*):

> Like snow in summer or rain in harvest,
>> so honor is not fitting for a fool. (Prov. 26:1)
> Like a dog that returns to its vomit
>> is a fool who reverts to his folly. (Prov. 26:11)

---

14. R. B. Y. Scott, *Proverbs, Ecclesiastes: A New Translation with Introduction and Commentary*, 2nd ed., AB 18 (Garden City: Doubleday, 1965), 5–8. See also R. B. Y. Scott, *The Way of Wisdom in the Old Testament* (New York: Collier, 1971), 59–63.

15. By Zimmerli's count, the admonition occurs only 25 times out of 402 sayings in the two main collections, i.e., Proverbs 10:1–22:16 and Proverbs 25–29; see Walther Zimmerli, "Concerning the Structure of Old Testament Wisdom," in *Studies in Ancient Israelite Wisdom*, ed. James L. Crenshaw (New York: Ktav, 1976), 182.

Other proverbs simply place two statements together without an explicit comparison:

> A door turns on its hinges,
>> a lazy person turns in bed. (Prov. 26:14, author's translation)
> One who takes a passing dog by the ears,
>> one who meddles in the quarrel of another. (Prov. 26:17, author's
>> translation)

Again, it is usually obvious what is a preferable course of action, but since it is not explicitly stated, the reader must decide what to do. This is especially so with those sayings that do not make the comparison explicit. When two observations are presented next to each other without the comparative *kî* ("like"), the reader has to determine the common element between the two halves. Unfortunately, this is undermined when modern translations add comparative words that are not present in the Hebrew. For instance, the NRSV inserts the word "so" in Proverbs 26:14b and "like" at 26:17a, imposing a correlation between the two parts that makes what was meant to be implicit into an explicit comparison and preventing the reader from participating in the pedagogical intent of the original sayings.

Another feature of the proverbs in this and other sections of the book is the presence of doublets, where sayings are repeated both within individual sections and across them.[16] Sometimes verbatim repetition occurs, as in the case of 14:12 and 16:25 ("There is a way that seems right to a person, / but its end is the way to death"). A comparable phenomenon is when the same idea is conveyed using different words, in a form of distant parallelism, such as:

> All one's ways may be pure in one's own eyes,
>> but the LORD weighs the spirit. (Prov. 16:2)
> All deeds are right in the sight of the doer,
>> but the LORD weighs the heart. (Prov. 21:2)

---

16. Complete lists of doublets in the book of Proverbs, with discussions, can be found in Daniel C. Snell, *Twice-Told Proverbs and the Composition of the Book of Proverbs* (Winona Lake, IN: Eisenbrauns, 1993); Knut Martin Heim, *Poetic Imagination in Proverbs: Variant Repetitions and the Nature of Poetry*, BBRSup 4 (Winona Lake, IN: Eisenbrauns, 2012).

Alternatively, comparable ideas can be expressed in different ways:

> The wise are cautious and turn away from evil,
>> but the fool throws off restraint and is careless. (Prov. 14:16)
> The clever see danger and hide;
>> but the simple go on, and suffer for it. (Prov. 22:3)

Other doublets display varying degrees of change from one to the other. For instance, they may have identical first lines while the second lines differ slightly:

> A false witness will not go unpunished,
>> and a liar will not escape. (Prov. 19:5)
> A false witness will not go unpunished,
>> and the liar will perish. (Prov. 19:9)

In some doublets, the second lines are so different that they have completely different conclusions:

> The wealth of the rich is their fortress;
>> the poverty of the poor is their ruin. (Prov. 10:15)
> The wealth of the rich is their strong city;
>> in their imagination it is like a high wall. (Prov. 18:11)

Proverbs 10:15 compares the rich and the poor but 18:11 indicates that the former's trust in their wealth is illusory. Similarly, compare the following proverbs:

> Those who oppress the poor insult their Maker,
>> but those who are kind to the needy honor him. (Prov. 14:31)
> Those who mock the poor insult their Maker;
>> those who are glad at calamity will not go unpunished. (Prov. 17:5)

The first contrasts two attitudes toward weaker members of society while the second affirms the punishment of those who oppress them. A different second line might even transform an indicative saying into a prohibition:

> A gossip goes about telling secrets,
>> but one who is trustworthy in spirit keeps a confidence. (Prov. 11:13)
> A gossip reveals secrets;
>> therefore do not associate with a babbler. (Prov. 20:19)

On the other hand, the opening lines in two doublets can differ while the second lines remain the same:

> The teaching of the wise is a fountain of life,
>> so that one may avoid the snares of death. (Prov. 13:14)
> The fear of the LORD is a fountain of life,
>> so that one may avoid the snares of death. (Prov. 14:27)

Diachronically, doublets indicate that some sayings circulated in different contexts before being combined into the final form of Proverbs.[17] But reading synchronically, these repeated sayings have two different effects. First, exact duplication and common ideas expressed through comparable words emphasize the duplication and suggest that their content is important enough to be repeated. Second, those that have different first or second lines indicate that sayings might not be universally applicable and the reader is left to decide which formulation applies in different contexts.

Proverbs 22:17–24:22

There are two indications that these verses constitute a distinct section. First, Proverbs 24:23 begins the subsequent section with "these also are sayings of the wise," and the word "also" points to a preceding reference to "the wise," namely in 22:17. Second, the form switches from the proverbs in the previous section to the Instruction genre, characterized by direct address in the form of commands and prohibitions followed by motives why the particular advice should be followed, introduced by "for," "because," "in order that," "lest," and so on.

There is a clear literary relationship between this section and the Egyptian *Instruction of Amenemope*.[18] There are extensive lexical similarities between

---

17. Snell, *Twice-Told Proverbs*, 10–14, 30–62; Heim, *Poetic Imagination in Proverbs*, 610–33.

18. For a treatment of this relationship as well as Proverbs's dependence on the *Instruction of Amenemope*, see Nili Shupak, "The Instruction of Amenemope and Proverbs 22:17–24:22 from the Perspective of Contemporary Research," in *Seeking Out the Wisdom of the Ancients: Essays Offered to Honor Michael V. Fox on the Occasion of His Sixty-Fifth Birthday*, ed. Ronald L. Troxel, Kelvin G. Friebel, and Dennis Robert Magary (Winona Lake, IN: Eisenbrauns, 2005), 203–20. She responds to challenges to the consensus view by R. N. Whybray, *Wealth and Poverty in the Book of Proverbs*, JSOTSup 99 (Sheffield: JSOT Press, 1990), 85–98; R. N. Whybray, *The Composition of the Book of Proverbs*, JSOTSup 168 (Sheffield: JSOT Press, 1994), 132–45.

Proverbs 22:17–18 and the beginning of *Amenemope*'s actual Instruction, appearing in the same order in both texts:[19]

PROVERBS 22:17–18	AMENEMOPE 3:9–11, 13, 16
The words of the wise:	
Incline your ear and hear my words,	Give your ears, hear the sayings,
and apply your mind to my teaching;	Give your heart to understand them;
for it will be pleasant if you	It profits to put them in your heart . . .
keep them within you,	let them rest in the casket of your belly . . .
if all of them are ready on your lips.	They'll be a mooring post for your tongue.

Proverbs 22:20–21 then refers to "thirty sayings" that will enable an appropriate response to "those who sent you," just as *Amenemope* has thirty chapters that serve the same purpose. In Proverbs this is followed by a sequence of sayings that share concepts and at times wording with *Amenemope*:[20]

1. Do not oppress the poor (Prov. 22:22–23; *Amen.* 4:4–5)
2. Avoid an angry/heated man lest he trap you (Prov. 22:24–25; *Amen.* 11:11–12)
3. Do not remove a landmark (Prov. 22:28; 23:10a; *Amen.* 7:12)
4. Skilled courtiers (Prov. 22:29; *Amen.* 27:16)
5. Dining etiquette with rulers (Prov. 23:1–3; *Amen.* 23:13)
6. Do not toil for wealth that flies away like a bird (Prov. 23:4–5; *Amen.* 9:14–15)
7. Do not eat the bread of the stingy/poor (Prov. 23:6–7; *Amen.* 14:5–6)
8. You will vomit (Prov. 23:8a; *Amen.* 14:8, 17)
9. And ruin your speech (Prov. 23:8b; *Amen.* 14:14)

19. The translation of the *Instruction of Amenemope* is from Miriam Lichtheim, *Ancient Egyptian Literature*, vol. 2: *The New Kingdom* (Berkeley: University of California Press, 2006), 149.

20. Cf. the charts in Shupak, "The Instruction of Amenemope," 218–19; Michael V. Fox, *Proverbs 10–31: A New Translation with Introduction and Commentary*, AB 18B (New York: Doubleday, 2009), 758–60.

10. Guard who you speak to, lest you lose their respect (Prov. 23:9; *Amen.* 22:11–12)
11. Do not enter the field of an orphan/another (Prov. 23:10b-11; *Amen.* 8:15)

A number of points indicate that Proverbs is dependent on *Amenemope* rather than the reverse. First, the *Instruction of Amenemope* was written during the thirteenth to eleventh centuries BCE, which means that this portion of Proverbs would have to have been compiled during the premonarchical period or even before the emergence of ancient Israel in order to have circulated to Egypt and influenced *Amenemope*. Second, the shared material is sequential in Proverbs but in different parts of *Amenemope*. There is no reason for *Amenemope* to disrupt the sequence in Proverbs; it makes more sense that Proverbs imposed order on an originally more haphazard collection of sayings. Third, the divergent locations in *Amenemope* and the fact that the parallels end at Proverbs 23:11 are best explained by the biblical author writing from memory and supplementing what he remembered in order to reach a total of thirty sayings. Fourth, some aspects of the common material are more at home in an Egyptian context than an Israelite one. For instance, the number thirty has little significance in Israel but it does in Egypt,[21] and although inclining the ear is a common biblical motif, it is not linked to "mind" elsewhere in the First Testament. Also, the Hebrew phrase translated "within you" (Prov. 22:18) is literally "in your belly" as in *Amenemope* rather than the usual Israelite idiom, "in your kidneys." Fifth, there are signs that some material has been adapted to an Israelite context: Proverbs 22:22 specifies the gate as the place of justice and Proverbs 23:10 links moving a landmark with injustice against an orphan, two frequent biblical motifs. Similar to the second point above, it makes more sense that the biblical author added these nuances than that the Egyptian author removed them.

The material that does not match *Amenemope* continues the Instruction form, with frequent calls for a child to listen to a father, and the content contains traditional wisdom themes such as the value of wisdom itself, the contrast between the wise and foolish as well as the wicked and the righteous, warnings against wicked women, and so on. As such, there are frequent points of contact with the rest of the book, such that this section serves as a bridge between the first part of Proverbs and its concluding sections. Proverbs 23:13–14 extols the educational benefits of physical discipline for children as in 13:24. Drunkenness and gluttony are dealt with in 23:19–21, anticipating

---

21. Fox, *Proverbs 10–31*, 711.

31:4–5, while 23:22–25 indicates the desirability of wisdom, echoing the first section of the book. Proverbs 23:29–35 discusses drunkenness at much greater length than 20:1; 21:17; 23:20–21; 31:4–5. The effect of the amusing opening rhyme in 23:29 (*lĕmî 'ôy lĕmî 'ăbôy*) can be conveyed as "who has shakes, who has aches" or "who moans, who groans." Additional questions lead to the identification of the drinker in v. 30, followed by the longest prohibition in Proverbs. The command to abstain from wine in v. 31 is followed in vv. 32–35a by the reasons it should be avoided, namely its hallucinatory effects and the attendant hangovers, and the passage ends (v. 35b) with the folly of someone who seeks another drink. The construction of a house by means of wisdom in Proverbs 24:3–4 points in both directions, back to Lady Wisdom's house in chapter 9 and the noble woman's household in 31:10–31. The rest of the section deals with typical wisdom contrasts between the wise and the foolish as well as good and evil doers, and concludes with an admonition to respect both God and the king. The implication is that the king cooperates with God in the administration of justice, and whatever the king misses, God will not. Moreover, the king could act as the agent of Yahweh's chastisement, or both may act independently.

Proverbs 24:23–34

This brief section is delineated by the new title at v. 23 ("these also are the sayings of the wise") and another for the next section at Proverbs 25:1. It contains two different subjects: honesty in speech (vv. 23–26, 28–29) and the value of work (vv. 27, 30–34). The first focuses on a legal context, instructing judges and witnesses not to pervert justice in the courts; v. 29 is a negative formulation of the Golden Rule. Proverbs 24:27 stresses the importance of work, while vv. 30–34 use an example story to drive the point home. Observation of a sluggard's property, with a run-down house and overgrown fields, provides an opportunity for instruction. The moral is found in vv. 33–34, which is identical to 6:10–11:

> A little sleep, a little slumber,
>> a little folding of the hands to rest,
> and poverty will come upon you like a robber,
>> and want, like an armed warrior.

Proverbs 25–29

The first two chapters of this section display greater thematic and structural coherence than the latter three.[22] After the section heading, Proverbs 25:2–27 is demarcated by a chiastic inclusio: the roots *kbd* ("glory") and *ḥqr* ("search") from v. 2b are repeated in the reverse order as "seek honor" in v. 27b. At the same time, the passage is subdivided by the semantic inclusio of "king" in v. 2 and "ruler" in v. 15, plus a chiastic inclusio created by reversing "honey" and "eat" in v. 16a as "eat . . . honey" in v. 27a. The first half of the chapter begins by contrasting the actions of God and the king; as God is to the king so the king is to the people. This is followed by a description of a metalsmith purifying silver for a vessel, which leads into the removal of the wicked as the dross of society. Proverbs 25:6–15 expands upon the two topics of interactions with kings and commoners. Verses 6–7b deal with keeping your proper place in the royal court when you come before the king. Proverbs 25:7c–10 switches to the law court, identifying first visual and then verbal matters: if you are unable to resolve a matter with a neighbor, then the judge ("one who hears"; v. 10) may rule against you. Verses 11–12 intermingle verbal expression with visual imagery using jewelry, still within a legal context: "speak a word" is used of rendering a decision (Judg. 11:11; 1 Sam. 20:23; 1 Kings 12:7; Isa. 8:10; 58:13; Hos. 10:4) and "rebuke" has a juridical sense (cf. Amos 5:10; Job 9:33). Weather imagery in Proverbs 25:13–14 conveys the positive status of a messenger and the negative status of a boaster, continuing the focus on speech. The subsection then returns to the ruler, summarizing the court and social conflicts from the preceding verses.

The second half of the chapter repeats elements from the first half in the same order. Verses 16–17 encourage restraint in both food and visiting others, echoing vv. 6–7b, while vv. 18–19 discourage "false witness against a neighbor" and misplaced trust, alluding to the legal concerns of vv. 7c-10. Improper speech in v. 20 contrasts with the proper speech from v. 11, the hope of reconciliation from v. 12 is repeated in vv. 21–22, and the weather imagery in vv. 13–14 is reflected in vv. 23–24, with the positive news and improper people from the same verses echoed in vv. 25 and 26 respectively.

Proverbs 26 divides into three parts focusing on three different topics. With the exception of v. 2, the first twelve verses all focus on fools. But v. 2 has structural and thematic links to vv. 1 and 3: each is a three-part saying describ-

---

22. My discussion of Proverbs 25–27 is indebted to Raymond C. Van Leeuwen, *Context and Meaning in Proverbs 25–27*, SBLDS 96 (Atlanta: Scholars Press, 1988).

ing what is fitting or unfitting, with vv. 1–2 having a common structure of "like ... like ... so" (the repetition of $k + k + k\bar{e}n$ in the two verses is not reflected in the NRSV) while vv. 2 and 3 both employ animal imagery. Apart from v. 2, the other sayings describe either someone relating to a fool (vv. 1, 3–6, 8, 10, 12) or the fool acting (vv. 7, 9, 11) and if the prohibition and admonition in vv. 4–5 are set aside, the remaining verses alternate their focus. Following that pattern, v. 2 would be the fool acting, specifically uttering a causeless curse. The juxtaposition of explicitly contrary advice in vv. 4 and 5 forces the reader to determine which is appropriate in any given situation. Some of the other sayings are notable for their dramatic (e.g., vv. 6, 7) or humorous (vv. 9, 11) content. The section ends by ranking "persons wise in their own eyes" as worse than fools (note the phrase in Prov. 26:5 as well).

Proverbs 26:13–16 is concerned with lazy people, as are the "sluggard" passages of 6:6–11; 24:30–34. Both of the latter tell a story and end with the same refrain: "A little sleep, a little slumber, / a little folding of the hands to rest, / and poverty will come upon you like a robber, / and want, like an armed man." Here, instead of a story there are three humorous sayings indicating how a lazy person invents excuses not to go out, doesn't get out of bed, and is even too lazy to eat. The final statement describing the lazy person as "wiser in self-esteem" is literally "more wise in his own eyes," echoing 26:12 and indicating that laziness and foolishness go hand in hand.

The concluding reference to those "who can answer discreetly" (26:16) leads into 26:17–28, which centers on the opposite, namely improper speech, with four inclusios. Verses 17–19 introduce two themes, namely a quarrel and the one who attacks another with words, and are set off by the repetition of "not": "a quarrel *not* his own" and "was I *not* joking?" Verses 20–22, which begin and end with a "whisperer," develop these two themes, since words can either maintain (26:20) or start (26:21) a quarrel and wound one's inner being. With "heart" forming a third inclusio (the NRSV's "within" in the latter is literally "in his heart"), 26:23–25 contrasts inner and outer attitudes. Verses 26–28, which are marked by the repetition of *śn'* ("hatred" and "hates"), indicate the external consequences, with an implicit warning to those who speak improperly.

The rest of this section has decreasing amounts of unity. Proverbs 27:1–22 contains disparate sayings that occasionally have verbal or thematic links. For instance, 27:1–2 rejects boasting in favor of another's praise, 27:4–5 deals with anger and rebuke, 27:13–14 discusses relationships, and 27:15–17 contrasts the grating effect of a "contentious wife" with the more positive honing effect of two people interacting. But more often the section simply moves to different topics in successive verses, although the theme of personal interactions does arise frequently (note the loud neighbor in the morning; 27:14), alongside topics from the preceding chapters like the fool (27:3, 12, 22) and the importance of wisdom (27:11). Proverbs 27:23–27 is more cohesive, dwelling on the importance of tending one's flocks in order to gain the benefit they bring, namely clothing and milk. Proverbs 28–29 consists primarily of antithetical proverbs, although their content is disjointed. The same contrasts encountered earlier in the book are present, for example, between the wicked and the righteous (28:1, 4, 5, 10, 12; 29:6, 7, 27; note especially the similar formulation of 28:12, 28; 29:2, 16), the foolish and the wise (28:26; 29:8, 9, 11), and the poor and the rich (28:6, 11). The problem of oppressive kings and other rulers appears frequently as well (28:3, 15–16; 29:4, 12, 14, 26).

Proverbs 30

This chapter is attributed to Agur, son of Jakeh, in its entirety, although the numerical sayings in 30:15–31 are distinct from Agur's words, based on their different form and content. The word *hammaśśā'* in v. 1 can be taken in two ways. Agur may be a Massaite, from the north Arabian tribe allegedly descending from a certain Massa (Gen. 25:14; 1 Chron. 1:30). Thus his words may represent international wisdom, even though the content is consistent with Israelite religious beliefs, including invoking the name Yahweh in v. 9. Alternatively, the word *hammaśśā'* means "the oracle," which indicates a prophetic revelation. Surprising for a wisdom text, he denies having any wisdom or knowledge of either human or divine things. No one can enter heaven or control nature (cf. Job 28; 38–39), but God is reliable, so Agur prays that he might have a moderate lifestyle so that he may not sin against God. The text then switches its form and focus to a prohibition against slandering a servant and a list of four unsavory kinds of people. The latter does not employ the x / x+1 formulation used by the numerical sayings in the rest of the chapter. Those x / x+1 sayings each describe four things that are, in turn, never satisfied (30:15–16), beyond understanding (30:18–19), unacceptable (30:21–23), small but wise (30:24–28), and stately when they walk (30:29–31). In most of these the connection among the items is clear, but the second (30:18–19) and fifth (30:29–31) sayings include a thematic twist when the way of an eagle, snake, and ship are linked to "the way of a man with a girl" and when a lion, rooster, and goat are followed a king. Each of the numerical sayings reflects the effort of the wise to categorize and classify human experience, and the divergent final element in those two cases provokes further reflection on how the items are connected. Interspersed among the numerical sayings are individual statements about disrespectful children (30:17), an adulterous woman (30:20), and those who provoke others (30:32–33).

Proverbs 31

The first nine verses contain the words taught to King Lemuel by his mother. As with Agur, either Lemuel is a Massaite who is otherwise unknown in history or the teaching is called an oracle. While not exactly the same, formally this passage mirrors an Instruction with an address to a son, admonitions, and motives. It contains warnings about women and alcohol, although the latter is recommended for the dying and depressed—a king must retain a clear mind in order to rule properly, but alcohol's sedative effect will help those suffering. The final exhortation is for the king to judge properly and to defend the destitute, poor, and needy.

This section ends with an acrostic poem about a "noble woman/wife" in which each of the successive twenty-two lines begins with the next letter of the Hebrew alphabet. Since there is no formal break with the preceding verses, the poem can be read as part of the teaching that Lemuel's mother conveyed to him. As such it balances the brief warning against women who could destroy him, just as the advice about alcohol is balanced with respect to the king and the suffering. The acrostic structure combined with its thematic content suggests that it serves as an intentional conclusion to the entire book, with the alphabetic acrostic further implying that it encompasses the totality of wisdom from A to Z.

The poem describes a woman who manages her family's internal and external affairs. Not only does she care for the needs of her "household," the traditional role of women in ancient Israel, which is mentioned three times (31:15, 21, 27), but she also takes on relations with the outside world. She engages in commercial ventures, importing food (31:14), buying a field then using the profit to plant a vineyard (31:16), and selling merchandise (31:18, 24), such that "her works praise her in the city gates" (31:31). Although there were exceptions, typically such activities were handled by the eldest male in the family, but her husband is only mentioned to indicate the benefits she brings to him (31:11–12), the leisure that allows him to enjoy respect among the regional elders in the city gate (31:23; cf. 31:31), and his effusive praise of her (31:28–29). In light of the description of the woman, the NRSV's translation as a "capable wife" in v. 10 does not do justice to the Hebrew word *ḥayil*, which connotes superior ability and even valor. Instead, it is more proper to characterize her as "strong" or even "noble."

Moreover, she is not just commercially successful; her very life is consistent with the rest of the book of Proverbs. She uses the products of her labor to provide for the poor and needy (31:19–20) and speaks not only wisdom but kindness (31:26), which demonstrate that she fears Yahweh (31:30). But in addition to reflecting wisdom teachings, she is also linked with Lady Wisdom.[23] The poem's opening question, "A noble wife, who can find?" echoes the statement in 18:22 that "he who finds a wife finds a good thing." But the reader was also regularly encouraged to "find" Wisdom (3:13; 8:17, 35). The similarity between 8:35 and 18:22 is especially instructive, in light of their identical second lines:

> For whoever finds me finds life
> > and obtains favor from the LORD. (Prov. 8:35)
> He who finds a wife finds a good thing,
> > and obtains favor from the LORD. (Prov. 18:22)

In other words, finding a wife is comparable to finding Wisdom. This link is reinforced by the fact that the noble wife is "far more precious than jewels" (31:10), which apart from the word "far" is said verbatim of Wisdom in 3:15 and in slightly different words in 8:11 ("wisdom is better than jewels").

But despite these parallels, the woman is not identified with Lady Wisdom. This is not Lady Wisdom, settled down and domesticated, as has been suggested.[24] The poem's opening question is not rhetorical, anticipating a negative answer, since it is followed by twenty-one verses describing a woman in terms that are far too concrete to represent the incarnation of the cosmic figure from Proverbs 8 now domesticated with husband and children, running a family business, managing her estate, and organizing her servants. This is not some unobtainable ideal held up as a model for the reader to emulate, but rather a real person who embodies all that Wisdom entails and promises.[25] This noble woman demonstrates that wisdom is not

23. For these and other parallels see Christine Roy Yoder, *Wisdom as a Woman of Substance: A Socioeconomic Reading of Proverbs 1–9 and 31:10–31*, BZAW 304 (Berlin: de Gruyter, 2001), 91–93.

24. Thomas P. McCreesh, "Wisdom as Wife: Prov. 31:10–31," *RB* 92 (1985): 25–46.

25. Al Wolters, "Ṣôpiyyâ (Prov 31:27) as Hymnic Participle and Play on *Sophia*," *JBL* 104 (1985): 577–87, argues that Prov. 31:27 provides a clue to this, where "she looks well (*ṣôpiyyâ*)

an abstract concept to be contemplated and admired, but a way of life, a principle by which one actually can organize and structure one's life. The combination of a concrete human being with identifiable allusions to Lady Wisdom illustrates that the ideals of the wisdom tradition can be successfully put into practice.

Summary

In light of the preceding it is now possible to identify a general overarching development across the book of Proverbs. In the first section, Lady Wisdom invites the reader to accept her as the guide to a successful life, as articulated in the Instructions. The subsequent sections contain shorter proverbial sentences, admonitions, and prohibitions that challenge the reader to make choices about various aspects of life. The final poem describes this wisdom embodied in the life of the noble woman who successfully runs her family's household and business while living a life that reflects wisdom's ethical and religious ideals.

FURTHER READING

Commentaries

Clifford, Richard J. *Proverbs: A Commentary*. OTL. Louisville: Westminster John Knox, 1999.

Cox, Dermot. *Proverbs, with an Introduction to the Sapiential Books*. OTM 17. Wilmington, DE: Glazier, 1982.

Farmer, Kathleen. *Who Knows What Is Good? A Commentary on the Books of Proverbs and Ecclesiastes*. ITC. Grand Rapids: Eerdmans / Edinburgh: Handsel, 1991.

Fox, Michael V. *Proverbs 1–9: A New Translation with Introduction and Commentary*. AB 18A. New York: Doubleday, 2000.

———. *Proverbs 10–31: A New Translation with Introduction and Commentary*. AB 18B. New York: Doubleday, 2009.

———. *Proverbs: An Eclectic Edition with Introduction and Textual Commentary*. Hebrew Bible 1. Atlanta: SBL Press, 2015.

---

to the ways of her household" plays on the Greek *sophia* ("wisdom"), such that "wisdom is the ways of her household."

Garrett, Duane A. *Proverbs, Ecclesiastes, Song of Songs*. NAC 14. Nashville: Broadman & Holman, 1993.

Hayes, Katherine M. *Proverbs*. New Collegeville Bible Commentary 18. Collegeville, MN: Liturgical Press, 2013.

Longman, Tremper, III. *Proverbs*. BCOTWP. Grand Rapids: Baker Academic, 2006.

Lucas, Ernest. *Proverbs*. THOTC. Grand Rapids: Eerdmans, 2015.

McKane, William. *Proverbs: A New Approach*. OTL. Philadelphia: Westminster, 1970.

Moss, Alan. *Proverbs*. Readings: A New Biblical Commentary. Sheffield: Sheffield Phoenix, 2015.

Murphy, Roland E. *Proverbs*. WBC 22. Nashville: Thomas Nelson, 1998.

Murphy, Roland E., and Elizabeth Huwiler. *Proverbs, Ecclesiastes, Song of Songs*. NIBCOT 12. Peabody, MA: Hendrickson, 1999.

Perdue, Leo G. *Proverbs*. Interpretation. Louisville: Westminster John Knox, 2000.

Scott, R. B. Y. *Proverbs, Ecclesiastes: A New Translation with Introduction and Commentary*. 2nd ed. AB 18. Garden City: Doubleday, 1965.

Steinmann, Andrew E. *Proverbs*. Concordia Commentary. St. Louis: Concordia, 2010.

Toy, C. H. *A Critical and Exegetical Commentary on the Book of Proverbs*. ICC. Edinburgh: T&T Clark, 1899.

Waltke, Bruce K. *The Book of Proverbs: Chapters 1–15*. NICOT. Grand Rapids: Eerdmans, 2004.

———. *The Book of Proverbs: Chapters 15–31*. NICOT. Grand Rapids: Eerdmans, 2005.

Whybray, R. N. *The Book of Proverbs*. CBC. Cambridge: Cambridge University Press, 1972.

———. *Proverbs*. NCB. Grand Rapids: Eerdmans, 1994.

Yoder, Christine Roy. *Proverbs*. AOTC. Nashville: Abingdon, 2009.

Other Works

Ansberry, Christopher B. *Be Wise, My Son, and Make My Heart Glad: An Exploration of the Courtly Nature of the Book of Proverbs*. BZAW 422. Berlin: de Gruyter, 2011.

Boström, Lennart. *The God of the Sages: The Portrayal of God in the Book of Proverbs*. ConBOT 29. Stockholm: Almqvist & Wiksell, 1990.

Camp, Claudia V. *Wisdom and the Feminine in the Book of Proverbs.* BLS 11. Sheffield: Almond Press, 1985.

Dell, Katharine J. *The Book of Proverbs in Social and Theological Context.* Cambridge: Cambridge University Press, 2006.

Estes, Daniel J. *Hear, My Son: Teaching and Learning in Proverbs 1–9.* Grand Rapids: Eerdmans, 1997.

Fontaine, Carole R. *Smooth Words: Women, Proverbs and Performance in Biblical Wisdom.* JSOTSup 356. Sheffield: Sheffield Academic, 2002.

———. *Traditional Sayings in the Old Testament: A Contextual Study.* BLS 5. Sheffield: Almond Press, 1982.

Forti, Tova L. *Animal Imagery in the Book of Proverbs.* VTSup 118. Leiden: Brill, 2007.

Frydych, Tomáš. *Living under the Sun: Examination of Proverbs and Qoheleth.* VTSup 90. Leiden: Brill, 2002.

Harris, Scott L. *Proverbs 1–9: A Study of Inner-Biblical Exegesis.* SBLDS 150. Atlanta: Scholars Press, 1995.

Hatton, Peter T. H. *Contradiction in the Book of Proverbs: The Deep Waters of Counsel.* SOTSMS. Burlington, VT: Ashgate, 2008.

Heim, Knut Martin. *Like Grapes of Gold Set in Silver: An Interpretation of Proverbial Clusters in Proverbs 10:1–22:16.* BZAW 273. Berlin: de Gruyter, 2001.

———. *Poetic Imagination in Proverbs: Variant Repetitions and the Nature of Poetry.* BBRSup 4. Winona Lake, IN: Eisenbrauns, 2012.

Kim, Seenam. *The Coherence of the Collections in the Book of Proverbs.* Eugene, OR: Pickwick, 2007.

Lang, Bernhard. *Wisdom and the Book of Proverbs: An Israelite Goddess Redefined.* New York: Pilgrim, 1986.

Lyu, Sun Myung. *Righteousness in the Book of Proverbs.* FAT/2 55. Tübingen: Mohr Siebeck, 2012.

McCreesh, Thomas P. *Biblical Sound and Sense: Poetic Sound Patterns in Proverbs 10–29.* JSOTSup 128. Sheffield: JSOT Press, 1991.

Miles, Johnny E. *Wise King—Royal Fool: Semiotics, Satire and Proverbs 1–9.* JSOTSup 399. London: T&T Clark, 2004.

Sandoval, Timothy J. *The Discourse of Wealth and Poverty in the Book of Proverbs.* BibInt 77. Leiden: Brill, 2006.

Schwáb, Zoltán S. *Toward an Interpretation of the Book of Proverbs: Selfishness and Secularity Reconsidered.* JTISup 7. Winona Lake, IN: Eisenbrauns, 2013.

Snell, Daniel C. *Twice-Told Proverbs and the Composition of the Book of Proverbs.* Winona Lake, IN: Eisenbrauns, 1993.

Stewart, Anne W. *Poetic Ethics in Proverbs: Wisdom Literature and the Shaping of the Moral Self.* Cambridge: Cambridge University Press, 2016.

Tan, Nancy Nam Hoon. *The 'Foreignness' of the Foreign Woman in Proverbs 1–9: A Study of the Origin and Development of a Biblical Motif.* BZAW 381. Berlin: de Gruyter, 2008.

Van Leeuwen, Raymond C. *Context and Meaning in Proverbs 25–27.* SBLDS 96. Atlanta: Scholars Press, 1988.

Washington, Harold C. *Wealth and Poverty in the Instruction of Amenemope and the Hebrew Proverbs.* SBLDS 142. Atlanta: Scholars Press, 1994.

Weeks, Stuart. *Instruction & Imagery in Proverbs 1–9.* Oxford: Oxford University Press, 2007.

Westermann, Claus. *Roots of Wisdom: The Oldest Proverbs of Israel and Other Peoples.* Translated by J. Daryl Charles. Louisville: Westminster John Knox, 1994.

Whybray, R. N. *The Book of Proverbs: A Survey of Modern Study.* HBIS 1. Leiden: Brill, 1995.

———. *The Composition of the Book of Proverbs.* JSOTSup 168. Sheffield: JSOT Press, 1994.

———. *Wealth and Poverty in the Book of Proverbs.* JSOTSup 99. Sheffield: JSOT Press, 1990.

———. *Wisdom in Proverbs: The Concept of Wisdom in Proverbs 1–9.* SBT 45. Naperville, IL: Allenson, 1965.

Williams, James G. *Those Who Ponder Proverbs: Aphoristic Thinking and Biblical Literature.* BLS 2. Sheffield: Almond Press, 1981.

Yoder, Christine Roy. *Wisdom as a Woman of Substance: A Socioeconomic Reading of Proverbs 1–9 and 31:10–31.* BZAW 304. Berlin: de Gruyter, 2001.

Zabán, Bálint Károly. *The Pillar Function of the Speeches of Wisdom: Proverbs 1:20–33, 8:1–36, and 9:1–6 in the Structural Framework of Proverbs 1–9.* BZAW 429. Berlin: de Gruyter, 2012.

CHAPTER 4

Job

The book of Job is more skeptical than the book of Proverbs. It deals with theodicy, the question of God's justice, through the story of an innocent individual who undergoes divinely sanctioned suffering. A lengthy poetic section has been inserted into that narrative, in which Job and three "friends" discuss his situation, with Job declaring his innocence while they vehemently insist that his suffering is justified. A pair of speeches by God conclude the book after some intervening material that we will discuss below. Central to the discussion is the theory of retribution, which holds that the good are blessed and the bad are punished.

Structure

A preliminary division can be made on the basis of the prose in Job 1–2 and 42:7–17 and the poetry in the intervening chapters. In addition to these different modes of expression, there are contradictions between the two sections. The poetry argues against the "reward and punishment" theory of retribution while the prologue presupposes it and the epilogue affirms it. The Job of the poetry is not the patient individual of the prologue and the epilogue's affirmation of Job's words seems inconsistent with his verbal attacks on God, while it is difficult to identify anything the friends said that justifies their condemnation. Finally, with the exception of Job 12:9, considered an insertion, the name Yahweh (NRSV "the LORD") is restricted to the prose material and the divine speeches of Job 38:1–42:6.[1] In contrast, the poetry

---

1. The standard phrase "fear of the Lord" in Job 28:28 uses the common noun "lord" (*'ădōnāy*) rather than the usual divine name.

uses El, Elohim, Eloah (different forms for "God") and Shaddai (NRSV "the Almighty"). In light of these inconsistencies and Job's legendary status in Ezekiel 14:14, 20, it appears that the author has inserted the poetry into a preexisting story about the righteous Job in order to provide the context for his discussion of theodicy.

The poetic section can be subdivided on the basis of its content. The section begins with Job cursing the day of his birth (Job 3). Job 4–27 consists of three cycles of speeches: in each, Eliphaz, Bildad, and Zophar take turns speaking, and Job responds in turn. Job 28 contains a poem about wisdom, Job 29–31 is Job's oath of innocence, Elihu intervenes in Job 32–37, and Yahweh gives two speeches in Job 38:1–42:6. The wisdom poem and Elihu's speech are usually considered later additions.

Orientation to the Book of Job	
Structure:	Job 1–2
	Job 3–27
	Job 28
	Job 29–31
	Job 32–37
	Job 38:1–42:6
	Job 42:7–17
Date:	sixth century BCE
Major Themes:	piety
	theodicy (divine justice)
	innocent suffering
	creation

Author and Date

Portions of the biblical book of Job, along with an Aramaic translation (targum), were discovered among the Dead Sea Scrolls. These texts date to the last few centuries BCE, supplying a final date before which Job must have been written. Identifying the author could help establish an earlier date, but in the absence of any concrete evidence from either the book or subsequent traditions, the search for a specific author is futile. Later Jewish writings demonstrate this. Some rabbis ascribe the book to Moses (B. Bat. 14b:17–18), but others in the same tractate say Job was a returnee from the Babylonian exile, placing it several centuries later (B. Bat. 15a:29). Investigations into the historical figure of Job, if ever there were such a figure, are equally unhelpful. Different rabbis quoted in B. Bat. 15b make Job a contemporary of the Israelites at the time of the exodus or of Ahasuerus (B. Bat. 15a) from the book of Esther, while still others date him to the time of Abraham (Bar Kappara) or the Queen of Sheba (cf. Job 1:16; 6:19). One of the most famous medieval rabbis, Rashi, dates Job to the reign of Nebuchadnezzar. One can infer from the variety of these identifications that trying to situate Job, either the book or the figure behind it, is largely guesswork.

It is possible, however, to determine an approximate date of composition from clues within this and other biblical books. There are no concrete historical references in the book; the narrative context reflects the patriarchal period, but that is a literary construct. Lacking such historical reference points, scholars look for periods when the issues addressed in Job were current. Although concern with individual suffering is ancient (cf. the extrabiblical parallels to Job in chapter 1 above), the book of Job challenges the doctrine of retribution, in which the good are blessed and the bad are punished. While this view has a long history in the ancient world, including in the biblical wisdom tradition, it was emphasized in the books of Jeremiah, Ezekiel, and the Deuteronomistic History (Joshua, Judges, 1–2 Samuel, and 1–2 Kings) as an explanation for the Babylonian conquest of Jerusalem and the deportation of leading citizens. But not all who experienced the conquest would have found retribution theology comforting, and it would also have been considered problematic in light of the early death of the righteous king Josiah, who promoted the deuteronomistic agenda.

The references to Job alongside Noah and Danel as models of righteousness in Ezekiel 14:14, 20 demonstrate that Job the individual was known around the time of the exile, but they are not evidence that the book itself existed. The figure of the satan may reflect Zoroastrian dualism, pointing to the Persian period, i.e., the latter sixth century BCE or later. The use of the definite article (it is always written "*the* satan" in Job) and the satan's subordination to Yahweh are consistent with Zechariah 3:1–2, from 520–518 BCE, rather than "a satan" (or perhaps "Satan") found in the later 1 Chronicles 21:1. There are parallels between Job 3:3–10 and Jeremiah 20:14–18 plus Job 7:17 and Psalm 8:4, and more generally between Job 38–39 and the trial speeches of Second Isaiah, but it is difficult to establish dependence in any of these situations. However, Job 3:3–10 is more clearly dependent on Genesis 1, which dates from the exilic period. This date is further supported by the book's language: its anomalies are deliberately archaic in keeping with the chronological setting of the narrative, but overall the Hebrew is consistent with a sixth-century BCE date.

Content

Job 1–2

This prose prologue provides the context for the poetic material, starting with the introduction of the central character, Job. The narrator describes Job's extensive livestock herds as well as the number and actions of his children and his regularly offered sacrifices just in case any of them sinned inadvertently. But the most important component for what follows is the narrator's fourfold description of Job himself: "That man was blameless and upright, one who feared God and turned away from evil" (1:1). In other words, unlike other humans, Job is sinless. The narrator's characterization of Job is repeated twice more by no less a figure than Yahweh (1:8; 2:3). Therefore, according to retribution theology, Job should not suffer.

The rest of the section alternates between scenes in heaven and on earth. In the first episode, the heavenly beings assembled in the presence of Yahweh. This is the divine council, known throughout the ancient Near East, wherein the gods gathered at the New Year to discuss earthly affairs and decide the fate of humans for the coming year.[2] It is described elsewhere in the First Testament at 1 Kings 22:19–23; Isaiah 6; Zechariah 3; Daniel 7; and perhaps Isaiah 40:1–11 (cf. also Jer. 23:18, 22; Amos 3:7; plus the divine references to "us" in Gen. 1:27; 3:22). One of the members is called "the satan." The definite article ("the") appears every time he is mentioned in Job 1–2, so because Hebrew grammar prohibits attaching an article to a name, this is not Satan, the devil found in later Jewish and Christian literature, but rather a noun indicating the character's title or role. The Hebrew noun *śāṭān* is derived from the verb meaning "to oppose, accuse," and that is precisely what he does in the narrative. Yahweh first directs the satan's attention to Job, repeating the narrator's fourfold characterization of him. Only then does the satan question the nature of Job's piety. Perhaps Job acts that way only because God protects him from harm, but if Yahweh (not the satan) were to afflict Job, then Job would curse Yahweh.[3] So Yahweh empowers the satan to afflict Job without affecting his body, and the satan departs.

The second scene (Job 1:13–22) describes what the satan does. A series of messengers arrive, one after another, to report to Job that Sabeans have stolen his oxen and donkeys and killed his servants who were with them, that his sheep and more servants were consumed by lightning, that his camels were captured and their herders killed by Chaldeans, and that all his children were killed when a windstorm caused the house they were in to collapse. But contrary to the satan's assertion, rather than curse Yahweh, Job responds by

2. The most recent full-length treatment of the biblical divine council is Ellen White, *Yahweh's Council: Its Structure and Membership*, FAT/2 65 (Tübingen: Mohr Siebeck, 2014).

3. The Hebrew in Job 1:5, 11; 2:5, 9 has "bless" but this is in order to avoid writing "curse God."

performing traditional mourning rituals and he speaks his famous words: "Naked I came from my mother's womb, and naked shall I return there; the LORD gave, and the LORD has taken away; blessed be the name of the LORD" (1:21). The narrator confirms that "in all this Job did not sin or charge God with wrongdoing" (1:22).

The third scene (Job 2:1–6) repeats the initial dialogue between Yahweh and the satan, to which Yahweh adds concerning Job, "He still persists in his integrity, although you incited me against him, to destroy him *for no reason*" (2:3; italics added), reaffirming that Job does not deserve what is happening to him. The satan retorts that Job would respond differently if he were physically afflicted ("Skin for skin!"; 2:4), and once again Yahweh empowers the satan to attack him; this time the satan can even touch Job's body, though he may not take his life.

The final scene (Job 2:7–13) returns to earth, where the satan has caused sores over Job's entire body. His wife tells him to "curse God and die" but Job rebukes her with his other famous words: "Shall we receive the good at the hand of God, and not receive the bad?" Once again the narrator attests that "in all this Job did not sin with his lips." Some take the final phrase as suggesting that Job did sin in his mind or heart, thereby justifying his suffering. But not only would that be inconsistent with the point of the book, the phrase comes *after* all Job's afflictions and therefore cannot be taken as justification for what happened *before* this point in the narrative. At the end of the chapter, Job is visited by three friends who sit with him in silence for seven days and nights, the traditional period of mourning before resuming one's participation in society.

The prologue establishes a point that is essential for the poetic dialogue to have any real significance: Job is a truly righteous individual who is completely innocent of any wrongdoing and therefore undeserving of what has happened to him, just as Yahweh said (2:3). Two other points must be added before considering the poetic section. First, neither Job nor his friends know what has happened during the heavenly scenes, and therefore they do not know why Job is suffering. Second, because they are ignorant of what has happened previously, their shared belief in the doctrine of retribution has not been challenged. Eliphaz, Bildad, and Zophar believe that good things happen to those who are good and bad things happen to those who are bad, and they can only conclude that because bad things have happened to Job, he must have done something wrong. Job shares their belief in the retribution doctrine but knows that he has not done anything wrong. His problem is not that he rejects the retribution theology of his friends. It is precisely because he still believes their doctrine of reward and punishment that he protests so vehemently in the following chapters: his personal experience of suffering does not fit his theological view. In fact, when the retribution system of reward and punishment breaks down, then God should step in to rectify the situation, but that has not happened in his case. Because Job's world no longer makes sense but he is unable to abandon his belief in retribution, the only thing left for him to do is to attack God for not doing God's job.

Job 3

In contrast to the patient individual in the prologue, Job opens the conversation with his friends by cursing the day of his birth and the night of his conception. Michael Fishbane has called the first part of the chapter a "counter-cosmic incantation," which, if put into effect, would return creation to the primordial darkness of Genesis 1:1–5.[4] Job's "let it be darkness" (*yěhî ḥōšek*; author's translation) in 3:4 is a direct reversal of the divine command "let it be light" (*yěhî 'ôr*; author's translation) from Genesis 1:3. This is reinforced by the five different nouns used for darkness overwhelming Job's birthday: "darkness" (NRSV "gloom") is repeated in 3:5 (the related verb also occurs in 3:9) alongside "deep darkness," "(dark) clouds," and "blackness," while "thick darkness" appears in v. 6. Job seeks to rouse Leviathan (3:8), the mythological symbol of chaos before creation, and asks that night never see the morning (3:9), which would destroy the ordered succession of night and day that was the basis of creation in Genesis 1:4–5. This is followed by Job lamenting that he had ever been born and then questioning the value of human existence itself.

Job 4–27

This section consists of three cycles of speech. Eliphaz, Bildad, and Zophar take turns addressing Job and he speaks after each of them. The friends begin gently but grow increasingly harsh and accusatory as they propose different expla-

4. Michael Fishbane, "Jeremiah IV 23–26 and Job III 3–13: A Recovered Use of the Creation Pattern," *VT* 21 (1971): 151–67. Cf. the related discussions of Leo G. Perdue, "Job's Assault on Creation," *HAR* 10 (1986): 295–315; Leo G. Perdue, *Wisdom in Revolt: Metaphorical Theology in the Book of Job*, JSOTSup 112 (Sheffield: JSOT Press, 1991), 91–108; Valerie Forstman Pettys, "Let There Be Darkness: Continuity and Discontinuity in the 'Curse' of Job 3," *JSOT* 98 (2002): 89–104.

nations for Job's suffering, trying to convince Job that he has done something wrong, while Job just as insistently stresses that he has not. This section is not really a dialogue: they do not actually talk with each other so much as talk at or even past one another. As we will see, the third cycle is corrupt.

Eliphaz (Job 4–5) begins the first cycle softly, asking for permission to speak, acknowledging Job's prior comfort of others and encouraging him to trust in God now. Eliphaz supports the traditional doctrine that the righteous will be protected and the wicked punished with appeals to nature, revelation, and his own observations. God is in control of the world and uses suffering to discipline people but ultimately restores them, as he will for Job. Job (Job 6–7) protests that no one understands the depths of his suffering and then affirms his innocence, which renders any attempt to correct him invalid. Human existence is like slavery and ends at death. God is attacking him, treating him like Sea/Dragon (i.e., Leviathan) and sending him nightmares. The idea of God's protective presence found in Psalm 8:4 is transformed into an image of divine oppression in Job 7:17–18, and Job wishes that God would leave him alone.

> What are human beings that you are mindful of them,
> > mortals that you care for them?
> Yet you have made them a little lower than God,
> > and crowned them with glory and honor. (Ps 8:4–5)
> What are human beings, that you make so much of them,
> > that you set your mind on them,
> visit them every morning,
> > test them every moment? (Job 7:17–18)

Bildad (Job 8) asserts that suffering is punishment for sin, which is why Job's children died. He appeals to the traditions of the ancestors and analogies from nature to demonstrate that the wicked will always be punished and the righteous rewarded, so if Job repents and appeals to God, then he will be restored to his previous state. Job (Job 9–10) acknowledges God's power, but God uses that power to overwhelm those like him who seek answers, crushing him with a "tempest" (9:17). Job longs for an "umpire" to stand between them, but since there is none, he complains about his situation and asks God to explain why he seems to take delight in afflicting humans (10:3). Why did God even bring him into existence?

Zophar (Job 11) objects to Job's protestations of innocence because Job deserves worse than he has received. God's ways are beyond us, but since God is just, Job should purify himself so that God might restore him. In reaction,

Job (Job 12–14) mocks their supposed wisdom ("wisdom will die with you"; 12:2), insists that he already knows their arguments, and denounces the easy ability of those in comfort to laugh at those who are not. Job acknowledges that God's power and wisdom are evident in nature and human affairs, but his friends are "worthless physicians" (13:4) who could only demonstrate their wisdom if they stopped talking. Instead, they are lying in defense of God, for which they will be punished, so Job begins to present his case directly to God, asking for a hearing now since he does not believe in an afterlife: "So mortals lie down and do not rise again; until the heavens are no more, they will not awake or be roused out of their sleep" (Job 14:12).

The conversation grows more heated in the second cycle, while also repeating ideas from the first cycle. Eliphaz (Job 15) starts by declaring that Job's accusations against God prove his wickedness. He mocks Job's claim to wisdom, asking if he is the primordial wise person (15:7–8; cf. Ezek. 28:1–19), when instead ancient traditions confirm Eliphaz's position. He then describes in sometimes gruesome detail the dismal fate of the wicked. Now that the gloves are off, so to speak, Job's next speech (Job 16–17) begins with some humorous insults: they are "miserable comforters" (16:2) afflicted with verbal diarrhea (16:3) and their platitudes are, in modern parlance, easy for them to say (16:4–5). More importantly, God continues to attack him, although Job has a heavenly witness who speaks on his behalf. But God also afflicts him through humans who mock him because God has clouded their minds, and Job has no hope against them. Bildad (Job 18) rejects Job's complaint against them and describes the terror of the wicked as they are captured by Death. Job (Job 19) repeats that the friends are condescending, and God has oppressed him and caused his family and friends to desert him. He invokes the Israelite concept of a *gō'ēl* (traditionally translated "redeemer"), a relative who will rescue him from debt or exact revenge if he is harmed (19:25), so they should be cautious. An agitated Zophar (Job 20) spends his whole speech reasserting the traditional view that the success of the wicked will be short-lived. Job (Job 21) ends this cycle by describing in detail how real experience contradicts the traditional doctrine; therefore, their "empty nothings" and lies fail to comfort him (21:34).

The text of the third cycle of speeches is obviously corrupt: Eliphaz and Job's initial back-and-forth is secure, but after that Bildad has only six verses and Zophar has none, while Job says things that would be more at home in the others' mouths. Some interpreters take this as a sign that the discussion has completely broken down and that a resolution is ultimately futile,[5] while

---

5. Cf. Carol A. Newsom, *The Book of Job: A Contest of Moral Imagination* (New York: Ox-

others rearrange portions of Job 24–27 in an attempt to reconstruct the cycle. The following are some examples:[6]

> Bildad: 25:1–6; 26:5–14; Job: 26:1–4; 27:1–12; Zophar: 27:13–23 (Gordis)
> Bildad: 25:1–6; 26:5–14; Job: 26:1–4; 27:1–7; Zophar: 27:8–23; 24:18–20, 22–25 (Pope)
> Bildad: 25:1–6; 26:5–14; Job 26:1–4; 27:1–12; Zophar: 27:13–23; 24 (Habel)
> Bildad: 25:1–6; 27:13–23; Job: 26:1–27:12; Zophar doesn't speak (Hartley)
> Bildad: 25:1–26:14; Job: 27:1–6, 11–12; Zophar: 27:7–10, 13–17; 24:18–24; 27:18–23 (Clines)

My own reading differs from all these to some degree. After asserting that no one can teach or benefit God, Eliphaz (Job 22) accuses Job of injustice toward others, which justifies Job's suffering. Like the wicked, Job erroneously thinks that God cannot see his deeds, but Eliphaz urges him to repent and be reconciled with God. Job (23:1–24:17) longs for a direct encounter with God, but although Job cannot find God, God does know his innocence; however, God ignores the oppressed and leaves the wicked unpunished. Bildad (Job 25:1–6; 26:5–14) states that because God is all-powerful, humans cannot be righteous before God. The shades cower before God, whose might is seen in creation: God's defeat of Sea, Rahab, and Leviathan ("the fleeing serpent"; 26:12–13), the mythological forces of chaos, is just a hint of God's power. Job (26:1–4) merely considers his friends poor counselors. Zophar (24:18–25; 27:7–21) insists that the prosperity of the wicked is short-lived and describes their horrible fate at

---

ford University Press, 2003), 164–68; V. Philips Long, "On the Coherence of the Third Dialogic Cycle in the Book of Job," in *Studies on the Text and Versions of the Hebrew Bible in Honour of Robert Gordon*, ed. Geoffrey Khan and Diana Lipton, VTSup 149 (Leiden: Brill, 2012), 113–25; Tremper Longman III, *Job*, BCOTWP (Grand Rapids: Baker Academic, 2012), 283; Lindsay Wilson, *Job*, THOTC (Grand Rapids: Eerdmans, 2015), 24, 116.

6. Robert Gordis, *The Book of God and Man: A Study of Job* (Chicago: University of Chicago Press, 1965), 98–99; Robert Gordis, *The Book of Job: Commentary, New Translation and Special Studies* (New York: The Jewish Theological Seminary of America, 1978), 534–35; Marvin H. Pope, *Job: A New Translation with Introduction and Commentary*, 3rd ed., AB 15 (Garden City: Doubleday, 1973), xx; Norman C. Habel, *The Book of Job: A Commentary*, OTL (Philadelphia: Westminster, 1985), 37–38; John E. Hartley, *The Book of Job*, NICOT (Grand Rapids: Eerdmans, 1988), 25–27; David J. A. Clines, *Job 21–37*, WBC 18A (Nashville: Thomas Nelson, 2006), 572–677. Some of them develop their position in greater detail in the commentary on the passages themselves. In these reconstructions, either Job does not speak after Zophar or chapters (28?)29–31 are Job's missing speech, except for Hartley, who thinks Zophar is silent here because he said all he had to say in the second cycle.

length. Job (27:1–6) ends the cycle by refusing to deny his righteousness, for to do so would be a lie.

Job 28

There is no indication of a new speaker in this chapter, which would make it part of Job's final speech. However, it is not addressed to either God or the friends and its content is distinct from the rest of the book, so most consider it an insertion, perhaps as an attempt to deal with the lack of wisdom in the preceding chapters. It begins by describing the great mining skill of humans, but despite this they do not know where to find wisdom. Wisdom is more valuable than all the precious items they might dig up (cf. Prov. 3:15; 8:11) and neither nature nor the underworld knows its location. In contrast, God does know where wisdom is and used it in creation (cf. Prov. 3:19–20; 8:22–31), but humans can only experience wisdom through "fear of the Lord" (28:28; cf. Prov. 1:7; 9:10, but note the different Hebrew words for "Lord/LORD").

Job 29–31

Having affirmed his innocence in 27:1–6, here Job takes an oath about it, with each chapter marking a stage in the process. He longs for the past when he was blessed by God, when he was respected and honored by others because he was generous and just, protecting the weak from the unrighteous and comforting others with his counsel. But now he is mocked and attacked, only to have God ignore and then oppress him; as a result he is depressed and bemoans his situation. Finally, he denies various types of wrongdoing and demands a hearing before God (31:35). With this, "the words of Job are ended" (31:40) and we expect God to answer his call for a hearing.

Job 32–37

Instead, Elihu speaks for five chapters, and his speeches seem like a secondary insertion. He appears nowhere else in the book—he was not mentioned in the prologue or in the preceding speeches and he is absent from the epilogue. Unlike the three "friends," Elihu quotes Job's own words extensively as if he had them before him as a written text, but Job does not answer him. Moreover, the

Hebrew of this section is from a later stage of the language than that in the rest of the book, and some parts of the content also signal that it dates from some time after the speeches: the meteorology of 36:27–29 is less mythological than that of the Yahweh speeches, Elihu's view of suffering as educating sinners is more advanced than Eliphaz's understanding of it as a test, and the angelology of this section is the most developed in the First Testament.[7] Therefore, this section was probably added later by someone upset that Job's friends had not refuted Job's claim to be just when God was not (Job 32:2–3).[8]

Elihu begins with a lengthy justification for intruding on the conversation, asserting his right, his duty, and his divine compulsion to speak. His self-description as an unvented wineskin about to burst (Job 32:17–19), or in other words a windbag, is comical after the rejection of windy words in Job 6:26; 8:2; 15:2; 16:3. He addresses Job's claim of innocence by arguing that God sends both dreams and suffering in order to make the wicked aware of their sin and turn back to God. Divine preservation of the cosmos illustrates God's essential justice, and Job has not received a response to his pleas because God only responds to those who submit to God's will. But although God wants sinners to repent, each individual is ultimately responsible for maintaining the proper relationship with God. Job 36:1–23 summarizes Elihu's preceding defense of God, while the creation hymn in 36:24–37:13 and the rhetorical questions of 37:14–20 anticipate the form and content of Yahweh's speeches.

Job 38:1–42:6

After this delay, Yahweh at last appears, speaking twice from a whirlwind, which earlier Job had feared God would use to crush him (9:17; cf. 30:22). Yahweh does not reveal his discussion with the satan in Job 1–2, nor does he address Job's righteousness or any of the other issues raised in the previous speeches. In fact, he only mentions humans tangentially in relationship to certain animals, but instead acts like a wisdom teacher, drawing lessons from nature.

In the first divine speech God asks Job a series of questions about his knowledge of various aspects of the natural world, reflecting the scribal chal-

7. Harold-Martin Wahl, *Der gerechte Schöpfer: Eine redaktions- und theologiegeschichtliche Untersuchung der Elihureden—Hiob 32–37*, BZAW 207 (Berlin: de Gruyter, 1993).

8. Alternatively, the Elihu speeches are seen as a comic interlude by W. Whedbee, "The Comedy of Job," in *Studies in the Book of Job*, ed. Robert M. Polzin and D. Robertson, Semeia 7 (Missoula: Scholars Press, 1977), 18–20; Habel, *Job*, 443–47; Hartley, *Job*, 427.

lenge to a rival.[9] These questions deal with three branches of creation: cosmology, meteorology, and zoology. The expectation is that Job cannot answer because he does not know about and cannot control these things, which is, in fact, the case. Instead, Job acknowledges his relative insignificance, covers his mouth and declines to speak further (40:3-5). Yahweh then questions him about Behemoth and Leviathan, mythological chaos monsters of the land and sea that Yahweh describes in detail. Once again the presupposition is that Job cannot control them but Yahweh can. Some identify them as the hippopotamus and crocodile respectively, but such natural creatures would not serve the same rhetorical purpose, since they do not represent the forces of chaos and humans actually can control them. More importantly, a crocodile does not breathe fire (41:19-21), but a dragon does.

Since they come at the end of the poetic material, one expects Yahweh's speeches to provide an answer to the issues raised in the book concerning the undeserved suffering of the righteous, and Job does seem satisfied in 42:1-6. Suggestions as to what the answer is include that (1) God is all-powerful, (2) some things are beyond human understanding or control, (3) God does not have to explain divine actions, or (4) God's justice and compassion in the natural world applies to the human world as well. Each of these finds some degree of support from 42:2-3, but subsequent verses suggest that for Job the answer was simply the encounter with God. In 42:5 he says, "I had heard of you by the hearing of the ear, but now my eye sees you," but the result of that encounter is not correctly conveyed in the NRSV translation of v. 6 as "therefore I despise myself, and repent in dust and ashes." First, the word "myself" is not present in the Hebrew. Second, instead of its frequent meaning of "upon," whenever the preposition 'al follows the verb nhm ("repent") it introduces the object of that repentance. This means that Job responds to his encounter with Yahweh by stating, "Therefore I despise and repent concerning dust and ashes."[10] In other words, Job stops lamenting his situation precisely because he has seen Yahweh, not because of anything that Yahweh said.

9. See Henry Rowold, "Yahweh's Challenge to Rival: The Form and Function of the Yahweh-Speech in Job 38-39," *CBQ* 47 (1985): 199-211, and the discussion of the form in chapter 2 above.

10. Dale Patrick, "The Translation of Job xlii 6," *VT* 26 (1976): 369-71.

Job 42:7–17

The prose epilogue returns to a world where retribution theology is the order of the day. Job offers sacrifice on behalf of Eliphaz, Bildad, and Zophar (Elihu is not mentioned) to compensate for them speaking incorrectly about God, unlike Job himself. Once Job does this he receives twice as much property as before and fathers the same number of sons and daughters as he had before his original children were killed in Job 1. Not only is this completely inconsistent with the whole point of the dialogue, it is also difficult to see why the friends' defense of God was incorrect but Job's attacks on the divine were correct, since the former reflects common theological perspectives and the latter does not. The best explanation is that in the original folktale Job continued to speak as in 1:21 and 2:10, but his three friends urged him to speak against God like Job's wife did in 2:9. In other words, it is likely that the epilogue originally concluded a much shorter story consisting of Job 1–2 plus the friend's negative words against God. A later author has replaced the friends' opposition to God with the poetic material that constitutes the bulk of the present book. Inserting the poetic material alters the referents and therefore the significance of God's denunciation of the friends' words and affirmation of Job's. In the final form of the book the friends' defense of retribution theology has been divinely discredited, along with the theory itself, while Job's protestations of innocence have been divinely affirmed. Their respective speeches should be read and used accordingly.

Summary

The book of Job challenges the traditional wisdom doctrine of retribution, that the good are blessed and the bad are punished in their lifetime. Job himself is a blameless individual who nonetheless experiences great suffering. In keeping with the doctrine of retribution, his three friends Eliphaz, Bildad, and Zophar as well as the interloper Elihu insist that he must have done something wrong, while Job insists just as strongly that he is innocent and therefore does not deserve what has happened to him. In the end, Yahweh appears in a whirlwind and asks Job about his ability to control various aspects of creation as well as the chaos monsters Leviathan and Behemoth. Job is comforted by his encounter with the divine, who pronounces him correct and his friends incorrect about God.

FURTHER READING

Commentaries

Alden, Robert L. *Job*. NAC 11. Nashville: Broadman & Holman, 1994.

Balentine, Samuel E. *Job*. SHBC 10. Macon, GA: Smyth & Helwys, 2006.

Boss, Jeffrey. *Human Consciousness of God in the Book of Job: A Theological and Psychological Commentary*. London: Continuum, 2010.

Clines, David J. A. *Job 1–20*. WBC 17. Waco, TX: Word, 1989.

———. *Job 21–37*. WBC 18A. Nashville: Thomas Nelson, 2006.

———. *Job 38–42*. WBC 18B. Nashville: Thomas Nelson, 2011.

Dhorme, Edouard. *A Commentary on the Book of Job*. Translated by Harold Knight. Nashville: Nelson, 1984.

Driver, Samuel Rolles, and George Buchanan Gray. *A Critical and Exegetical Commentary on the Book of Job*. ICC. 1921; reprinted Edinburgh: T&T Clark, 1977.

Estes, Daniel J. *Job*. Teach the Text Commentary Series. Grand Rapids: Baker Academic, 2013.

Fokkelman, Jan P. *The Book of Job in Form: A Literary Translation with Commentary*. SSN 58. Leiden: Brill, 2012.

Gordis, Robert. *The Book of Job: Commentary, New Translation and Special Studies*. New York: The Jewish Theological Seminary of America, 1978.

Gray, John. *The Book of Job*. Text of the Hebrew Bible 1. Sheffield: Sheffield Phoenix, 2010.

Guinan, Michael D. *Job*. Collegeville Bible Commentary 19. Collegeville: Liturgical Press, 1986.

Habel, Norman C. *The Book of Job*. CBC. Cambridge: Cambridge University Press, 1975.

———. *The Book of Job: A Commentary*. OTL. Philadelphia: Westminster, 1985.

Hartley, John E. *The Book of Job*. NICOT. Grand Rapids: Eerdmans, 1988.

Janzen, J. Gerald. *Job*. Interpretation. Atlanta: John Knox, 1985.

Kissane, Edward Joseph. *The Book of Job*. New York: Sheed & Ward, 1946.

Longman, Tremper, III. *Job*. BCOTWP. Grand Rapids: Baker Academic, 2012.

O'Connor, Kathleen M. *Job*. Collegeville Bible Commentary 19. Collegeville, MN: Liturgical Press, 2012.

Pope, Marvin H. *Job: A New Translation with Introduction and Commentary*. 3rd ed. AB 15. Garden City: Doubleday, 1973.

Rowley, Harold Henry. *The Book of Job*. 2nd ed. NCBC. Grand Rapids: Eerdmans, 1978.

Scheindlin, Raymond P. *The Book of Job: Translation, Introduction and Notes*. New York: Norton, 1998.

Selms, Adrian van. *Job: A Practical Commentary*. Translated by John Vriend. Text and Interpretation. Grand Rapids: Eerdmans, 1985.

Seow, Choon-Leong. *Job 1–21: Interpretation and Commentary*. Illuminations. Grand Rapids: Eerdmans, 2013.

Simundson, Daniel J. *The Message of Job: A Theological Commentary*. Augsburg Old Testament Studies. Minneapolis: Augsburg, 1986.

Tur-Sinai, N. H. *The Book of Job: A New Commentary*. Rev. ed. Jerusalem: Kiryath Sepher, 1967.

Whybray, Norman. *Job*. Readings: A New Biblical Commentary. Sheffield: Sheffield Academic, 1998.

Wilson, Gerald H. *Job*. NIBCOT. Peabody: Hendrickson / Milton Keynes: Paternoster, 2007.

Wilson, Lindsay. *Job*. THOTC. Grand Rapids: Eerdmans, 2015.

Other Works

Aufrecht, Walter E., ed. *Studies in the Book of Job*. SR Supplement 16. Waterloo: Wilfred Laurier, 1985.

Balentine, Samuel E. *Have You Considered My Servant Job?: Understanding the Biblical Archetype of Patience*. SPOT. Columbia: University of South Carolina Press, 2015.

Beuken, W. A. M., ed. *The Book of Job*. BETL 114. Leuven: Leuven University Press, 1994.

Brown, Ken. *The Vision in Job 4 and Its Role in the Book: Reframing the Development of the Joban Dialogues*. FAT/2 75. Tübingen: Mohr Siebeck, 2015.

Burrell, David D., and A. H. Johns. *Deconstructing Theodicy: Why Job Has Nothing to Say to the Puzzled Suffering*. Grand Rapids: Brazos, 2008.

Ceresko, Anthony R. *Job 29–31 in the Light of Northwest Semitic: A Translation and Philological Commentary*. BibOr 36. Rome: Biblical Institute Press, 1980.

Cheney, Michael. *Dust, Wind and Agony: Character, Speech and Genre in Job*. ConBOT 36. Stockholm: Almqvist & Wiksell, 1994.

Cotter, David W. *A Study of Job 4–5 in the Light of Contemporary Literary Theory*. SBLDS 124. Atlanta: Scholars Press, 1992.

Course, John E. *Speech and Response: A Rhetorical Analysis of the Introductions to the Speeches of the Book of Job (Chaps. 4–24)*. CBQMS 25. Washington, DC: Catholic Biblical Association of America, 1994.

Cox, Dermot. *The Triumph of Impotence: Job and the Tradition of the Absurd.* AnGreg 212. Rome: Universita Gregoriana, 1978.

Crossan, John Dominic, ed. *The Book of Job and Ricoeur's Hermeneutics.* Semeia 19. Chico, CA: Scholars Press, 1981.

Dell, Katharine J. *The Book of Job as Sceptical Literature.* BZAW 197. Berlin: de Gruyter, 1991.

Dell, Katharine J., and William L. Kynes, eds. *Reading Job Intertextually.* New York: Bloomsbury, 2013.

Doak, Brian R. *Consider Leviathan: Narratives of Nature and the Self in Job.* Minneapolis: Fortress, 2014.

Duquoc, C., and C. Floristan, eds. *Job and the Silence of God.* New York: Seabury, 1983.

Fisher, Loren R. *The Many Voices of Job.* Eugene, OR: Cascade, 2009.

Girard, René. *Job: The Victim of His People.* Stanford: Stanford University Press, 1987.

Good, Edwin M. *In Turns of Tempest: A Reading of Job, with a Translation.* Stanford: Stanford University Press, 1990.

Gordis, Robert. *The Book of God and Man: A Study of Job.* Chicago: University of Chicago Press, 1965.

Grabbe, Lester L. *Comparative Philology and the Text of Job.* SBLDS 34. Missoula: Scholars Press, 1977.

Guillaume, Alfred. *Studies in the Book of Job, with a New Translation.* Leiden: Brill, 1968.

Habel, Norman C. *Finding Wisdom in Nature: An Eco-Wisdom Reading of the Book of Job.* EBC 4. Sheffield: Sheffield Phoenix, 2014.

Hoffman, Yair. *A Blemished Perfection: The Book of Job in Context.* JSOTSup 213. Sheffield: Sheffield Academic, 1996.

Hyun, Seong Whan Timothy. *Job the Unfinalizable: A Bakhtinian Reading of Job 1–11.* BibInt 124. Leiden: Brill, 2013.

Iwanski, Dariusz. *The Dynamics of Job's Intercession.* AnBib 161. Rome: Pontifical Biblical Institute, 2006.

Janzen, J. Gerald. *At the Scent of Water: The Ground of Hope in the Book of Job.* Grand Rapids: Eerdmans, 2009.

Johnson, Timothy Jay. *Now My Eye Sees You: Unveiling an Apocalyptic Job.* Hebrew Bible Monographs 24. Sheffield: Sheffield Phoenix, 2009.

Jones, Scott C. *Rumors of Wisdom: Job 28 as Poetry.* BZAW 398. Berlin: de Gruyter, 2009.

Kynes, Will. *My Psalm Has Turned into Weeping: Job's Dialogue with the Psalms.* BZAW 437. Berlin: de Gruyter, 2012.

Lo, Alison. *Job 28 as Rhetoric: An Analysis of Job 28 in the Context of Job 22–31*. VTSup 97. Leiden: Brill, 2003.

Low, Katherine. *The Bible, Gender, and Reception History: The Case of Job's Wife*. LHBOTS 586. London: Bloomsbury T&T Clark, 2013.

Lugt, Pieter van der. *Rhetorical Criticism and the Poetry of the Book of Job*. OTS 32. Leiden: Brill, 1995.

Mathewson, Dan. *Death and Survival in the Book of Job: Desymbolization and Traumatic Experience*. LHBOTS 450. London: T&T Clark, 2006.

McKibben, Bill. *The Comforting Whirlwind: God, Job, and the Scale of Creation*. Grand Rapids: Eerdmans, 1994.

Michel, Walter L. *Job in the Light of Northwest Semitic I: Prologue and First Cycle of Speeches, Job 1:1–14:22*. BibOr 42. Rome: Biblical Institute Press, 1987.

Murphy, Roland E. *The Book of Job: A Shorter Reading*. New York: Paulist, 1999.

Nam, Duck-Woo. *Telling about God: Job 42:7–9 and the Nature of God in the Book of Job*. Studies in Biblical Literature 49. New York: Peter Lang, 2003.

Neiman, D. *The Book of Job: A Presentation of the Book with Selected Portions Translated from the Original Hebrew Text*. Jerusalem: Massada, 1972.

Nelson, Alissa Jones. *Edward Said, Contrapuntal Hermeneutics and the Book of Job: Power, Subjectivity and Responsibility in Biblical Interpretation*. Bible World. London: Equinox, 2011.

Newsom, Carol A. *The Book of Job: A Contest of Moral Imagination*. Oxford: Oxford University Press, 2003.

Ngwa, Kenneth Numfor. *The Hermeneutics of the 'Happy' Ending in Job 42:7–17*. BZAW 354. Berlin: de Gruyter, 2005.

Noegel, Scott B. *Janus Parallelism in the Book of Job*. JSOTSup 223. Sheffield: JSOT Press, 1996.

O'Connor, D. *Job: His Wife, His Friends, and His God*. International Scholars Publications, 1995.

Oeming, Manfred, and Konrad Schmid. *Job's Journey: Stations of Suffering*. CSHB 7. Winona Lake, IN: Eisenbrauns, 2015.

Pelham, Abigail. *Contested Creations in the Book of Job: The-World-as-It-Ought-and-Ought-Not-to-Be*. BibInt 113. Leiden: Brill, 2012.

Penchansky, David. *The Betrayal of God: Ideological Conflict in Job*. Literary Currents in Biblical Interpretation. Louisville: Westminster John Knox, 1990.

Perdue, Leo G. *Wisdom in Revolt: Metaphorical Theology in the Book of Job*. JSOTSup 112. Sheffield: JSOT Press, 1991.

Perdue, Leo G., and W. Clark Gilpin, eds. *The Voice from the Whirlwind: Interpreting the Book of Job*. Nashville: Abingdon, 1992.

Pyeon, Yohan. *You Have Not Spoken What Is Right about Me: Intertextuality and the Book of Job.* Studies in Biblical Literature 45. New York: Peter Lang, 2003.

Schifferdecker, Kathryn. *Out of the Whirlwind: Creation Theology in the Book of Job.* HTS 61. Cambridge, MA: Harvard University Press, 2008.

Shugart, H. H. *Foundations of the Earth: Global Ecological Change and the Book of Job.* New York: Columbia University Press, 2014.

Terrien, Samuel. *Job: Poet of Existence.* Indianapolis: Bobbs-Merrill, 1957.

Thomason, Bill. *God on Trial: The Book of Job and Human Suffering.* Collegeville, MN: Liturgical Press, 1997.

Ticciati, Susannah. *Job and the Disruption of Identity: Reading Beyond Barth.* London: T&T Clark, 2005.

Verbin, N. *Divinely Abused: A Philosophical Perspective on Job and His Kin.* London: Continuum, 2010.

Wahl, Harold-Martin. *Der gerechte Schöpfer: Eine redaktions- und theologiegeschichtliche Untersuchung der Elihureden—Hiob 32–37.* BZAW 207. Berlin: de Gruyter, 1993.

Ward, W. A. *Out of the Whirlwind: Answers to the Problem of Suffering from the Book of Job.* Richmond: John Knox, 1958.

Weiss, Meir. *The Story of Job's Beginning. Job 1–2: A Literary Analysis.* Jerusalem: Magnes, 1983.

Westermann, Claus. *The Structure of the Book of Job: A Form-Critical Analysis.* Translated by Charles A. Muenchow. Philadelphia: Fortress, 1981.

Wolfers, David. *Deep Things out of Darkness: The Book of Job. Essays and a New English Translation.* Kampen: Kok Pharos / Grand Rapids: Eerdmans, 1995.

Zerafa, P. P. *The Wisdom of God in the Book of Job.* Studia Universitatis S. Thomae in Urbe 8. Rome: Herder, 1978.

Zuck, Roy B., ed. *Sitting with Job: Selected Studies on the Book of Job.* Grand Rapids: Baker Books, 1992.

Zuckerman, Bruce. *Job the Silent: A Study in Historical Counterpoint.* Oxford: Oxford University Press, 1991.

CHAPTER 5

Qoheleth

The book of Qoheleth, often called Ecclesiastes in English Bibles (see "Title" below), provides another example of the skeptical strain of Israelite literature, similar to Job. The author reviews multiple aspects of human existence, including wisdom itself, and finds them all to be *hebel*. The Vulgate, an early translation of the Bible into Latin, translated the Hebrew term *hebel* with *vanitas*, which led to the traditional rendering as "vanity" found in English Bibles both old (e.g., the KJV) and new (e.g., the NRSV). Many scholars have challenged the use of "vanity" to convey the biblical writer's point, however, and alternative suggestions have included "absurd," "incomprehensible," "enigmatic," and many more.[1] But Qoheleth frequently exhorts the reader to seek joy, and even though joy also falls under the assertion that "all is *hebel*," joy is not absurd, incomprehensible, or enigmatic. However, joy can be cut short by Qoheleth's other major concern, death. The fact that no one can know when death will come vexes Qoheleth. The term *hebel* literally means "breath" or "vapor," neither of which last, and in the first half of Qoheleth the term frequently appears with the expression "a chasing after wind," so translating the word as "transitory" is consistent with *hebel*'s root meaning as well as how the word is used in the book.[2]

---

1. For surveys of the history of interpretation of *hebel* see Russell L. Meek, "The Meaning of הבל in Qohelet: An Intertextual Suggestion," in *The Words of the Wise Are Like Goads: Engaging Qohelet in the 21st Century*, ed. Mark J. Boda, Tremper Longman III, and Cristian G. Rata (Winona Lake, IN: Eisenbrauns, 2013), 241–45; Antoon Schoors, *Ecclesiastes*, HCOT (Leuven: Peeters, 2013), 40–47.

2. Thus Daniel C. Fredericks, *Coping with Transience: Ecclesiastes on Brevity in Life*, BibSem 18 (Sheffield: JSOT Press, 1993); Ethan Dor-Shav, "Ecclesiastes, Fleeting and Timeless," *Azure* 18 (2004): 67–87; cf. R. B. Y. Scott, *Proverbs, Ecclesiastes: A New Translation with Intro-*

Unity and Structure

After the superscript to the book, Qoheleth 1:2 says "totally transitory, says Qoheleth, totally transitory. All is transitory," and 12:8 repeats "totally transitory, says Qoheleth. All is transitory." While the term *hebel* occurs thirty-eight times in the book, the superlative construct form *hăbēl hăbālîm* occurs only in these two verses, marking them as an inclusio encompassing Qoheleth's own words and setting 12:9–14 off as a later addition.[3] Within that inclusio, some earlier scholars suggested that individual verses or parts thereof are "pious glosses" inconsistent with the general tenor of Qoheleth himself. But this imposes a modern view of "consistency" on an ancient work, and more recent interpreters tend to see such "contradictions" as Qoheleth's citation of traditional views in order to refute them, or as reflecting his own internal struggle to reconcile himself with established wisdom, or both.[4]

> **Orientation to Qoheleth**
>
> | Structure: | Qoheleth 1:1–11 |
> | --- | --- |
> | | Qoheleth 1:12–6:9 |
> | | Qoheleth 6:10–8:17 |
> | | Qoheleth 9:1–11:6 |
> | | Qoheleth 11:7–12:8 |
> | | Qoheleth 12:9–14 |
> | Date: | third century BCE |
> | Major Themes: | everything is transitory (*hebel*) |
> | | everyone dies |
> | | the time of death is uncertain |
> | | enjoy whatever pleasure God might provide |

With respect to the book's structure (or its lack thereof) there are almost as many proposals as there are interpreters.[5] Often this is simply a matter of listing the successive topics that Qoheleth addresses. In contrast, Addison G.

---

duction and Commentary, 2nd ed., AB 18 (Garden City: Doubleday, 1965), 209. For Douglas Miller, "transient" is one of three metaphorical nuances for the term, the others being "insubstantial" and "foul"; see his *Symbol & Rhetoric in Ecclesiastes: The Place of* Hebel *in Qohelet's Work*, SBLAB 2 (Atlanta: Society of Biblical Literature, 2002). The evaluation of things as "transitory" extends beyond the phrase "a chasing after wind."

3. The construction "X of Xs" indicates the superlative in Biblical Hebrew, that is, the fullest example of something. Examples include "Song of Songs," "king of kings," and "lord of lords."

4. Michael V. Fox, *Qohelet and His Contradictions*, JSOTSup 71 (Sheffield: JSOT Press, 1989).

5. For a convenient survey see David Beldman, "Framed! Structure in Ecclesiastes," in *The Words of the Wise Are Like Goads: Engaging Qohelet in the 21st Century*, ed. Mark J. Boda, Tremper Longman III, and Cristian G. Rata (Winona Lake, IN: Eisenbrauns, 2013), 137–43.

Wright focuses on repeated vocabulary in distinct portions of the book.[6] The phrase "a chasing after wind" occurs in 1:14, 17; 2:11, 17, 26; 4:4, 6, 16; 6:9 (all except 1:17; 4:6 are preceded by *hebel*), but not afterwards. Instead, the phrases "not find/found" and "who can find" occur in 7:14, 24, 28 (2×); 8:17 (3×), with the final three instances forming an ABA pattern: the NRSV translates "no one can find"—"will not find"—"cannot find," but the first and last phrases are the same in the Hebrew. Similarly, "not know" is found in 9:12; 10:14, 15; 11:2, 5. The last two of these occurrences are surrounded by "there is no knowledge for you," forming another ABA pattern comparable to 8:17, although the NRSV obscures the mirror pattern by translating the A phrase as "you do not know" both times, making it indistinguishable from the B element.

Wright claimed that these repeated phrases marked the end of sections, with eight each in Qoheleth 1:12–6:9 and 6:10–11:6, but not all repetitions appear at the end of topics (e.g., 1:14, 17; 4:4; 7:28). Nevertheless, the repeated phrases do govern their respective portions of the book, establishing major thematic divisions. To these Wright added some numerical and structural features. First, Qoheleth 6:9 marks the halfway point of the book, with 111 verses in both 1:1–6:9 and 6:10–12:14. Second, the book begins with a poem plus an introduction to the first theme of the book, with that introduction divided into two sections, marked by two prose verses plus a poetic proverb (1:12–15, 16–18). The book ends with a poem plus a prose epilogue consisting of two parts, also with three verses each (12:9–11, 12–14). Moreover, both the opening and closing portions of the book consist of eighteen verses, producing a balanced inclusio around the entire book.

Based on the preceding, the book of Qoheleth can be outlined as follows:

A Poem on the nature of life + two-part introduction to Theme 1 (1:1–18)
    B Theme 1: "A chasing after wind" (1:12–6:9)
    C Theme 2: "One cannot find" (6:10–8:17)
    D Theme 3: "One cannot know" (9:1–11:6)
A' Poem on the uncertain time of death + two-part epilogue (11:7–12:14)

6. Addison G. Wright, "The Riddle of the Sphinx: The Structure of the Book of Qoheleth," *CBQ* 30 (1968): 313–34; Addison G. Wright, "The Riddle of the Sphinx Revisited: Numerical Patterns in the Book of Qoheleth," *CBQ* 42 (1980): 38–51.

Author and Date

Qoheleth 1:1 introduces "the words of Qoheleth, the son of David, king in Jerusalem." The phrase "son of David" only occurs in this opening title, which is not from the author, and could indicate any king in Judah descended from David. Qoheleth identifies himself simply as "king over Israel in Jerusalem" in 1:12, and while 2:7, 9 imply that there were more than one before him, the description of his wealth and wisdom in chapter 2 indicates that Solomon is the implied author. But this royal persona is not invoked from chapter 3 on, where Qoheleth is powerless to control things (3:16; 4:1; 5:8; 10:5–7) and frequently speaks as if he is not a king (see 4:13, 15; 5:9; 8:2–4; 9:14; 10:16, 17, 20).

Moreover, a number of considerations date the composition of the book well past the time of Solomon, or any other king in Jerusalem. To begin with, the book must be dated after the beginning of Persian control (ca. 539 BCE) in light of two loanwords: *pardēsîm* ("gardens") in 2:5 and *pitgām* ("sentence") in 8:11. In addition, the description in 5:8 of government as a series of ascending bureaucratic layers reflects the Persian Empire, as do "the eyes and ears of the king" who reported to the emperor directly concerning the satraps and governors.

There is no direct influence from Greek language, but there is evidence that Qoheleth was familiar with various aspects of Greek philosophy, even if he did not always agree with it. Many of these parallels are found in 1:4–7:

> [4] A generation goes, and a generation comes,
>   but the earth remains forever.
> [5] The sun rises and the sun goes down,
>   and hurries to the place that it rises.
> [6] The wind blows to the south,
>   and goes around to the north;
> round and round goes the wind,
>   and on its circuits the wind returns.
> [7] All streams run to the sea,
>   but the sea is not full;
> to the place where the streams flow,
>   there they continue to flow.

The passage mentions earth (1:4), air ("wind"; 1:6), and water (1:7), and if one links the sun (1:5) with fire, the result is the four elements from pre-Socratic thought. The description of continuous movement is also similar to Heraclitus's insistence that everything is in flux, with 1:7 in particular evoking his famous claim, "No one ever steps in the same river twice." (Both Heraclitus's emphasis on alteration and his categorization of everything as opposites may also be reflected in the alternating "times" in Qoheleth 3:1–9.) The Stoics' view of life as cyclical is also echoed in Qoheleth 1:4–7, but not their deterministic interpretation of life as a succession of ages.

Other passages in Qoheleth reflect Greek thought as well. Qoheleth 1:9 claims, "What has been is what will be, and what has been done is what will be done; there is nothing new under the sun," which recalls Parmenides's assertion that nothing changes. Qoheleth's regular exhortations to enjoyment (2:24; 3:12–13, 22; 5:17–18; 8:15; cf. 11:9) bring to mind the Epicurean focus on pleasure but without the latter's hedonism; apart from 3:22, Qoheleth's exhortations always identify such enjoyment as God's gift, and God will hold us accountable for how we use it. At the same time, enjoying life was a common theme throughout the Semitic world (see especially the discussion of Gilgamesh in chapter 1 above). In 3:21, Qoheleth pleads ignorance whether human spirits ascend and animal spirits descend, suggesting knowledge of Plato's doctrine of the soul but a reluctance to accept it—at the very least this is not the Epicureans' dogmatic denial of immortality. Qoheleth 7:16–18 argues against being too righteous, wise, wicked, or foolish, concluding, "It is good that you should take hold of the one, without letting go of the other," much like the Greek "golden mean" of moderation. Finally, Qoheleth works by "adding one thing to another to find the sum" (7:27), much like the philosophers' inductive method.

These similarities between Qoheleth and Greek thought are general enough that they do not require direct dependence of one on the other, but they do indicate enough familiarity with Greek ideas to situate the book of Qoheleth some time after Alexander the Great's conquest of the region in 333 BCE and his promotion of Hellenism to unify his expanding empire. This is reinforced by the book's language, which is late in the chronological development of Biblical Hebrew.[7] The latest possible date is established by portions of Qoheleth 5:14–16; 6:3–8; and 7:7–9 among the Dead Sea Scrolls, dating to the middle of the second century BCE. The book's content does not reflect any awareness of the persecutions by Antiochus IV and the ensuing Maccabean

---

7. Charles Francis Whitley, *Koheleth: His Language and Thought*, BZAW 148 (Berlin: de Gruyter, 1979), 136–48; Antoon Schoors, *The Preacher Sought to Find Pleasing Words: A Study of the Language of Qoheleth*, Part I: *Grammatical Features*, OLA 41 (Leuven: Peeters, 1992), especially 221–24; and Antoon Schoors, *The Preacher Sought to Find Pleasing Words: A Study of the Language of Qoheleth*, Part II: *Vocabulary*, OLA 143 (Leuven: Peeters, 2004), especially 499–502. Contrast Daniel C. Fredericks, *Qoheleth's Language: Re-Evaluating Its Nature and Date*, ANETS 3 (Lewiston, NY: Edwin Mellen, 1988), who considers it preexilic.

revolt, pointing to a time before 167 BCE. Ben Sira, composed between ca. 190 and 180 BCE (see the following chapter), alludes to Qoheleth, which pushes the date of composition further back, while the sense of political stability reflects the period of the Ptolemies rather than the Seleucids, i.e., before 198 BCE. Allowing time for the book to circulate and gain sufficient importance to be used by Ben Sira and preserved at Qumran, this suggests a date in the early to mid-third century BCE.

To summarize, Qoheleth was a third-century BCE sage whom the epilogue characterizes as a teacher and a writer (12:9–10). Many of his observations are consistent with a Judean setting (e.g., the decay of a cistern in 12:6), and his familiarity with Jerusalem, the temple sacrifice, etc., point to him living there, perhaps as the head of a school like Ben Sira (Sir. 51:23).

Title

The title Qoheleth comes from the Hebrew word *qōhelet*, a singular feminine participle from the root *qhl*. A singular feminine participle often indicates a title for a role or position, and the definite article before *qôhelet* in Qoheleth 12:8 understands it as such (i.e., "the *qôhelet*"). However, the four instances of the word in the body of the book (1:1, 2, 12; 7:27) do not have the definite article and appear to use the word as a proper name.[8] The difference can be attributed to Qoheleth 12:8 being a later addition to form an inclusio with Qoheleth 1:2 and attributing a role to the book's author. The term also appears subsequently in Qoheleth 12:9 and 10, where it may be either a title or a name. The verb *qhl* means "assemble, gather, collect," and is always associated with people. This points to Qoheleth as someone who gathered together people, probably students, which is reflected in the epilogue's description of Qoheleth as someone who taught and perhaps wrote (12:9–10). This leads to the Greek and Latin titles for the book, which are the basis for the traditional English title Ecclesiastes (Greek *ekklēsiastēs*, "gatherer," translates the Hebrew word *qōhelet*). But this can easily be confused with Ecclesiasticus, the alternative name of Ben Sira (see chapter 6), especially when they are abbreviated (Eccl. and Ecclus.), so many contemporary scholars use Qoheleth to refer to both the book and its author.

---

8. For feminine participles used as titles and then names see Ezra 2:55 // Neh 7:57 (the scribe) and Ezra 2:57 // Neh 7:59 (the binder of gazelles), each of which retains the article. The Greek translation of Qoh. 7:27 does have a definite article, but not the Hebrew.

Content

Qoheleth 1:1–11

The first two verses of the book contain the superscription and motto, respectively. Qoheleth 1:1 sets up the persona of a king, probably Solomon, which dominates for the first two chapters but is dropped after that. This literary fiction's purpose is to establish Qoheleth as someone who had sufficient wealth to experience every possible earthly pleasure so that he could then pronounce that "all is transitory" in v. 2 without anyone objecting that perhaps he missed something. At the same time, the traditional association of Solomon with wisdom means that he also experienced wisdom to the fullest, which gives full weight to his evaluation of wisdom as also transitory.

Qoheleth 1:3–11 provides a general evaluation of human existence that will be developed further in the following chapters. The opening rhetorical question asks whether people gain anything from human existence that happens "under the sun." Despite the passage of generations, the earth remains the same, locked into unending repetition of the same things. This is the first hint that Qoheleth will diverge from the wisdom tradition. The latter often celebrated the regularity and order in nature, but Qoheleth sees this as a negative thing. Since there is "nothing new under the sun" (1:9), human existence is tiresome and therefore those who experience it are not worth remembering.

Qoheleth 1:12–6:9—Theme 1: "A Chasing after Wind"

Qoheleth 1:12 switches to first-person reflections, with Qoheleth describing himself as "king over Israel in Jerusalem," as is common in ancient Near Eastern royal introductions.[9] Verses 12–18 introduce a new dual focus, Qoheleth's exploration of what is done on earth alongside his devotion to wisdom. Two proverbs summarize the dispiriting findings: the first indicates that humans can change nothing (1:15), the second shares the negative results of wisdom ("those who increase knowledge increase sorrow"; 1:18). These verses also introduce the larger theme of the first half of the book, namely that everything is transitory and "a chasing after wind." Chapter 2 develops these points by describing the author's actual experience with pleasure and wisdom. He em-

9. Y. V. Koh, *Royal Autobiography in the Book of Qoheleth*, BZAW 369 (Berlin: de Gruyter, 2006).

phasizes that he did not spare himself any indulgence, but neither did he abandon his wisdom (2:10): he erected buildings and lavish gardens, had slaves to meet his needs, owned flocks, amassed gold and silver, and surrounded himself with entertainers and concubines. He lacked for nothing and yet found it all unsatisfying. So he then considered the value of wisdom over folly, but even though wisdom was preferable, the wise and the foolish experience the same end. Both die alike and are forgotten by future generations. Moreover, all his possessions will be inherited by others, and he will have no control over how they use them. He concludes his reflections by asserting that if God gives one the opportunity to enjoy life, one should do so, but not even that has lasting significance. It too is "transitory and a chasing after wind" (2:26).

Qoheleth 3:1–15 deals with whether or not we can determine the right time to act. It begins with the statement that everything has "a season" and "a time," which implies that everything is already determined. This is followed by a series of fourteen opposites, each of which may be a merismus encompassing everything in between as well, but since each opposite has its own time, they also cancel each other. Rather than a haphazard listing, the pairs are arranged according to their presumed desirability: the first two list the positive element first and the negative element second, the next four have the negative action followed by the positive one, the next four reverse that order with the positive before the negative, and the next two reverse the initial two opposites with a negative and a positive. This creates a mirror pattern of 2 + 4 + 4 + 2, which is followed by a chiastic arrangement of positive plus negative in 3:8a and negative plus positive in 3:8b.[10] Each of the pairs occurs within the parameters of the first set: birth and death.[11]

Opposites in Qoheleth 3		
2	be born	die
	plant	pluck up
3	kill	heal
	break down	build up
4	weep	laugh
	mourn	dance
5	throw away stones	gather stones together
	embrace	refrain from embracing
6	seek	lose
	keep	throw away
7	tear	sew
	keep silence	speak
8	love	hate
	war	peace

10. J. A. Loader, *Polar Structures in the Book of Qohelet*, BZAW 152 (Berlin: de Gruyter, 1979), 11–13.

11. Addison G. Wright, "'For Everything There Is a Season': The Structure and Meaning of

QOHELETH 3	FOCUS
v. 2a	birth and death
vv. 2b–3	construction and destruction
v. 4	reactions to these
vv. 5–7a	combining and separating
v. 7b	reaction to these
v. 8a	love and hate (which result in)
v. 8b	war or peace

The final two chiastic pairs identify the larger framework within which the previous individual actions take place: love and hate plus their fullest expression in either war or peace.

The second part of this unit reflects on the previous list, but as with 1:4–7, Qoheleth does not celebrate the order and balance that they express. Instead, he concludes that workers gain nothing from their effort and then explains why. He acknowledges that God has given everyone a task with a "suitable . . . time," but God does not give people the ability to determine what those predetermined tasks are. God has put '*lm* into their minds (3:11); the NRSV renders the Hebrew word as "a sense of past and future" and many interpreters opt for "eternity." But the same Hebrew root also has the nuance of "darkness" (cf. Qoh. 12:5, 14; Job 28:21; 42:3), which is more consistent with the second part of the verse, in which "they cannot find out what God has done."[12] God is responsible for this lack of human insight, and we cannot change what God has done, but this very fact reinforces Qoheleth's advice to enjoy God's gift of pleasure.

Qoheleth 3:16–4:6 addresses the problem of human oppression. One expects justice and righteousness in the law courts, but the opposite prevails. Recalling God's predetermined times in the previous section, Qoheleth says, at least in his heart, that God will judge according to the "time" that God has appointed "for every matter." In light of his complaints later in the book that there is no retribution in this life (see 7:15; 8:14), he may have as little hope of

---

the Fourteen Opposites (Ecclesiastes 3, 2–8)," in *De la tôrah au messie: mélanges Henri Cazelles*, ed. Joseph Doré, Pierre Grelot, and Maurice Carrez (Paris: Desclée, 1981), 321–28.

12. For an evaluation of ten different understandings of the word here, with a defense of it meaning "darkness," see Brian P. Gault, "A Reexamination of 'Eternity' in Ecclesiastes 3:11," *BSac* 165 (2008): 39–57. Cf. also the earlier study of Francis T. Holland, "Heart of Darkness: A Study of Qohelet 3.1–15," *PIBA* 17 (1994): 81–101, especially his contextual and semantic arguments on pp. 98–101.

actually seeing God's judgment as he had of finding out what God wants us to do. He believes that human injustice is God's way of demonstrating that humans are no different than animals. Because both die and decompose in the dust, humans are no better off than the animals. Qoheleth asks whether human "spirits" go up and those of animals go down, but the form of the question anticipates a negative answer. As a result, humans should enjoy their work, because they have no insight into what happens after they die.

Turning to a more general consideration, Qoheleth notes the distress that the oppressed experience because their oppressors are powerful. He does not propose any solution to the oppression or even that the sufferers can be comforted, not because he approves of the situation but because he is unable to change it. As a result, the dead are actually better off because they can no longer be oppressed, and the unborn even more so because they have not yet experienced the "evil deeds" that mark human existence "under the sun." Qoheleth concludes that these evil deeds are rooted in envy. The section ends with two proverbs. In 4:5 the laziness of fools means they will waste away, reminiscent of Proverbs 19:24; 26:15. Qoheleth 4:6 also echoes a sentiment common in Proverbs (e.g., Prov. 15:16, 17; 17:1), namely that is better to have a little in calmness than more with stress, to which Qoheleth adds "and a chasing after wind."

The next unit, 4:7–16, includes another instance of *hebel*, this time referring to individuals without a family ("sons or brothers"; 4:8). Such solitary people have no one with whom to share the results of their efforts, and therefore they are never satisfied. In contrast, two people working together make a job easier, produce more than either individually, and if one falls then the other can lift her, unlike someone working alone. Verse 11 moves to two sleeping together and keeping each other warm, revealing that Qoheleth has probably been speaking about a married couple. In keeping with this, two can resist a single attacker better than an individual acting alone, while a three-ply cord is hard to break (see chapter 1 above for the appearance of a nearly identical expression in the Gilgamesh epic). This may be an image for a family comprising a mother, father, and child.

This leads into consideration of a successor in 4:13–16. The details of this passage are obscure; if it is an historical allusion, the specifics are lost to us and no attempt at identification has been convincing. It is more likely an example story, although one that reverses the typical evaluation of youth and age, where wisdom is traditionally associated with age. But Qoheleth advises that one should follow a wise young person rather than a foolish old king, regardless of the former's age, because even a lowborn former prisoner can rule well. But the youth who replaced the king will also be replaced (contrary to the NRSV, a better rendering of v. 15b is, "with the youth is a second who will stand in his place") and the people will transfer their allegiance. There is an advantage in a stable succession but a disadvantage in the lack of loyalty. Moreover, since those who come after do not praise him, the youth's wisdom has no lasting value. It is "transitory and a chasing after wind" (4:16).

Qoheleth 4:17–5:7 deals with worship. One should approach the temple carefully, where being attentive is preferred over foolish sacrifices (cf. 1 Sam. 15:22; Prov. 15:8; 21:3; 21:17; Hos. 6:6); unthinking participation in the cult is not advisable. Qoheleth repeats traditional advice against rash speech, then extends it to prayer as well. This is because there is a distance between God in heaven and humans on earth, which implies a distant God. Within this context, the dreams in 5:3 are revelatory, but they bring their own problems; Qoheleth compares them to the unguarded speech of fools, a very negative analogy in the wisdom tradition.

Related to worship are religious vows, which Qoheleth insists must be fulfilled quickly. The first half of Qoheleth 5:4 resembles Deuteronomy 23:21a, but one variation between the two stands out. Qoheleth replaces "Yahweh your God" with simply "God." This is in keeping with the general lack of references to Israel's religious traditions in the early wisdom literature, and it also reflects Qoheleth's view of a distant impersonal deity. He goes on to say that it would be better not to make a vow to God than to leave it unfulfilled, which is an inexcusable sin that will provoke divine anger. At that point it will be too late to admit one's "mistake" (šĕgāgâ) to "the messenger." The Hebrew word for "mistake" is used in priestly legislation about inadvertent sin (Num. 15:22–31; Lev. 4:2–5), so the "messenger" here is probably a priest seeking the fulfillment of a vow rather than a heavenly messenger. However, the precepts concerning unintentional violation of the law will not help in this case because one is fully conscious of a vow and the obligation to fulfill it. The unit ends with a variation on Qoheleth 5:3, with the added command to "fear God."

The final unit in this section, 5:8–6:9, presents a series of reflections on money and possessions. The opening verses note the oppression of the "poor" in the "province," which differentiates it from 3:16–4:6. The latter deals with the law courts and oppression of the weak, but here the author is concerned specifically with the poor, who overlap with but are not identical to the weak. The term "province" plus the subsequent description of a system of increasing oversight indicate that this is a political and bureaucratic matter. Qoheleth says one should not be surprised at the oppression of the poor, so this is not a case of higher officials correcting their subordinates; rather, they expect a share of the financial exploitation. Oppression is built into the system of overseers, with each level taking money from those lower down in order to pay those higher up, so there's no sense getting upset. The precise meaning of 5:9 is not clear. It seems to indicate that a king could be a corrective to this problem, but since Israel did not have its own king at this point in time, that is not a realistic hope for Qoheleth.

Qoheleth 5:10 moves from official to private wealth, while also introducing a subsection that extends to the end of the unit. There are two overlapping structural patterns in Qoheleth 5:10–6:9.[13] The first is a mirror pattern that presents material in the second half in the reverse order to the first half, as follows:

A Limits to Satisfaction (5:10–12)
    B Coming and Going in Darkness (5:13–17)
        C God's Blessing or Curse (5:18–20)
        C' God's Blessing or Curse (6:1–2)
    B' Coming and Going in Darkness (6:3–6)
A' Limits to Satisfaction (6:[5], 7–9)

At the same time, topics are developed in parallel order in the two halves of the subsection. Qoheleth 5:10–12 introduces the four topics discussed in the subsequent verses: (1) The Wealthy; (2) Temporary Property; (3) What Advantage?; and (4) Contentment. These are then developed twice in three movements:

I. There Is an Evil: Riches Possessed and Lost (5:13–14a // 6:1–2)
II. Begetting: Having Nothing Plus Coming and Going (5:14b–16a // 6:3–6)
III. What Advantage from Toil? No Satisfaction versus Contentment (5:16b–20 // 6:7–9)

This unit completes Qoheleth's discussion of the first theme with a final repetition of the phrase "transitory and a chasing after wind."

---

13. The following summarizes the far more detailed analysis in Daniel C. Fredericks, "Chiasm and Parallel Structure in Qoheleth 5:6–6:9," *JBL* 108 (1989): 17–35. The section and topic labels are Fredericks's.

Qoheleth 6:10–8:17—Theme 2: "One Cannot Find"

Qoheleth 6:10–12 marks the start of the second half of the book in terms of the number of verses (111 in each half) as well as a transition to the second and third themes in the book. Verses 10–11 summarize the preceding chapters with the announcement that everything is determined ("named")—nothing is new and any human attempt to dispute with God ("the one who is stronger" [a more accurate translation than "those who are stronger" in the NRSV]) is transitory and without benefit. Verse 12 anticipates the two themes that will dominate the following chapters, namely that humans can know neither what to do ("what is good") in their short and empty lives nor what will come afterward on this earth ("under the sun").

In 7:1–14 the author begins his discussion of the difficulty in knowing what is "good"—the Hebrew word occurs seven times in these fourteen verses—with six "better" sayings (7:1, 2, 3, 5, 8 [2×]), each of which is accompanied by his commentary calling into question the traditional wisdom concerning what is and is not good. The first better saying asserts the importance of a good name over fine oil, and the poetic symmetry, alliteration, and assonance of 7:1a (*ṭôb šēm miššemen ṭôb*) suggest it was a popular proverb. One's reputation is important in wisdom literature (cf. Prov. 22:1), but Qoheleth qualifies this in 7:1b by preferring the day of one's death over the day of one's birth, since only after death is one's reputation secure from change. Qoheleth elaborates the point in 7:2–4, starting with another better saying in 7:2. The reference to "death" in 7:1b links with "the house of mourning" repeated in vv. 2 and 4, while "oil" anticipates "the house of feasting/mirth," in the same two verses. Once again Qoheleth prefers the negative "house of mourning" over the positive "house of feasting/mirth" because death is the common end of all. The sorrow that accompanies death is better than laughter, because that makes one glad, a counterintuitive conclusion at odds with Proverbs 15:13a ("a glad heart makes a cheerful countenance"). The wise recognize that all will arrive at the house of mourning when they die, in contrast to fools who focus on mirth now. Therefore, the rebuke of the wise is preferable to fools singing in "the house of mirth," which is like the popping sound of burning thorns.

Nevertheless, wisdom itself is transitory because it can be corrupted by strength or bribery. Instead, the proper evaluation can only be made after something is completed (cf. 7:1b), so patience is preferable to pride. In other words, do not boast before successfully completing a task (cf. 1 Kings 20:11). At the same time, do not respond to such injustices with anger, in contrast to fools who "nurse" their anger, which in turn gnaws at them. Contrary to wisdom's reliance on insights from the past, Qoheleth encourages the reader to live in the present, which yields wisdom that is more useful than money, because it results in life. But this is also relativized by the fact that we cannot change what God has done, which could be a blessing or a curse, nor can humans find out which they will experience.

Qoheleth next explores injustice and wickedness (7:15–24). The opening observation conflicts with the typical wisdom view of retribution, namely that the righteous are blessed and the wicked punished. As a result, he advises against excessive desire for either option, as well as the wisdom and folly that are normally associated with each. Instead, one should hold the two in balance. So a god-fearer will succeed in pursuing wickedness, as long as he doesn't do so excessively. After a proverb about the relative value of wisdom, he notes that even the righteous sin, so do not pay equal attention to everything that is said. In particular, servants may be overheard cursing their masters, just as we all have often cursed others, if only internally ("your heart knows"). Qoheleth sought to understand these things by wisdom (cf. 1:13) but failed because it was inaccessible, as in Job 28:12–22; Prov. 30:1–4. In the words of his thematic phrase for this section, "Who can find it?"

Following this, 7:25–29 deals with human beings, specifically females and males. In his search for wisdom Qoheleth discovered that "wickedness is folly," which in turn is "madness." An example of such wickedness is the adulterous woman "who is a trap" to sinners. The adulterous woman is a common theme in the wisdom literature, as in Proverbs 2:16–19; 5:1–23; 6:20–35; 7:1–27 (see chapter 3 above). After extensive reflection Qoheleth found only one man in a thousand, but no women. The text does not evaluate the genders or state what they do, other than to say that males are rare and females nonexistent, but the context suggests a moral consideration. Regardless, both sexes fall under his conclusion that humans in general deviate from God's plan for them.

Qoheleth 8:1–9 reflects upon human and divine authority. The implied answer to the opening questions is that "no one" can compare with the wise person, which is followed by a description of wisdom's benefits. However, these benefits can be circumscribed by the need to obey one's vows to the king— prudence is in order because no one can challenge the king. The sages sought to teach one how to operate within the royal court, knowing "the time and the way" (cf. 3:1–9), but once again Qoheleth calls that into question, because humans do not know the future and cannot control the wind, death, battle, or wickedness. But people do have power over others, and that power can be exercised with negative effects.

This leads to the issue of retribution in 8:10–17. Because the wicked frequented "the holy place" and were honored in the city, their lack of punishment encourages people to continue their evil deeds. Even though Qoheleth recognizes that sinners live long lives, he states the traditional doctrine that they will not, while god-fearers will experience happiness. But since the reality is the opposite, Qoheleth repeats his exhortation to enjoy oneself if God gives the opportunity. Reiterating his examination of everything that is done, especially unending toil, he concludes that no one can "find out" what God would have us do. The final verse closes the second theme through a repetition of the verbal root *mṣ'* ("find out") in an ABA mirror pattern as an infinitive, an imperfect, and another infinitive.

Qoheleth 9:1–11:6—Theme 3: "One Cannot Know"

The first unit in the book's third section is enclosed by the negated root *yd'* in Qoheleth 9:1 and 12 ("one does not know" and "no one can anticipate" in the NRSV) as well as the root *qrh* in 9:2 and 11 ("fate" and "happen" in the NRSV). The good are in God's hand, but one cannot tell whether God will favor them or not. Rather, contrary to the usual wisdom teaching, Qoheleth asserts that everyone experiences the same fate regardless of one's deeds. He identifies seven pairs of individuals, listing the positive and then the negative, except for the last pair, which are reversed, ending with the positive. This leads to evil and madness, followed by death, but the living have the advantage that they know they will die, whereas the dead know nothing. Knowledge, no matter how unpleasant, is better than ignorance, and consciousness is better than nonexistence. The dead have no further participation in this world: human passion fades, and by implication it is constitutive of existence. The human emotions of love and hate in 9:6 recall the divine love and hate in 9:1 and form an inclusio marking the end of a subsection.

With greater urgency than his previous recommendations of enjoyment, Qoheleth here commands it: "Go, eat your bread with enjoyment, and drink your wine with a merry heart" (9:7). He urges the comfort of white clothes in a hot climate, oil to combat dry skin, and enjoying life with one's spouse. Do everything with enthusiasm, because humans are on their way to Sheol, where "there is no work or thought or knowledge or wisdom" (9:10)—the last three terms emphasize a lack of intellectual activity. There is no advantage in five traditionally positive attributes because of the role of chance, coupled with the fact that no one can know ("anticipate") disaster. The images of fish and birds being caught suggest a reference to death, which comes suddenly.

Qoheleth 9:13–10:15 contains reflections on the inability of wisdom to provide insight into what will happen next. It begins with an example story describing how a wise man defended a city against a great king, only to have his efforts forgotten. Qoheleth acknowledges the relative value of wisdom, but the fact that this man's wisdom was not remembered leads to two sayings that note the worth of wise words and how they are delivered, only to be undermined by a "bungler." A comparison from the natural world follows in 10:1, noting that just as a little folly can negate wisdom, so small things can destroy great good. The section concludes with a series of elaborations about how a fool demonstrates his folly.

Qoheleth admonishes one to remain calm in the face of a ruler's anger (10:4), then describes "an evil" that is as bad as if it came from a ruler, namely the reversal of traditional social roles. Verses 8–9 repeat traditional wisdom teaching about reaping the consequences of one's actions—in particular, falling into the very pit that one digs (10:8a) is also found at Proverbs 26:27; Psalms 7:15; 57:6; Sirach 27:26. Digging through the wall implies theft, which is punished by a snake hiding in the spaces between the wall's stones (10:8b; cf. Amos 5:19). Even normal chores like quarrying or chopping logs can be dangerous. Verses 10 and 11 both begin with "if" and deal with the need to use expertise before beginning a task. The unit ends with a contrast between the benefit derived from the words of the wise and the fact that despite the destructive effects of their words, fools don't know enough to be silent. The final verse mocks their expenditure of energy when they do not even know the goal.

The next unit (10:16–11:2) combines reflections on royal leadership with two sayings about the uncertainty of commercial ventures. According to Proverbs 19:10; 30:21–23, the lower class was not meant to govern, and Isaiah 5:11 condemns early morning feasts. For Qoheleth, in contrast to commoners, the nobility would not be swayed by the assumption of power and would feast at the right time and for the right reason, whereas drunkards do not make necessary repairs. Qoheleth repeats the value of feasts with wine, which are made possible by the nobles' wealth. At the same time, one should guard one's thoughts and words even in private, lest any negative comments be reported to the king and the rich associated with him. Attached to this are two directives concerning business transactions, both of which begin with a command followed by a motive clause starting with "for" (*ki*). Sending out "bread upon the waters" (11:1) probably refers to grain being traded overseas with the expectation that one will get its value back again. Moreover, it should be divided among a number of boats as a hedge against misfortune, which one does not know about in advance. This marks the end of the unit, reflecting the concern over the lack of knowledge about what will happen that runs through this portion of Qoheleth.

Reflections on humanity's lack of knowledge concerning agricultural activity in 11:3–6 close the book's third theme. We cannot know for sure when the clouds produce rain or when trees fall; the context suggests that the trees are felled by the wind, in which case the wind and clouds are repeated in the reverse order in the unit's second verse. Qoheleth's point is that excessive concern for the elements will prevent a farmer from accomplishing any work: fear that wind may blow away seeds delays sowing, while focusing on possible rain may interfere with the harvest. God's ways are as mysterious as the beginning of life, and since one does not know the outcome, one should sow twice. As with 8:17, 11:6 has an ABA pattern using a participle, an imperfect, and another participle to assert that one does "not know," thereby reinforcing the end of Qoheleth's third theme.

Qoheleth 11:7–12:8

A poem serves as the final unit of Qoheleth's own words, balancing the poem at the beginning of the book. The final verse here, 12:8, also forms an inclusio with 1:2. This concluding poem reinforces two points made frequently throughout the book, namely the need to enjoy life now before death makes that impossible. After an introductory statement about the value of being alive ("see the sun"; 11:7), 11:8 specifies the preceding with a chiastic pattern surrounding the twin imperatives of the poem, to rejoice and remember (in the sense of "be aware"):

> Even those who live <u>many years</u> should **rejoice** in them all;
> yet let them **remember** that the <u>days</u> of darkness will be <u>many</u>.

These are mutually interpretive: the exhortation to remember is the motivation for rejoicing. The "days of darkness" are death (cf. 6:4), not old age; they are contrasted with the many years of life. Not everyone will experience old age, nor has it been a concern previously in the book, whereas the universality and suddenness of death make it the best candidate for a motivating factor in one's youth. Therefore, everything that comes is transitory (*hebel*).

The command to rejoice is elaborated in 11:9–10, with the urgency to do so "while you are young" reinforced by the series of imperatives in both verses. The time for this rejoicing is indicated by the mirror pattern of "youth . . . heart

... mind ... youth" unifying these verses. God will judge how we have used the divine gift of joy, because that is God's will. Since youth is transitory and there is no certainty that anything else will follow, in 11:10 Qoheleth urges that one reject negative things, reiterating the positive formulation of 11:9 through its opposite.

The imperative to remember is developed in 12:1–7, which is a single sentence in the Hebrew. Qoheleth commands the reader to "remember ... in the days of your youth." The references to "days" and "years" in the reverse order of 11:8 link this to the emphasis on youth in the preceding verses, while the lengths of the two sections reinforce the relative lengths of youth and death: the discussion of transitory youth comprises just two verses (11:9–10), while the finality of death is treated over seven verses (12:1–7). According to the preserved Hebrew text, Qoheleth issues an order to remember "your creator," but since the other forty references to God in the book always use *'ĕlōhîm*, most interpreters assume that the text is corrupt. A small emendation of the Hebrew, from *bôr'eykâ* to *bôrĕkâ*, yields "your pit," so Qoheleth likely instructs his audience to remember the grave. This is in keeping with the previous contrast between youth and death as well as the content of the following verses. These verses have often been understood as either metaphorical, in which old age is described in terms of the deterioration of a household, or allegorically, whereby the "women who grind" (12:3) equals the teeth, "those who look through the windows ... dimly" (12:3) refers to fading eyesight, and so on. Neither approach can be maintained consistently, and both fail to take into account the contrast between youth and death in the first part of the poem, the absence of old age from the rest of the book, and the details of 12:1–7.

This remembering is to take place "before" three different events, introduced in verses 1, 2, and 6. The first is the coming of "the days of trouble," echoing "the days of darkness" in 11:8 and death as "the evil time" in 9:12. This will be a time with no pleasure, just as there is no pleasure in Sheol (9:10). The second "before" governs 12:2–5, which consists of three subsections. The first contains the image of a storm, although the obliteration of light may be a secondary allusion to death, in contrast to light as life in 11:7. The second subsection is further specified as occurring "when" (*bayyôm šĕ-*; NRSV "in the day") in 12:3a, which is matched by another "when" (*b-*; NRSV "and") in 12:4a, and this temporal inclusio encompasses a discussion of human affairs. The guards and female grinders are servants while the strong men and the women looking through windows are the upper class, and the actions of all four are explained by the central phrase of the section, "because they are few," referring to a reduction in the number of humans on the estate. The death of some or many members of the household explains a number of their actions. The movements of the males suggest mourning, the women at the window either wear black or have a gloomy demeanor, and the grinders have fewer to provide for and therefore work less. As a result, the mill is silent and the doors are closed because normal activity ceases during mourning. The third subsection begins with 12:4c and extends up to the concluding "because" in 12:5. The repetition of "sound" in 12:4b and 12:4c links this subsection to the previous description of the reduced activity in the household. However, this portion deals with the natural realm, much of which is diminished, and it is also the realm in which the storm in the first "before" section occurred (12:1b), establishing an inclusio around the discussion of the effect of death on human affairs. This is reinforced by the end of 12:5, which specifies that all this is because everyone goes to the grave ("their eternal home") accompanied by mourners. Thus, events in nature reflect those in the world of humans.

The final "before" section encompasses 12:6–7 and employs four images for death: a snapped cord, a broken bowl, a broken pitcher, and a broken pulley at a cistern. These verses are united by an intricate pattern: "broken" is repeated in both halves of 12:6, the prepositions 'al and 'el occur in the same order in 12:6b (NRSV has "at" for both) and 12:7 (both are "to" in the NRSV), and "returns" is found in both halves of 12:7. The subsection ends with a reference to returning to dust, echoing Genesis 3:10 (see also Ps. 104:29; Job 34:14–15), presenting an image of dissolution, not immortality. Qoheleth 12:8 concludes the main book through an inclusio with Qoheleth 1:2, while also negating any possibility of hope from 12:7.

Qoheleth 12:9–14

The final six verses of Qoheleth are marked off as a later addition not only by their location after the inclusio of Qoheleth 12:8 with 1:2, but by their content, which is dramatically different from the rest of the book. This section has affinities with both Proverbs and Sirach,[14] and it appears to be an attempt to render the book more orthodox by adding a positive evaluation of Qoheleth's efforts and some concluding pious comments. It evenly divides into two sub-

---

14. See Gerald H. Wilson, "'The Words of the Wise': The Intent and Significance of Qohelet 12:9–14," *JBL* 103 (1984): 175–92; and Gerald T. Sheppard, *Wisdom as a Hermeneutical Construct: A Study in the Sapientializing of the Old Testament*, BZAW 151 (Berlin: de Gruyter, 1980), 121–29, respectively.

sections of three verses each through the repetition of "in addition" in 12:9 and 12:12. The first half begins with a third-person description of Qoheleth's social location and activity as a sage, in contrast to his first-person speech in the preceding chapters. He did not restrict himself to the elite, the normal audience of the wise, but he also taught "the people" with carefully considered proverbs that were well expressed. The first subsection ends with a reference to sages in the plural, not just Qoheleth; their efforts are meant to prod the reader, which makes Qoheleth's critiques more acceptable. The second half of the epilogue shifts from Qoheleth to the intellectual process itself. This is the only instance in the book of "my son," the typical address of a teacher to a student, and the use of imperatives rather than the indicative give a sense of urgency. The comment that "of making many books there is no end" (12:12) is frequently cited in books about Qoheleth, but ironically it does not prevent their production. The negative evaluation of study also seems counterintuitive in a wisdom book and may be a critique of Qoheleth's efforts. The book ends with two thoughts that are inconsistent with Qoheleth's own ideas, namely that people should fear God and obey the commandments and that God will judge everyone according to their deeds.

Summary

Qoheleth reflects on human experience and finds that everything, including Israel's wisdom traditions, lacks lasting significance. Instead, in his experience everything is "transitory" (*hebel*). Moreover, death will come to everyone, but no one can predict when she or he will die. Therefore, the only thing that Qoheleth can recommend is that if God provides an opportunity for pleasure, then we should enjoy that experience now and not put it off, since we might die and miss the opportunity.

FURTHER READING

Commentaries

Bartholomew, Craig G. *Ecclesiastes*. BCOTWP. Grand Rapids: Baker Academic, 2009.

Barton, George Aaron. *A Critical and Exegetical Commentary on the Book of Ecclesiastes*. ICC. Edinburgh: T&T Clark, 1912.

Bergant, Dianne. *Job, Ecclesiastes.* OTM 18. Wilmington, DE: Glazier, 1982.

Bollhagen, James. *Ecclesiastes.* ConcC. Saint Louis: Concordia, 2011.

Brown, William P. *Ecclesiastes.* Interpretation. Louisville: Westminster John Knox, 2000.

Crenshaw, James L. *Ecclesiastes: A Commentary.* OTL. Philadelphia: Westminster, 1987.

Enns, Peter. *Ecclesiastes.* THOTC. Grand Rapids: Eerdmans, 2011.

Farmer, Kathleen. *Who Knows What Is Good? A Commentary on the Books of Proverbs and Ecclesiastes.* ITC. Grand Rapids: Eerdmans / Edinburgh: Handsel, 1991.

Fox, Michael V. *A Time to Tear Down and a Time to Build Up: A Rereading of Ecclesiastes.* Grand Rapids: Eerdmans, 1999.

———. *Ecclesiastes* קהלת: *The Traditional Hebrew Text with the New JPS Translation.* JPS Bible Commentary. Philadelphia: Jewish Publication Society, 2004.

———. *Qohelet and His Contradictions.* JSOTSup 71. Sheffield: JSOT Press, 1989.

Fredericks, Daniel C., and Daniel J. Estes. *Ecclesiastes & the Song of Songs.* ApOTC 16. Nottingham: Apollos / Downers Grove, IL: InterVarsity Press, 2010.

Garrett, Duane A. *Proverbs, Ecclesiastes, Song of Songs.* NAC 14. Nashville: Broadman & Holman, 1993.

Krüger, Thomas. *Qoheleth: A Commentary.* Translated by O. C. Dean Jr. Hermeneia. Minneapolis: Fortress, 2004.

Lohfink, Norbert F. *Qoheleth.* Translated by Sean E. McEvenue. CC. Minneapolis: Fortress, 2003.

Longman, Tremper, III. *The Book of Ecclesiastes.* NICOT. Grand Rapids: Eerdmans, 1998.

Moore, David George, and Daniel L. Akin. *Ecclesiastes, Song of Songs.* Holman Old Testament Commentary. Nashville: Broadman & Holman, 2003.

Murphy, Roland E. *Ecclesiastes.* WBC 23a. Waco, TX: Word, 1992.

Murphy, Roland E., and Elizabeth Huwiler. *Proverbs, Ecclesiastes, Song of Songs.* NIBCOT 12. Peabody: Hendrickson, 1999.

Nowell, Irene. *Song of Songs, Ruth, Lamentations, Ecclesiastes, Esther.* New Collegeville Bible Commentary 24. Collegeville, MN: Liturgical Press, 2013.

Ogden, Graham S. *Qoheleth.* 2nd ed. Readings: A New Biblical Commentary. Sheffield: JSOT Press, 2007.

Perry, T. A. *Dialogues with Kohelet: The Book of Ecclesiastes: Translation and Commentary.* University Park: Pennsylvania State University Press, 1993.

Schoors, Antoon. *Ecclesiastes.* HCOT. Leuven: Peeters, 2013.

Scott, R. B. Y. *Proverbs, Ecclesiastes: A New Translation with Introduction and Commentary.* 2nd ed. AB 18. Garden City: Doubleday, 1965.

Seow, Choon-Leong. *Ecclesiastes: A New Translation with Introduction and Commentary.* AB 18C. New York: Doubleday, 1997.

Whybray, R. N. *Ecclesiastes.* NCBC. Grand Rapids: Eerdmans, 1989.

Other Works

Anderson, William H. U. *Qoheleth and Its Pessimistic Theology: Hermeneutical Struggles in Wisdom Literature.* Mellen Biblical Press Series 54. Lewiston, NY: Mellen, 1997.

———. *Scepticism and Ironic Correlations in the Joy Statements of Qoheleth?* Gorgias Dissertations in Biblical Studies 44. Piscataway, NJ: Gorgias, 2010.

Barbour, Jennie. *The Story of Israel in the Book of Qohelet: Ecclesiastes as Cultural Memory.* Oxford Theology and Religion Monographs. Oxford: Oxford University Press, 2012.

Bartholomew, Craig G. *Reading Ecclesiastes: Old Testament Exegesis and Hermeneutical Theory.* AnBib 139. Rome: Biblical Institute Press, 1998.

Berlejung, A., and P. van Hecke, eds. *The Language of Qohelet in Its Context: Essays in Honour of Prof A. Schoors on the Occasion of His Seventieth Birthday.* OLA 164. Leuven: Peeters, 2007.

Boda, Mark J., Tremper Longman III, and Cristian G. Rata, eds. *The Words of the Wise Are Like Goads: Engaging Qohelet in the 21st Century.* Winona Lake, IN: Eisenbrauns, 2013.

Bundvad, Mette. *Time in the Book of Ecclesiastes.* Oxford: Oxford University Press, 2015.

Burkes, Shannon. *Death in Qoheleth and Egyptian Biographies of the Late Period.* SBLDS 170. Atlanta: Society of Biblical Literature, 1999.

Christianson, Eric S. *A Time to Tell: Narrative Strategies in Ecclesiastes.* JSOTSup 280. Sheffield: Sheffield Academic, 1998.

Crenshaw, James L. *Qoheleth: The Ironic Wink.* SPOT. Columbia: University of South Carolina Press, 2013.

Dell, Katharine J. *Interpreting Ecclesiastes: Readers Old and New.* CSHB 3. Winona Lake, IN: Eisenbrauns, 2013.

Dell, Katharine J., and William L. Kynes, eds. *Reading Ecclesiastes Intertextually.* LHBOTS 587. London: Bloomsbury T&T Clark, 2014.

Ellul, Jacques. *Reason for Being: A Meditation on Ecclesiastes.* Translated by Joyce Main Hanks. Grand Rapids: Eerdmans, 1991.

Fredericks, Daniel C. *Coping with Transience: Ecclesiastes on Brevity in Life*. Bib-Sem 18. Sheffield: JSOT Press, 1993.

————. *Qoheleth's Language: Re-Evaluating Its Nature and Date*. ANETS 3. Lewiston, NY: Mellen, 1988.

Frydych, Tomáš. *Living under the Sun: Examination of Proverbs and Qoheleth*. VTSup 90. Leiden: Brill, 2002.

Fuhr, Richard Alan, Jr. *An Analysis of the Inter-Dependency of the Prominent Motifs within the Book of Qohelet*. Studies in Biblical Literature 151. New York: Peter Lang, 2013.

Geering, Lloyd. *Such Is Life! A Close Encounter with Ecclesiastes*. Salem, OR: Polebridge, 2010.

Gordis, Robert. *Koheleth—The Man and His World: A Study of Ecclesiastes*. 3rd augmented ed. New York: Schocken, 1968.

Ingram, Doug. *Ambiguity in Ecclesiastes*. LHBOTS 431. London: T&T Clark, 2006.

Isaksson, Bo. *Studies in the Language of Qoheleth, with Special Emphasis on the Verbal System*. Acta Universitatis Upsaliensis. SSN 10. Stockholm: Almqvist & Wiksell, 1987.

Kamano, Naoto. *Cosmology and Character: Qoheleth's Pedagogy from a Rhetorical-Critical Perspective*. BZAW 312. Berlin: de Gruyter, 2002.

Koh, Y. V. *Royal Autobiography in the Book of Qoheleth*. BZAW 369. Berlin: de Gruyter, 2006.

Koosed, Jennifer. *(Per)Mutations of Qohelet: Reading the Body in the Book*. LHBOTS 429. London: T&T Clark, 2006.

Lee, Eunny P. *The Vitality of Enjoyment in Qohelet's Theological Rhetoric*. BZAW 353. Berlin: de Gruyter, 2005.

Leithart, Peter K. *Solomon among the Postmoderns*. Grand Rapids: Brazos, 2008.

Limburg, James. *Encountering Ecclesiastes: A Book for Our Time*. Grand Rapids: Eerdmans, 2006.

Loader, J. A. *Polar Structures in the Book of Qohelet*. BZAW 152. Berlin: de Gruyter, 1979.

Miller, Douglas B. *Symbol & Rhetoric in Ecclesiastes: The Place of Hebel in Qohelet's Work*. AcBib 2. Atlanta: Society of Biblical Literature, 2002.

Mills, Mary E. *Reading Ecclesiastes: A Literary and Cultural Exegesis*. Heythrop Studies in Contemporary Philosophy, Religion and Theology. Burlington, VT: Ashgate, 2003.

Perry, T. A. *Book of Ecclesiastes (Qohelet) and the Path to Joyous Living*. Cambridge: Cambridge University Press, 2015.

Rudman, Dominic. *Determinism in the Book of Ecclesiastes*. JSOTSup 316. Sheffield: Sheffield Academic, 2001.

Salyer, Gary D. *Vain Rhetoric: Private Insight and Public Debate in Ecclesiastes.* JSOTSup 327. Sheffield: Sheffield Academic, 2001.

Schoors, Antoon. *The Preacher Sought to Find Pleasing Words: A Study of the Language of Qoheleth. Part I: Grammar.* OLA 41. Leuven: Peeters, 2004.

———. *The Preacher Sought to Find Pleasing Words: A Study of the Language of Qoheleth. Part II: Vocabulary.* OLA 143. Leuven: Peeters, 1992.

Shields, Martin A. *The End of Wisdom: A Reappraisal of the Historical and Canonical Function of Ecclesiastes.* Winona Lake, IN: Eisenbrauns, 2006.

Sneed, Mark R. *The Politics of Pessimism in Ecclesiastes: A Social-Science Perspective.* AIL 12. Atlanta: Society of Biblical Literature, 2012.

Tamez, Elsa. *When the Horizons Close: Rereading Ecclesiastes.* Translated by Margaret Wilde. Maryknoll, NY: Orbis Books, 2000.

Weeks, Stuart. *Ecclesiastes and Scepticism.* LHBOTS 541. London: T&T Clark, 2012.

———. *The Making of Many Books: Printed Works on Ecclesiastes 1523–1875.* Winona Lake, IN: Eisenbrauns, 2014.

Whitley, Charles Francis. *Koheleth: His Language and Thought.* BZAW 148. Berlin: de Gruyter, 1979.

Zuck, Roy B., ed. *Reflecting with Solomon: Selected Studies on the Book of Ecclesiastes.* Grand Rapids: Baker Books, 1994.

CHAPTER 6

Ben Sira

The Wisdom of Ben Sira, also known as just Ben Sira, Sirach, and Ecclesiasticus, is one of the deuterocanonical books—it is not part of the Jewish canon and therefore not in Protestant Bibles, but it is accepted by Roman Catholics and many Eastern Christian communities. The prologue indicates that it was written in Hebrew and translated into Greek by the author's grandson, but for most of its history it was known only through Greek, Latin, and Syriac versions. In 1898 CE, however, portions from five different medieval Hebrew manuscripts surfaced in the genizah, a storage room for worn-out texts, in a Cairo synagogue. Since then, Hebrew fragments of Sirach 6:20–31 plus 51:13–20 and 30 have been found among the Dead Sea Scrolls, and Sirach 39:27–44:71 at Masada. Together these constitute about two-thirds of the book in Hebrew, which is supplemented by the Greek.

The name Ben Sira comes from Sirach 50:27, where the author refers to himself as "Jesus son of (*ben*) Eleazar son of (*ben*) Sira." It is also known as Sirach, his grandfather's name in Greek, and Ecclesiasticus ("of the church"), due to its popularity in the early church. We follow scholarly convention in this book by using Ben Sira generally and Sirach with citations. Both of these are preferable to Ecclesiasticus, which is easily confused with Qoheleth/Ecclesiastes.

The book consists primarily of proverbial sayings, like much of Proverbs and with many of the same concerns, but unlike Proverbs, Job, and Qoheleth, Ben Sira refers to events and individuals from Israel's history, cites or alludes to significant parts of the biblical canon, and identifies Lady Wisdom with Torah. This is consistent with the purpose of the book, which is to respond to the promotion of Greek culture by Alexander the Great and his successors after 333 BCE. That included the promotion of Greek philosophy ("love of wisdom"), with all its skeptical elements but without Israel's experience of a special relationship with Yahweh. Ben Sira compiled material consistent with earlier Israelite wisdom texts but with the added perspective that true wisdom was to be found not in Greek philosophy but in God's interaction with and revelation to Israel, culminating in the Torah.

Unity and Structure

The first ten verses of the book introduce wisdom as being derived from the Lord, followed by a twenty-two-line poem in praise of Lady Wisdom. The poem is balanced by a twenty-three-line acrostic at Sirach 51:13–30 also praising wisdom, forming an inclusio around the book as a whole. The extra line in the concluding poem starts with the letter *peh*, so that together with the first line beginning with an *aleph* and the middle line beginning with a *lamed*, they spell the verb *'lp*, "to learn." Sirach 24 contains a third poem about Lady Wisdom: the chapter has thirty-five lines, as does Proverbs 8, which is also about Wisdom, and Wisdom herself gives a twenty-two-line speech in Sirach 24:3–22. The two twenty-two-line Lady Wisdom poems initiate major sections of the book, with a third section comprising Sirach 44:1–50:24, titled "Praise of the Ancestors" in most Greek manuscripts, as well as the Latin and Syriac versions (NRSV has "Hymn in Honor of our Ancestors"). The third section surveys major figures from Israel's history, followed by a laudatory description of Simon II, the Jewish high priest from 219 to 196 BCE. Following this, the numerical saying in Sirach 50:25–26 is anticlimactic and Ben Sira's autobiographical statement in 50:27–29 reads like a conclusion. Chapter 51 is

---

Orientation to Ben Sira

Structure:	Section I: 1:1–23:27
	A. 1:1–4:10
	B. 4:11–6:17
	C. 6:18–14:19
	D. 14:20–23:27
	Section II: 24:1–43:33
	E. 24:1–32:13
	F. 32:14–38:23
	G. 38:24–43:33
	Section III: 44:1–50:24
	Appendixes: 50:26–51:30
Author:	Jesus ben Eleazar ben Sira (50:27)
Date:	ca. 190–180 BCE
Major Themes:	Lady Wisdom is equated with Torah
	Israel's religious history
	advice about women
	various kinds of personal relationships
	true and false friendship
	the use of Scripture

appended to this, with a personal prayer of thanks (51:1–12) and the concluding acrostic poem about wisdom (51:13–30). One of the Cairo manuscripts inserts between them an exhortation for communal worship that is modeled on Psalm 136 but is not found in any of the versions.

The first two major sections can be further subdivided on the basis of repeated wisdom poems. The first section has poems about Lady Wisdom in both the introduction and the immediately following section (1:1–30) as well as in 4:11–19; 6:18–37; 14:20–15:10. Sirach 24 marks the beginning of the second major section with an introduction, a twenty-two-line speech by Lady Wisdom and an autobiographical comment by Ben Sira. This is the final poem by or about Lady Wisdom in the book proper, but poems about wisdom in general appear in 32:14–33:18 (using the synonym "instruction" in 32:14; 33:17) and 38:24–39:12, both of which end with additional biographical notes. Taking these seven wisdom poems as the start of individual units yields the following structure:[1]

Section I (1:1–23:27)
    A. 1:1–4:10   Understanding Wisdom
    B. 4:11–6:17   Applying Wisdom Personally
    C. 6:18–14:19   Applying Wisdom Socially
    D. 14:20–23:27   Applying Wisdom to Speech and Thought
Section II (24:1–43:33)
    E. 24:1–32:13   Applying Wisdom to the Covenant Community
    F. 32:14–38:23   Using Wisdom to Make Good Decisions
    G. 38:24–43:33   Demonstrating the Results of Wisdom
Section III (44:1–50:24)   In Praise of Devout Ancestors
Appendixes (50:26–51:30)

---

1. Wolfgang M. W. Roth, "On the Gnomic-Discursive Wisdom of Jesus Ben Sirach," *Semeia* 17 (1980): 59–79; Patrick W. Skehan and Alexander A. Di Lella, *The Wisdom of Ben Sira: A New Translation with Notes, Introduction and Commentary*, AB 39 (New York: Doubleday, 1987), xiii–xvi; John D. Harvey, "Toward a Degree of Order in Ben Sira's Book," *ZAW* 105 (1993): 52–62. The section titles are slightly modified from Harvey. They do not indicate exclusive content in each section (see the distribution of individual topics across multiple sections in Skehan and Di Lella, *Ben Sira*, 4–5), but that does not negate the structuring function of the wisdom poems.

Author and Date

As noted above, the author provides his name in 50:27, and refers to writing his wisdom in the book, followed by a blessing on those who study his sayings and put them into practice. Three autobiographical passages provide further insight into the author's self-understanding as a teacher. After comparing Lady Wisdom to six great rivers, in 24:30–34 Ben Sira describes himself as a channel for that water, gushing forth in his instruction for the sake of others. Sirach 33:16–18 repeats that his search for wisdom was for the benefit of others, and in the book's concluding poem (51:13–30) he again describes his efforts to gain wisdom and invites the reader to enter his school ("house of instruction") to receive his teaching. Assuming that Ben Sira would identify with the sage in 38:34–39:11, this further confirms him as a scholar and teacher, as in his grandson's description of Ben Sira's efforts in his prologue.

The grandson says that he moved to Egypt "in the thirty-eighth year of the reign of Euergetes," which is 132 BCE, so Ben Sira worked some two generations prior to that date. The description of the high priest Simon II, the son of Onias, is in the past tense, so Ben Sira must have been writing after Simon's death in 196 BCE, but there is no indication in the book of the persecution under Antiochus IV Epiphanes (175–164 BCE). Therefore, the book probably dates to ca. 190–180 BCE. Moreover, the description of Simon sounds like an eyewitness, so Ben Sira probably wrote in Jerusalem.

Content

Like the book of Proverbs, much of Ben Sira consists of two-line aphorisms. They are better organized in Ben Sira, however, and often collected into sets of twenty-two lines, reflecting the number of letters in the Hebrew alphabet. Some sets are organized simply by catchwords while others have greater thematic unity, and Ben Sira often repeats forms as well as topics in different parts of the book. Both Lady Wisdom and Israel's history play important roles in the book, and the author also makes extensive use of earlier biblical material.

Catchwords

Some sayings in Ben Sira are grouped on the basis of catchwords. Sometimes they occur frequently in a passage, but unlike keywords (see chapter 2 above) catchwords do not create a thematic unity. For instance, "do not" is repeated frequently in Sirach 7:1–20, sometimes matched by a reason in the second half of the verse, but what is forbidden in each case has little correlation with the prohibitions in other verses. Similarly, the question "do you have?" is found in 7:22–26 and the phrase "with all" repeats in 7:27–30, although both clusters have little internal coherence. Other times catchwords function like a hinge, appearing at the end of one section and the beginning of the next, linking larger portions of the book that deal with distinct topics. Sirach 8:1–19 discusses relations with others, with "do not" again dominating, and ends with the word "heart" (NRSV "thoughts"). Sirach 9:1–9 turns to the topic of women, with "do not" beginning each of vv. 1–7, but the passage as a whole links to the preceding one with its opening reference to "the wife of your heart" (NRSV "bosom"). Sirach 9:1–9 ends by mentioning "wine" in 9:9, which recurs in 9:10 at the start of a passage dealing with relationships (9:10–16). This is followed by a reflection on rulers (9:17–10:5), with the two units linked by the word "intelligent" in 9:15 and its synonym "wise" in 9:17.

Thematic Passages

Sometimes the correlation among individual sayings goes beyond simple catchphrases to broader themes. These include works of mercy (7:32–36), rulers (9:17–10:5), disciplining the tongue (23:7–15), three positive or negative things (25:1–2), forgiveness (28:1–7), charity (29:1–20), disciplining children (30:1–17), table manners (31:12–18), dreams (34:1–8), sacrifices (34:21–35:13), counselors (37:7–15), and the human condition and various problems of life (40:1–41:13); the last passage includes a subsection listing two things followed by a third that is "better than either" (40:18–27).

Some topics display significant internal development. For instance, Sirach 25:16–26:18 concerns women, a topic Ben Sira addresses elsewhere as well. He begins by discussing how living with an "evil woman" has negative effects on her husband (25:16–26), then reviews the positive effects of a "good wife" (26:1–4), before returning to the unfavorable aspects of a bad wife (26:5–9). This is followed by a discussion of the need to protect a daughter's virtue (26:10–12; cf. 7:24–25; 42:9–14), before Ben Sira once again praises the advantages of a charming wife. Similarly, "shame" is introduced in 41:14–16, followed by lists of things one should (41:17–42:1a) and should not (42:1b-8) be ashamed of, culminating with the possibility of a daughter's disgrace (42:9–14) and repeating the term "shame" in the final verse. A third extended section is the comparison between the vocation of the scribe with various other occupations in 38:24–39:11. This is often compared with the Egyptian *Satire of the Trades* (see chapter 1 above), although Ben Sira does not mock the trades as the *Satire* does, but rather laments the fact that their jobs do not allow them the time needed for study. The farmer (38:25–26), artisan (38:27), smith (38:28), and potter (38:29–30) all do important work that is essential to society (38:31–34a). Although not included here, the physician receives similar praise in 38:1–15. But "the one who devotes himself to the study of the law of the Most High" receives greater praise (39:1–11) for studying "wisdom" and "prophecies" (39:1) in order to be of service to leaders (39:4) and to convey his learning to others (39:6–11). In contrast to Proverbs and Qoheleth, both of which derived their collected wisdom through reflection on human experience, here Ben Sira equates wisdom with revelation through Scripture, in keeping with his equation of Lady Wisdom with Torah (see further below).

Repeated Forms

Some material is unified by means of specific forms. For instance, Ben Sira arranges some sections with graduated numerical sayings comparable to those in Proverbs 30. They deal with nine/ten things that are blessed (25:7–11), three/four things that frighten him (26:5–6, with the fourth element developed at length in 26:7–9), two/three things that anger him (26:28), and two/three nations he despises (50:25–26). Related to these are a simple grouping of three things he likes alongside three that he dislikes in 25:1–2.

Another repeated form in Ben Sira is the hymn, an innovation within the wisdom literature that stems from his introduction of explicitly religious matters into the book. All the hymns praise God for creation, although each focuses on a different aspect. Sirach 1:1–10 acclaims the Lord as the source of Wisdom, who was created before everything else and was poured out on the earth and its inhabitants. Sirach 16:24–17:10 celebrates the order reflected in the creation of the sky and its lights followed by the creation of the earth and human beings, and culminating in God's selection of Israel. Sirach 18:1–14 also extols divine majesty reflected in creation, describes humanity's comparative insignificance, and acknowledges God's patience with them. In Sirach 39:12–15 the author calls his disciples to sing a hymn of praise, while 39:16–31 provides the words to be used: God has created everything in an orderly manner for a purpose, namely to serve as a blessing for the good but punishment for the bad. The passage ends with Ben Sira's summary of the preceding verses and another exhortation to sing God's praises (39:32–35). Sirach 42:15–43:33 contains even more detailed praise of God's works, extolling the divine omniscience reflected in the ordered harmony of creation; the itemization of the elements of creation that are above and below in 43:1–26 recalls God's questions about creation in Job 38–39 in particular (see also Job 28; 36:24–37:13; Ps. 148). Finally, there are doxological calls to praise at Sirach 45:26; 50:22–24, and communal praise comparable to Psalm 136 that is inserted between Sirach 51:12 and 13 in one of the Hebrew manuscripts from the Cairo Genizah.

A related liturgical form in Ben Sira is the prayer of petition and thanksgiving that shares features with some psalms.[2] Sirach 22:27–23:6 asks God to protect him from those who would bring about his downfall, but unlike the psalms that seek help against human enemies, Ben Sira's opponents are his own lips and desires that could lead him into sin. Sirach 36:1–22 is more consistent with the communal petitions in the psalms, calling upon God to intervene against the nation's enemies and invoking God's prior selection of Israel and his presence in the temple as motivation for divine intervention. In the appendix, Sirach 51:1–12 corresponds to individual psalms of thanksgiving, acknowledging the Lord's already accomplished deliverance and promising to offer public praise.

Repeated Topics

Ben Sira returns to some topics more than once. As noted above, one of Ben Sira's repeated topics is women, in keeping with the preoccupation with them in ancient wisdom literature in general. Sirach 25:16–26:18, the structure of which was outlined above, concerns itself with good and bad wives as well as daughters. Sirach 42:9–14 singles out a daughter as a particular means by which a father might be shamed, discussing her at much greater length (six verses) than any of the other possible sources of shame mentioned in the larger unit (41:14–42:14). Sirach 9:1–9 encompasses a number of possible dangers with respect to women: being jealous of one's wife or allowing her power over you (9:1–2), loose women in general (9:3–4), virgins (9:5), harlots (9:6–7), and the potential for adultery with another man's wife (9:8–9). After 23:16–21 condemns men who commit incest or adultery, 23:22–27 discuss the adulterous

2. On the latter see Erhard S. Gerstenberger, *Psalms: Part 1 with an Introduction to Cultic Poetry*, FOTL 14 (Grand Rapids: Eerdmans, 1988); Erhard S. Gerstenberger, *Psalms: Part 2, and Lamentations*, FOTL 15 (Grand Rapids: Eerdmans, 2001).

wife impregnated by her lover, who will be judged "before the assembly," her children rejected, and her reputation disgraced. Finally, 36:26–31 discusses the advantages of gaining an attractive, well-spoken wife, followed by a warning that unmarried men become wanderers whom others will not trust.

Relationships are an even more frequent concern of Ben Sira. Sirach 7:18–28 contains a series of exhortations concerning maintaining positive relationships with members of one's household, including friends, a wife, slaves and workers, children (especially a daughter), and parents. This is followed in 7:29–8:19 by advice about dealing with a number of different outsiders, such as priests and God, those in need (the poor, the deceased, mourners, and the sick), the rich and powerful, the old and dying, sages, sinners, ambushers, borrowers, judges, "the reckless," quarrelers, and fools. Sirach 9:10–16 prefers old friends to new ones, warns against envying sinners and avoiding those who can kill, then concludes by recommending the company of the wise and righteous, surrounding the reflections on undesirable people (9:11–13) with reflections on positive companions (9:10, 14–16).

Underlying the preceding passages is the nature of true friendship, which Ben Sira examines in detail.[3] For instance, 6:5–17 advises that one be selective in choosing friends, because some will stick by you only when things go well but will abandon you if your fortunes change, in contrast to faithful friends, who are a gift from God. The same point is made in 37:1–6, which has a number of lexical contacts with 6:5–17[4] and also warns about fair-weather friends, who are contrasted with faithful companions. Sirach 11:29–13:24 is similar, providing an extended reflection about opposites types of people. Inviting strangers into your home invites danger, so instead help the devout but not sinners. Enemies cannot be trusted, even when they act friendly in good times, because they will abandon you in adversity. So too the rich, who will exploit your prosperity only to laugh at you after they have stolen what you had; therefore, be cautious when invited to join them. Since people are known by the company they keep, you should be cautious about your associates. Ben Sira ends the passage by returning to the rich person, who has many come to his aid when he experiences difficulty, but the poor and humble are ignored when they need help. Sirach 19:13–17 counsels discussing perceived grievances in case a friend did not actually commit the offense and the relationship can

3. For a detailed discussion see Jeremy Corley, *Ben Sira's Teaching on Friendship*, BJS 316 (Providence: Brown University Press / Atlanta: Society of Biblical Literature, 2002). In addition to longer treatments of the topic in Ben Sira, Corley surveys eighteen "incidental references to friendship" on pp. 219–27.

4. Corley, *Ben Sira's Teaching on Friendship*, 63–64.

be preserved, and 22:19–26 argues that a friendship can survive harsh words and even violence but not a betrayal, a point that 27:16–21 develops at greater length. Finally, in keeping with the advice in 6:6 that one can have many friends but that "advisors be one in a thousand," 37:7–15 elaborates on who one should accept as a counselor. Those who put themselves forward should be treated with suspicion, and Ben Sira lists nine people who cannot be expected to offer unbiased advice about specific topics ("a woman about her rival," "a coward about war," etc.). Instead, deal with "a godly person," be attentive to your own opinion, and remember that God is the most important advisor.

Lady Wisdom

Another important theme for Ben Sira is wisdom, both in terms of intellectual capacity in general and Lady Wisdom in particular. The book opens by linking both wisdom and Lady Wisdom with God, asserting that all wisdom comes from the Lord and that he created Lady Wisdom in the beginning (1:4; cf. Prov. 8:32). But just as the created world is beyond human comprehension, so too wisdom/Lady Wisdom is known only to the Lord (1:6–8; cf. Job 28:12–28) and those with whom God shares it/her. This is followed by a twenty-two-line poem linking Lady Wisdom with the fear of the Lord. Sirach 1:11–13 introduces the positive results that derive from fearing the Lord, before asserting in 1:14 that "to fear the Lord is the beginning of wisdom," repeating the phrase from Proverbs 1:7; 9:10; Psalm 111:10; Job 28:28. Ben Sira links fear of the Lord to the fact that Wisdom is with humans from the womb, then adds that fear of the Lord is also "fullness of wisdom" (1:16), just as she fulfills their needs with fruits (cf. Prov. 8:19) and other produce, as well as "the crown of wisdom" (1:18), just as her knowledge brings glory. Verse 20 proclaims that "to fear the Lord is the root of wisdom, and her branches are long life," the final image echoing Proverbs 3:15. "Fear of the Lord" also repels anger and allows self-control (1:21–24), gives wisdom through following God's commandments (1:25–27), and prevents hypocrisy (1:28–30).

Lady Wisdom appears three other times in the first part of the book, starting with 4:11–19, which indicates that if her children seek and hold fast to her she will put them to the test but reward those who endure. Sirach 6:18–31 elaborates on her discipline at greater length, but ends once again with the reward that results from submitting to her yoke. The third Lady Wisdom passage is Sirach 14:20–15:10. The first half describes the one who searches for Wisdom like a hunter (cf. 51:13–20) and ends by linking such actions to fear of the Lord and a commitment to the law. The second half expounds the benefits of doing so: she will be both a mother and a bride to him, providing food and drink, supporting and exalting him, and inspiring his speech so that he gains a "crown" and "an everlasting name" (15:6). In contrast, fools, sinners, the arrogant, and liars cannot enter into a relationship with her, for they are not fit to be in the Lord's presence.

Lady Wisdom makes her final appearance in the book, apart from the appendix, in chapter 24, which contains a significant development of her persona. The poem has thirty-five lines, as does Proverbs 8, the earlier extended presentation of Lady Wisdom. Proverbs 8 consists of Lady Wisdom's self-description in relationship to Yahweh and the created world and its inhabitants, and she gives a speech (of twenty-two lines) in Sirach 24:3–22 as well. The speech in Ben Sira echoes a number of features from Proverbs 8 but also goes well beyond it. She originated from God's own mouth like a mist covering the earth (24:3; cf. Gen. 1; 2:6), being created "in the beginning" (24:9; cf. Sir. 1:4; Prov. 8:22–26). But while Proverbs 8:27–31 depicts Lady Wisdom as a passive observer of Yahweh's creative activity who simply delights with God in the world and its inhabitants, in Sirach 24 she is more directly involved in the world (24:4–7), culminating in the divine command to take up residence within the holy tent in Jerusalem (24:8, 10–12). Expanding on the image of wisdom as a tree of life in Proverbs 3:18, Lady Wisdom uses imagery of fragrant majestic plants to describe her expansion throughout the traditional territory of Israel.[5] She then issues an invitation for the reader to come to her (24:19–22; cf. Prov. 8:32–36), promising food, drink, and honor (cf. Prov. 9:1–6).

The chapter concludes with Ben Sira's remarks on her speech, starting with his identification of Lady Wisdom with "the book of the covenant . . . the law that Moses commanded us" (24:23; cf. Bar. 4:1 and the wording of Deut. 33:4). Earlier in the book Wisdom was linked with obeying the law (Sir. 1:26; 15:1; 19:20; 21:11), but here Lady Wisdom is equated with the Torah itself, which he describes as gushing forth like the mighty rivers of the ancient Near East: the Pishon, Tigris, Euphrates, Jordan, Nile, and Gihon. Ben Sira himself is a channel, funneling the water of the Torah to his readers like a prophet. He is the conduit that marks the transition from the cosmic Lady Wisdom to a wisdom teacher, and his instruction is full of the wisdom contained in the Torah.

---

5. Coming after Lebanon and Hermon in the north plus Ein-Gedi and Jericho in the south, "the field" and "water" in 24:14 probably allude to the coastal plain in the west and the Jordan River in the east.

Praise of the Ancestors

The longest cohesive composition in Ben Sira is titled "Praise of the Ancestors" in the ancient versions and spans Sirach 44:1–50:24. Thomas R. Lee analyzed the passage in terms of the ancient *encomium*, a work in praise of a person or thing, in this case the high priest Simon II.[6] Lee divides the section into four parts: (1) an introduction (44:1–15); (2) Simon's ancestry (44:16–49:16); (3) his deeds (50:1–21); and (4) a concluding doxology (50:22–24). Jeremy Corley builds upon the subdivision of the second part by Lee and others based on the doxologies in 45:26 and 50:22–24, both of which come after a description of the actions of the high priests Aaron (plus a brief description of Phinehas) and Simon II. Corley proposes a different fourfold division: (1) a prologue (44:1–15); (2) from Noah to Phinehas (44:17–45:26); (3) from Joshua to Nehemiah (plus Enoch to Adam) (46:1–49:16); and (4) praise of Simon (50:1–24).[7] The resulting subdivisions correlate to the divisions of the Jewish canon alluded to in the grandson's prologue.[8] The heroes in 44:16–45:26 are taken in sequence from the Torah, and those in 46:1–49:13 appear in sequence from the Former and Latter Prophets and the Writings. Additional references to Enoch, Joseph, Shem, Seth, and Adam in Sirach 49:14–16 recall humankind's beginnings. The composition ends with the lengthy extended commendation of Simon II.

Burton Mack has gone beyond the basic encomium features of the poem and identified seven components in the review of the ancestors: (1) designation of an office; (2) divine approval or election; (3) a covenant; (4) the individual's character or piety; (5) his deeds; (6) the historical setting; and (7) rewards.[9]

---

6. Thomas R. Lee, *Studies in the Form of Sirach 44–50*, SBLDS 75 (Atlanta: Scholars Press, 1986).

7. Jeremy Corley, "A Numerical Structure in Sirach 44:1–50:24," *CBQ* 67 (2007): 45–46; he deletes the reference to Enoch in 44:16 as secondary. He supports this structure with an arithmetical pattern among the divisions: Part 1 has eighteen bicola, which is half the thirty-six in Part 4, while Part 2 has sixty-four bicola, half as many as the 128 bicola in Part 3 (pp. 56–62). On the structural significance of the doxologies see O. Rickenbacher, *Weisheitsperikopen bei Ben Sira*, OBO 1 (Freiburg: Universitätsverlag / Göttingen: Vandenhoeck & Ruprecht, 1973), 194–95; Lee, *Sirach 44–50*, 6, 20; P. C. Beentjes, "The 'Praise of the Famous' and Its Prologue: Some Observations on Ben Sira 44:1–15 and the Question on Enoch in 44:16," *Bijdragen* 45 (1984): 379–80.

8. Cf. Alon Goshen-Gottstein, "Ben Sira's Praise of the Fathers: A Canon-Conscious Reading," in *Ben Sira's God: Proceedings of the International Ben Sira Conference, Durham-Ushaw College 2001*, ed. Renate Egger-Wenzel, BZAW 321 (Berlin: de Gruyter, 2002), 235–67.

9. Burton L. Mack, *Wisdom and the Hebrew Epic: Ben Sira's Hymn in Praise of the Fathers* (Chicago: University of Chicago Press, 1985).

Not every component is explicitly mentioned for every named individual, but the components are sometimes implied, and taken together they are frequent enough to constitute an overall pattern. Mack also identifies five different offices: father (Noah, Abraham, Isaac, Jacob), priest (Aaron, Phinehas, Samuel, Joshua, Simon), judge (Joshua, Caleb, "the judges"), prophet (Samuel, Nathan, Elijah, Elisha, Isaiah, Jeremiah, Ezekiel, "the Twelve") and king (David, Hezekiah, Josiah, and "the kings of Judah" are named, but Saul, Rehoboam, and Jeroboam are alluded to negatively). No office is explicitly attributed to Moses, but Mack argues that he exercises prophetic roles in that he performs miracles and stands against kings (45:3) and anoints Aaron (45:15), a view that is reinforced by 46:1, which says that Joshua was "the successor of Moses in the prophetic office."[10]

All seven individuals in the first part of the praise of the heroes (44:17–45:26) are linked with a covenant. This is explicit in the case of Noah (44:17), Abraham (44:20), Jacob (44:23), Aaron (45:15), and Phinehas (45:24). In addition, Isaac is given "the same assurance" as Abraham, and therefore receives a covenant implicitly (44:23), while Moses receives the covenant from the Lord and passes it on to the people. Covenants are not mentioned after this section, except for one with David in 45:25.[11] David is out of place chronologically, but the reference provides an analogy between the royal succession and the restriction of the priesthood to Aaron's descendants. But at the same time, referring to David's covenant here means that four of the five offices, excluding the transitional judges, are linked to a covenant.

The Praise of the Ancestors can be divided into four historical periods. The first section deals with figures from the Pentateuch, from Noah to Phinehas, and was the time of covenants for four of the five offices. The period of the conquest encompasses Joshua and Judges, while the history of the kings and prophets spans Samuel to Ezekiel. The restoration after the Babylonian Exile is summarized through brief references to Zerubbabel, Joshua the priest, and

---

10. Mack, *Wisdom and the Hebrew Epic*, 31. Mack also views Moses as a teacher (45:5; a role that is subsumed by Aaron and the priests in 45:17) and as a ruler (Mack, *Wisdom and the Hebrew Epic*, 30, 32). The latter is based on Mack's translation of 45:3c as "God put him in command of the people," which the NRSV translates, "he gave him commandments for his people."

11. The NRSV translates 47:11 with "a covenant of kingship," following the Greek, but the Hebrew has *ḥoq* ("statute") rather than *bĕrît* ("covenant") as in 45:26; *ḥoq* is the basis for "the rights of royalty" in the NABRE and Skehan and Di Lella, *Ben Sira*, 523; cf. Benjamin G. Wright, *No Small Difference: Sirach's Relationship to Its Hebrew Parent Text*, SCS 26 (Atlanta: Scholars Press, 1989), 297 n. 122. In any case, the phrase occurs in the concluding summary about David and is not the focus of the section dealing with him.

Nehemiah, followed by singular references to six more individuals from the Pentateuch, linking back to the initial period of the poem. Following this, the extended description of Simon II officiating in the temple serves as the culmination of the section.[12] The clearest indication of this is the numerous parallels between Simon and the earlier description of Aaron, as well as between the colophon naming Phinehas (Sir 45:23) and the one near the end of the book (Sir. 50:22-23), thereby linking Simon to the two priests associated with the initial priestly covenant.[13] Sirach 50:1-4 also describes Simon's building and repair efforts, a role attributed in the earlier material to kings (Solomon and Hezekiah) and similar leaders (Zerubbabel, Joshua the priest, and Nehemiah). In addition, Lee sees a cultic connection for Joshua son of Nun, Samuel, David, Solomon, and Josiah, with the result that all Simon's predecessors in the Praise of the Ancestors except the prophets are "types" of the high priest.[14] For Lee, the Praise of the Ancestors is an encomium exalting Simon II as a model of priestly leadership to which his son and successor, Onias III, should conform.[15] Mack seeks to incorporate the prophets as well through the doxology's reference to "growth from birth" (50:22). Mack links this to Jeremiah's consecration in the womb in 49:7 and then argues that Simon also fulfills the offices of king and prophet.[16] While the prophetic role is forced, Mack's view that the Praise of the Ancestors is a "mythic charter for Second Temple Judaism"[17] is otherwise persuasive.

Ben Sira's Use of Scripture

The Praise of the Ancestors demonstrates that Ben Sira was familiar with significant portions of what became the First Testament, bringing together material from the Pentateuch, Joshua, the books of Samuel and Kings, probably Chronicles (for his view of David and Solomon), Ezra-Nehemiah, Isaiah, Jeremiah, Ezekiel, Haggai/Zechariah, and Malachi. He also mentions the judges

---

12. For a detailed treatment of the topic see Otto Mulder, *Simon the High Priest in Sirach 50: An Exegetical Study of the Significance of Simon the High Priest as Climax to the Praise of the Fathers in Ben Sira's Concept of the History of Israel*, JSJSup 78 (Leiden: Brill, 2003).

13. For the lexical details see Lee, *Sirach 44-50*, 6, 13-15.

14. Lee, *Sirach 44-50*, 12-19, 213.

15. Lee, *Sirach 44-50*, 210, following Ulrich Kellerman, *Nehemiah: Quellen, Überlieferung und Geschichte*, BZAW 102 (Berlin: Töpelmann, 1967), 112-15.

16. Mack, *Wisdom and the Hebrew Epic*, 36.

17. Mack, *Wisdom and the Hebrew Epic*, 56.

(46:11–12), proverbs by Solomon (47:14–17) and the Twelve Prophets (49:10), which does not necessarily reflect knowledge of the scrolls by those names (although see below concerning Proverbs). Other passages also indicate that Ben Sira knew earlier biblical literature. For instance, Sirach 16:6–10 alludes to five different episodes, two repeated in the Praise of the Ancestors, that are linked by the theme of sin and rebellious people, although not in their current canonical order: the rebellion by Korah, Dathan, and Abiram in the desert (Num. 16; Sir. 45:18–19), the giants (Gen. 6:1–4), Sodom and Gomorrah (Gen. 19), the Canaanites (the book of Joshua), and the 600,000 Israelites in the desert (Exod. 12:37; Num. 11:21; Sir. 46:8). Similarly, Sirach 16:26–17:24 mixes together details from the two creation stories in Genesis 1–2 and combines them with the giving of the covenant at Sinai and its attendant obligations.

Sometimes the wording of individual passages in Ben Sira is close enough to those elsewhere in the Jewish canon to indicate direct quotation.[18] James Crenshaw notes that Sirach 2:18 cites 2 Samuel 24:14 for its emphasis on divine mercy over that of humans.[19] In addition to this, the reference to Elijah's return in Sirach 48:10b echoes Malachi 4:5, while the wording of Sirach 48:10c more closely matches Malachi 4:6a; the intentional correspondence is confirmed by "it is written" in Sir. 48:10a. Other verses in Ben Sira also seem to be citing, or at least paraphrasing, biblical texts, although less explicitly than the preceding example. Sirach 15:17 says, "Before each person are life and death" and adds the need to choose, which corresponds to Moses's statement, "I have set before you life and death. . . . Choose life" in Deuteronomy 30:19. The statement that "he appointed a ruler for every nation, but Israel is *the Lord's portion*" (Sir. 17:17; emphasis added) calls to mind Elyon's allocation of the nations in Deuteronomy 32:8–9, especially v. 9 ("*the Lord's own portion* was his people"; emphasis added). The image of humans as clay in the hands of the divine potter in Sirach 33:13 is worded much like Yahweh's declaration of the same point in Jeremiah 18:6.

More frequently, Ben Sira alludes to portions of the First Testament, reflecting an awareness of canonical texts without necessarily citing them verbatim. Obviously, the Praise of the Ancestors falls into this category, but so do individual verses in Ben Sira. Space does not permit a complete listing of the numerous parallels, and two representative examples must suffice.[20] "The

---

18. Notwithstanding the cautions in John G. Snaith, "Biblical Quotations in the Hebrew of Ecclesiasticus," *JTS* NS 18 (1967): 1–12.

19. James L. Crenshaw, *Old Testament Wisdom: An Introduction*, 3rd ed. (Louisville: Westminster John Knox, 2010), 156.

20. See the itemization in Crenshaw, *Old Testament Wisdom*, 156, and the essays on Ben

Lord created human beings out of earth and makes them return to it again" (Sir. 17:1; see also 33:10) clearly alludes to Genesis 3:19, while "water made sweet with a tree" (Sir. 38:5) points to Moses's purification of the water at Marah in Exodus 15:25.

As one would expect, Ben Sira is in dialogue with earlier Israelite wisdom literature, especially Qoheleth and Proverbs, with which it shares the use of proverbial material to reflect upon common human experience. On a thematic level, Gerald Sheppard has drawn a link between the emphasis on fearing God and keeping the commandments in Qoheleth 12:13 and the link between wisdom and Torah in Sirach 1 and elsewhere. Sheppard thinks the epilogue was added to Qoheleth after Ben Sira was written, which would negate any influence from the former to the latter, but Katharine Dell argues cogently for the chronological priority of Qoheleth 12:9-14 as an earlier stage in the development of Ben Sira's combination of wisdom and Torah.[21] Individual verses in Ben Sira echo those in Qoheleth as well, such as the common wisdom motif of someone digging a pit then falling into it, found in Sirach 27:26 and Qoheleth 10:8 (and Prov. 26:27). Sirach 33:15 and 42:24 both note that things come in opposing pairs, a point developed at length in Qoheleth 3:1-9. Sirach 40:11 states that "all that is of earth returns to earth, and what is from above returns above," reflecting the assertion in Qoheleth 12:7 that "the dust returns to the earth as it was, and the breath returns to God who gave it."

There are extensive points of contact between Ben Sira and the book of Proverbs.[22] The elaboration of the concept of fear of the Lord as well as the correlations between Lady Wisdom in Sirach 24 and Proverbs 8 are noted above. Other shared themes appearing frequently in both books include retribution, respect for parents, and both positive and negative descriptions of women. The two books have many specific points of contact as well, of which the following is a sampling. Both Sirach 2:5 and Proverbs 17:3 use smelting

---

Sira and Gen. 1–11, Exodus, the book of Kings, the prophets and Proverbs in *Intertextual Studies in Ben Sira and Tobit: Essays in Honor of Alexander A. Di Lella, O.F.M.*, ed. Jeremy Corley and Vincent Skemp, CBQMS 38 (Washington: Catholic Biblical Association, 2004), 89–182. For Chronicles see John G. Gammie, "The Sage in Sirach," in *The Sage in Israel and the Ancient Near East*, ed. John G. Gammie and Leo G. Perdue (Winona Lake, IN: Eisenbrauns, 1990), 361–64.

21. Gerald T. Sheppard, *Wisdom as a Hermeneutical Construct: A Study in the Sapientializing of the Old Testament*, BZAW 151 (Berlin: de Gruyter, 1980), 126–29; Katharine J. Dell, "Ecclesiastes as Wisdom: Consulting Early Interpreters," *VT* 44 (1994): 313.

22. See the list in Gammie, "The Sage in Sirach," 359, and the fuller discussion in Jeremy Corley, "An Intertextual Study of Proverbs and Ben Sira," in *Intertextual Studies in Ben Sira and Tobit: Essays in Honor of Alexander A. Di Lella, O.F.M.*, ed. Jeremy Corley and Vincent Skemp, CBQMS 38 (Washington, DC: Catholic Biblical Association of America, 2004), 155–82.

imagery to describe how God tests people in order to purify them. Sirach 3:18 and Proverbs 3:34 insist that the great must be humble in order to find favor with God. Sirach 4:1 and Proverbs 17:5 both speak against mocking the poor. Sirach 13:8–10; 29:26–27 advise choosing a less important place at the table in the hopes of being invited higher rather than being shamed into taking a lower place after sitting down in a prominent seat, as does Proverbs 25:6–7.

Ben Sira does not just cite or allude to biblical texts; he also interprets them.[23] This is the case with the Praise of the Ancestors, where Ben Sira mentions some events from Israel's history and says nothing about others.[24] The flood, the reception of the Law at Sinai, the conquest of Canaan, the Assyrian conquest of the Northern Kingdom, and the Babylonian destruction of Jerusalem and the temple all receive merely passing reference, and even then the emphasis is on the associated individuals rather than the events themselves. At the same time, the exodus, the Babylonian exile, and the subsequent return are all passed over in silence. This is consistent with Ben Sira's focus on the heroes of the past, but even so there are notable omissions. Obviously not every ancient leader could be included, but only five people prior to Noah are named, and only in a summary listing in 49:14–16. Similarly, Ben Sira notes that Jacob's heritage was divided among the twelve tribes but names only Joseph of all his children. He is also selective about which kings and prophets he names, and to the surprise of most commentators he does not mention Ezra at all.[25] This demonstrates that Ben Sira does not simply repeat everything that is in his sources but rather selects what is useful to his purpose and remains silent about the rest. In doing so he shapes his review of Israel's past in order to provide models for his contemporary audience.

Ben Sira's interpretive stance with respect to earlier material is not restricted to the final major section of the book. His intermingling of details from the two creation stories of Genesis 1–2, rather than presenting them sequentially, is probably an attempt to harmonize the differences between them. Sirach 3:1–16 elaborates in detail on the commandment to honor one's parents (Exod. 20:12; Deut. 5:16), in part by alluding to numerous other biblical texts as well.[26] He also gives some biblical texts a different nuance or even

23. See also Benjamin G. Wright III, "Biblical Interpretation in Ben Sira," in *A Companion to Biblical Interpretation in Early Judaism*, ed. Matthias Henze (Grand Rapids: Eerdmans, 2012), 363–88.

24. See the discussion in Mack, *Wisdom and the Hebrew Epic*, 49–52.

25. For possible explanations see Mack, *Wisdom and the Hebrew Epic*, 119; Crenshaw, *Old Testament Wisdom*, 158, and the literature they cite.

26. Skehan and Di Lella, *Ben Sira*, 41–42.

a completely different meaning.[27] For instance, Proverbs 3:5–6 exhorts the reader to trust in the Lord, who "will make straight your paths," while Sirach 2:6 urges people to trust in God as well, but also to make their ways straight themselves, then elaborates on what that means in 2:7–9. Deuteronomy 6:5 commands the Israelites to love the Lord "with all your soul, and with all your strength," to which Sirach 7:29–30 adds the requirement to "revere his priests" and "not neglect his ministers" respectively. In Job 29:21, people used to listen in silence to Job's counsel; in Sirach 13:23 people are silent when a rich man speaks, praising his words, to which Ben Sira adds the comment that they also dismiss what a poor person says. Similarly, Yahweh provides "joy and gladness" to Zion in Isaiah 51:3, which Sirach 15:6 adapts so that wisdom will provide "gladness and a crown of rejoicing" to the one who fears the Lord (see also Sir. 1:10).

In sum, Ben Sira did not simply reproduce what he found in his biblical sources; he used it for his own purposes. He was selective in the material he chose, adapting it to the points he wanted to make by omitting some elements and emphasizing others. Sometimes he expanded on what he found in the biblical texts and other times he reinterpreted it. This indicates that while he considered the biblical material important enough to be a major source for his reflections, he was not constricted by its content but rather felt free to utilize it as he saw fit. In doing so he confirmed his grandson's note in the prologue that Ben Sira "devoted himself especially to the reading of the Law and the Prophets and the other books of ancestors," while he fulfilled the role of the scholar who "seeks out the wisdom of the ancients" in order to "pour forth words of wisdom of his own" (Sir. 39:1, 6).

Summary

Ben Sira responds to the influx of Hellenism into Israel by compiling his wisdom teachings in order to attract students to his school. For Ben Sira, Greek philosophy is unnecessary because Israel has its own wisdom traditions. But unlike the earlier Israelite wisdom authors, Ben Sira does not just deal with general human experience but also includes Israel's specific religious traditions in his reflections. To that end he alludes to and even elaborates on the existing Israelite Scriptures, and he equates Lady Wisdom with the Torah. His review of significant individuals from Israel's history culminates in a

27. Skehan and Di Lella, *Ben Sira*, 40–41.

description of the high priest Simon II presiding over worship in the Jerusalem temple. Simon combines the various roles of Israel's ancestral heroes in a single individual, reflecting Ben Sira's vision of the nation being led by the Jewish high priest.

FURTHER READING

Commentaries

Coggins, Richard J. *Sirach.* Guides to Apocrypha and Pseudepigrapha. Sheffield: Sheffield Academic, 1998.

Corley, Jeremy. *Sirach.* New Collegeville Bible Commentary 21. Collegeville, MN: Liturgical Press, 2013.

MacKenzie, R. A. F. *Sirach.* OTM 19. Wilmington, DE: Glazier, 1983.

Skehan, Patrick W., and Alexander A. Di Lella. *The Wisdom of Ben Sira: A New Translation with Notes, Introduction and Commentary.* AB 39. New York: Doubleday, 1987.

Snaith, John G. *Ecclesiasticus, or, The Wisdom of Jesus, Son of Sirach.* Cambridge: Cambridge University Press, 1974.

Other Works

Balla, Ibolya. *Ben Sira on Family, Gender, and Sexuality.* DCLS 8. Berlin: de Gruyter, 2011.

Beentjes, Pancratius C. *Happy the One Who Meditates on Wisdom (Sir. 14,20): Collected Essays on the Book of Ben Sira.* CBET 43. Leuven: Peeters, 2006.

Beentjes, Pancratius C., ed. *The Book of Ben Sira in Modern Research: Proceedings of the First International Ben Sira Conference, 28–31 July 1996, Soesterberg, Netherlands.* BZAW 255. Berlin: de Gruyter, 1997.

Calduch-Benages, N., and J. Vermeylen, eds. *Treasures of Wisdom: Studies in Ben Sira and the Book of Wisdom: Festschrift M. Gilbert.* BETL 143. Leuven: Leuven University Press, 1999.

Corley, Jeremy. *Ben Sira's Teaching on Friendship.* BJS 316. Providence: Brown University; Atlanta: Society of Biblical Literature, 2002.

Corley, Jeremy, and Vincent Skemp, eds. *Intertextual Studies in Ben Sira and Tobit: Essays in Honor of Alexander A. Di Lella, O.F.M.* CBQMS 38. Washington, DC: Catholic Biblical Association of America, 2004.

Egger-Wenzel, Renate, ed. *Ben Sira's God: Proceedings of the International Ben Sira Conference, Durham-Ushaw College 2001.* BZAW 321. Berlin: de Gruyter, 2002.

Ellis, Teresa Ann. *Gender in the Book of Ben Sira: Divine Wisdom, Erotic Poetry, and the Garden.* BZAW 473. Berlin: de Gruyter, 2013.

Goering, Greg Schmidt. *Wisdom's Root Revealed: Ben Sira and the Election of Israel.* JSJSup 139. Leiden: Brill, 2009.

Lee, Thomas R. *Studies in the Form of Sirach 44–50.* SBLDS 75. Atlanta: Scholars Press, 1986.

Mack, Burton L. *Wisdom and the Hebrew Epic: Ben Sira's Hymn in Praise of the Fathers.* Chicago: University of Chicago Press, 1985.

Mulder, Otto. *Simon the High Priest in Sirach 50: An Exegetical Study of the Significance of Simon the High Priest as Climax to the Praise of the Fathers in Ben Sira's Concept of the History of Israel.* JSJSup 78. Leiden: Brill, 2003.

Sanders, Jack T. *Ben Sira and Demotic Wisdom.* SBLMS 28. Chico: Scholars Press, 1983.

Trenchard, Warren C. *Ben Sira's View of Women: A Literary Analysis.* BJS 38. Chico: Scholars Press, 1982.

Wright, Benjamin G. *No Small Difference: Sirach's Relationship to Its Hebrew Parent Text.* SCS 26. Atlanta: Scholars Press, 1989.

CHAPTER 7

The Wisdom of Solomon

The Wisdom of Solomon is a first-century CE book that uses Greek language, style, ideas, and mythology to encourage Alexandrian Jews to persevere in their ethical life and worship of Israel's God, in contrast to the idolatry of their Egyptian neighbors. It combines an appeal to rulers to obtain wisdom and rule justly, thereby eliminating persecution, with an exposition of the value of Lady Wisdom for Jews in general and an elaboration of her role in salvation history.

Structure

The book can be divided into three main sections according to content and some structural features. Wisdom 1:1–6:21 deals with the suffering of the righteous and punishment of the ungodly, and is marked off by an inclusio created by the address to rulers in Wisdom 1:1 and 6:21. The second section, 6:22–10:21, shifts from third- to first-person speech and focuses on Lady Wisdom. Finally, the third section comprises Wisdom 11–19, which deals with God's contrasting dealings with the Israelites and Egyptians during the exodus and wilderness periods. This section includes digressions dealing with divine mercy (11:15–12:22) and idolatry (13:1–15:17).

Date and Location

The uncertainty concerning the authorship of the Wisdom of Solomon does not provide any help in narrowing down the date or place of composition.[1] The literary features and ideas suggest that the book was written after the establishment of Greek rule over Israel, which means after Alexander the Great's conquest of the area in 333 BCE. The book's use of the LXX of Isaiah moves the date forward to at least the second century BCE and may indicate a location in Egypt in general if not Alexandria in particular. The use of Isis mythology for the portrait of Wisdom is not decisive for an Egyptian provenance since her cult was popular throughout the Greek and Roman worlds, but an Egyptian location is supported by the focus on the Egyptians in Wisdom 11–19. The "judges of the ends of the earth" (6:1) who are distant (14:17) presumably refers to the Romans, who conquered Egypt in 30 BCE. The Wisdom of Solomon has affinities with the work of Philo of Alexandria, a philosopher who wrote in the first half of the first century CE, which might indicate that the author of Wisdom and Philo were contemporaries. The presence of terminology that is unattested before the first century CE further supports a date after the turn of the millennium. The contrast of the wicked and the righteous, combined with the annihilation of the former, suggests a period of persecution, and a good possibility is under the reign of Caligula (37–41 CE). Riots in Alexandria in 38 CE destroyed synagogues and Jews were declared aliens, a decree rescinded in 41 CE by Claudius.

> **Orientation to the Wisdom of Solomon**
>
> | | |
> |---|---|
> | Structure: | Wisdom 1:1–6:21 |
> | | Wisdom 6:22–10:21 |
> | | Wisdom 11:1–19:22 |
> | Date: | ca. 35–40 CE |
> | Location: | Alexandria, Egypt |
> | Major Themes: | persecution of the righteous |
> | | immortality of the soul |
> | | the fate of the wicked |
> | | Lady Wisdom's role in Israel's history |
> | | contrasts between Israel and Egypt |
> | | divine mercy |
> | | idolatry |

---

1. For the following see David Winston, *The Wisdom of Solomon: A New Translation with Introduction and Commentary*, AB 43 (Garden City: Doubleday, 1979), 20–25.

Author

The author of the Wisdom of Solomon is never identified, although the prayers for wisdom in 7:1–14 and 8:17–9:18 reflect Solomon's prayer in 1 Kings 3:6–9 and are the basis for attributing the book to that king. However, this attribution is demonstrably fictional. First, Wisdom was clearly written in Greek, which would have been unknown to King Solomon. Second, although the text has some Hebrew aspects, it also uses later Greek rhetorical features, such as *diatribe*, quoting an opponent's views in order to dispute them (2:1–20); *sorites*, a sequence of propositions in which the conclusion of one is the premise for the next (6:17–20); *aretology*, a recitation of a subject's virtues (7:22–8:8); and *synkrisis*, an extended series of contrasts, here between the fate of Israelites and Egyptians (Wis. 11–19). It also reflects Greek ideas, including the immortality of the soul (3:1–4, etc.), the four cardinal virtues of self-control, prudence, justice, and courage (8:7), and Isis mythology in the presentation of Lady Wisdom. This, plus the fact that the probable date of composition and the background situation presuppose a much later period than Solomon, means that the work is pseudepigraphic and the actual author is unknown.

Content

Wisdom 1:1–6:21

The first section of the Wisdom of Solomon concerns itself with the suffering of the righteous. It opens with an exhortation for rulers to "love righteousness" and to "think of" and "seek" God, followed by reasons for doing so: God is present to those who trust but Lady Wisdom avoids sinners. The latter point is expanded on in 1:6–11, while 1:12–15 introduces a central motif of the book, namely that sin brings death, contrary to the divine plan for the world, but "righteousness is immortal" (1:15).

Wisdom 1:16–2:24 deals with the fate of the ungodly. "Their words and deeds summoned death . . . because they are fit to belong to his company" (1:16). The words of the ungodly are quoted in Wisdom 2:1–20, but they "reasoned unsoundly" (2:1). Since they do not believe that there is an afterlife, they encourage each other to enjoy themselves, which includes oppressing the righteous poor. While they claim that might makes right (2:11), the real issue is that the lifestyle of the righteous challenges their unrighteous actions, so they persecute and even kill the righteous individual to see if his expectation of divine protection will be fulfilled. Wisdom 2:21–24 summarizes and evaluates their words. Their wickedness blinds them to the divine plan for humans, especially the reward that awaits the righteous. God intended all people for "incorruption" (2:23) but death came into the world through the devil and is experienced by those who "belong to his company"; this phrase forms an inclusio with the same phrase in 1:16. The implication is that only the devil's companions experience this death, and that they do so because of their words and deeds. Their "death" is contrasted with the fate of the righteous in Wisdom 3–5, which means that this is not physical death, which is experienced by all, but rather spiritual death.

Wisdom 3:1–9 describes the actual fate of the righteous, namely that their souls are with God. Although they appear to have died, the reality is the exact opposite: "their hope is full of immortality" (3:4). Their suffering was a test, and having passed that test they will live with God forever. The ungodly, on the other hand, will be treated according to their reasoning. Since they reasoned that there was no afterlife, that is exactly what they will experience; unlike the hope of the righteous, "their hope is vain" (3:11). Moreover, their wives are "foolish" and their offspring "evil" and "accursed" (3:12–13), unlike both the barren but undefiled woman and the righteous eunuch who will enter the temple, contrary to his exclusion in Deuteronomy 23:1. The fate of the latter two is also contrasted with that of children of adulterers (3:16–19; 4:3–6), for "the memory of virtue is immortality" (4:1). The true value for humans is not long life but rather wisdom, and an early death frees one from suffering.

The judgment of the ungodly is described at some length in Wisdom 4:16–5:14. The righteous dead will condemn the wicked living, because the latter cannot comprehend the divine reward that the righteous have received. But once the wicked die they will confront the righteous, at which point they will realize they were wrong: they thought that they could condemn the righteous without any repercussions because they thought there was no afterlife. But now that they themselves have died, they see that the righteous have been rewarded by God, which means they will not be rewarded. The ungodly will be forced to acknowledge that the things they valued have passed away, and 5:14 conveys the emptiness of their "hope" through four images of transitoriness: thistledown on the wind, frost driven by a storm, smoke blown away, and a guest who leaves after one day. In contrast to this fleeting hope, "the righteous live forever" (5:15), and they will be rewarded with crowns and divine protection. God puts on armor (compare Wis. 5:16b–20a with Isa. 59:16–17) and creation itself fights against God's enemies (Wis. 5:20b–23; cf. Josh. 10:12–13; Judg. 5:20–21). The end result is that "evildoing will overturn the thrones of rulers" (Wis. 5:23).

This leads to the final address to rulers ("kings" and "judges" in 6:1 and "monarchs" in 6:21), introducing the conclusion to be drawn from the preceding discussion of the righteous and the wicked. "Therefore" is repeated in vv. 1, 11 and 21, reinforcing the semantic inclusio of rulers in 6:1 and 6:21, with "therefore" in 6:11 marking a subdivision. The author tells them that their position comes from God but because they fail to rule correctly, God will punish them. He encourages them to gain wisdom so that they might be sanctified. "Therefore" they should pay attention to his words. A glowing description of Wisdom herself follows. She is easily accessible to those who sincerely seek her, since she goes out actively looking for those worthy to receive her. Wisdom 6:17–20 is a *sorites*, a series of linked propositions that start with wisdom, which leads to instruction, then to love of her, to keeping her laws, and to immortality, which results in proximity to God, who, as 6:3 indicated, is the one who gave rulers their kingdoms. The result is that "desire for wisdom leads to a kingdom" (6:20). Along the way, those who seek wisdom are reminded that following her laws and living righteously "is assurance of immortality" (6:18), which is reinforced by the section's conclusion in 6:21: if they seek wisdom they will reign forever.

To summarize, this section deals with the traditional wisdom issue of the contrasting fates of the righteous and the wicked, but it provides a new answer to the problem. The ungodly claim that there is no afterlife, and by living wickedly they align themselves with the devil, who brings death. Their fate is consistent with their thoughts: having reasoned that there is nothing to come after this earthly existence, that is exactly what will happen to them—they will cease to exist. In contrast, the righteous will be given immortality as a reward for their pious lives. This means that while everyone has a soul, immortality is not inherent to all souls but rather is a reward given *only* to the righteous; the souls of the wicked will pass out of existence while the souls of the righteous will reign with God. Thus, in this section death is spiritual, not physical, and if the rulers wish to rule forever, they must seek wisdom and embody justice in their earthly reigns.

Wisdom 6:22–10:21

The second section of the book, dealing with the nature of Wisdom and Solomon's quest for her, follows from the end of the previous section, the exhortation to gain wisdom. King Solomon is not named but the content of 7:1–14 and 8:17–9:18 reflects his prayer for wisdom in 1 Kings 3. After indicating that he will speak about Wisdom's nature and origins, he describes his own mortal nature, with all its limitations. This led him to pray for Wisdom rather than riches or power; he received those gifts as well, but most importantly he obtained Wisdom, which leads to "friendship with God" (7:14). But he needs God's help in order to do justice to the topic of Wisdom, since God guides both Wisdom and the wise. God gave him all fields of knowledge (physics, chemistry, history, astronomy, zoology, psychology, botany), but in 7:22 Solomon says that "Wisdom, the fashioner of all things, taught me." This will not be the only time that he seems to equate Wisdom with God.

He then praises Wisdom's virtues, in terms that reflect the Isis cult. The Greek and Roman world adored this Egyptian deity, who was described as a savior, a revealer and patron of kings, and who was linked to wisdom.[2] Wisdom 7:22-23 lists twenty-one qualities of her spirit that enable her to interact with everything, followed by five metaphors linking her to God: she is God's breath, emanation, reflection, spotless mirror, and image. She can do all things, including making "holy souls . . . into friends of God and prophets" (7:27) because God loves those who remain with wisdom. She is superior not only to the light sources but to light itself, and she encompasses the entire world.

From his youth Solomon desired to marry her because then he would benefit from the various aspects of her nature; this includes the fact that "the fashioner of what exists" (8:6; cf. 7:22) is best suited to impart understanding of the created world and that she brings immortality (8:17). But he realizes that he needs God's help to possess her and so he offers an extended prayer (Wis. 9) to that end. He asks for the wisdom that is next to God's throne (9:4, 10; cf. Prov. 8:30) so that he may rule properly, guided by Wisdom to govern Israel justly. Only Wisdom can overcome the limitations of human beings so that they can know what God desires for the world. In fact, people "were saved by Wisdom" (9:18).

This last phrase leads into a recitation of Wisdom's saving power during Israel's early history in chapter 10. The righteous and ungodly of Wisdom 1-5 are now linked to concrete historical individuals, but unlike in Ben Sira's Praise of the Ancestors, the individuals are not named. Instead the author appeals to the reader's ability to determine who is meant, but anyone familiar with the biblical traditions would easily recognize the descriptions of Adam, Cain,

2. John S. Kloppenborg, "Isis and Sophia in the Book of Wisdom," *HTR* 75 (1982): 57-84; Alice M. Sinnott, *The Personification of Wisdom*, SOTSMS (Aldershot: Ashgate, 2005), 144-50. Sinnott lists forty-one instances of vocabulary shared by the Wisdom of Solomon and Isis texts on p. 145.

Noah, Abraham, Lot, Jacob, Joseph, and the Israelites in succession. The most striking element of this chapter is that Lady Wisdom takes on the roles that are attributed to Yahweh elsewhere in Israelite tradition.

Wisdom 11–19

Lady Wisdom's salvific role continues into the opening verse of the book's third division, where she inspires Moses ("a holy prophet"), but the next two verses describe the Israelites in the wilderness without referring to her. Then, in 11:4 they call out to God, who is the agent of salvation throughout the rest of the book. This transition completes the earlier equation of Lady Wisdom with God through her saving deeds: she was described as distinct from God while at the same time fulfilling God's roles, and here the focus switches to God without drawing attention to the switch. This links these final chapters with what preceded by continuing the review of salvation history but also distinguishes the two sections by changing the agent of salvation. The contrast between the Israelites and Egyptians, emphasized in the remainder of the book, reinforces this.

Wisdom 11:5 spells out the principle by which the contrasts are organized: "For through the very things by which their enemies were punished / [the Israelites] themselves received benefit in their need." There are seven contrasts in all, starting with God providing water from a rock in the desert for the Israelites versus the Nile river turning to blood before the exodus. The Israelites' thirst highlights how the Egyptians were punished with undrinkable water, but while God was testing the former during their enslavement, like a parent, he judged the Egyptians so they might see that the Israelites received a benefit through their punishment.

At this point the contrasts are interrupted by two digressions, starting with one dealing with God's mercy in 11:15–12:22. This introduces a second principle that is picked up again in the contrasts, namely that "one is punished by the very things by which one sins" (11:16). In keeping with this principle, the Egyptians were afflicted by plagues of the things they worshiped. God, being all-powerful, could have sent them much worse afflictions, but God judges slowly in order to allow time for repentance. This is seen through God's subsequent treatment of the Canaanites, whose sins included sorcery, unholy rituals, infanticide, and cannibalism. God could have wiped them out, but instead God sent wasps ahead of the Israelites to give the Canaanites an opportunity to repent, demonstrating both the power and the righteousness of God. This also serves as a lesson for the Israelites, whom God will also correct when they sin. The point of the digression is summarized in the concluding verses of the section (12:23–27): God uses the things through which people sin to punish them with the hope that they will reject those things, repenting and recognizing the true God.

The second digression, on the foolishness of idolatry (13:1–15:17), follows immediately after the first. People should have recognized God in nature (cf. Wis. 13:1–9 with Rom. 1:18–23), but instead they worship lifeless statues, for which they will be judged. Idols did not always exist, and the author provides two explanations for their origins. The author first asserts that a father made an image to commemorate a deceased child, honoring it as a deity and passing the rituals on to his descendants (14:15–16). Second, he explains that people honored distant rulers with statues that they eventually deified (14:17–21). Either way, the resulting idols became the basis for a catalogue of evil and depravity, which will result in punishment. In contrast, the righteous do not sin because they know God's power, knowing which "is the root of immortality" (15:3). On the other hand, the potter knows that idolatry is a sin since he has made the idols from the same clay that he used for ordinary vessels (cf. Isa. 44:12–20), and Israel's oppressors are also accountable for worshiping those lifeless objects.

The Egyptians also worshiped loathsome animals, which is the basis for the second contrast between them and the Israelites. The former were plagued by such creatures in Egypt, whereas the Israelites were miraculously fed with quail in the desert. Similarly, the Israelites were saved from fiery serpents but the Egyptians experienced plagues of locusts and flies, constituting the third contrast. The other contrasts follow, each emphasizing that the negative events that the Egyptians experienced were meant to make them recognize their sins, while the Israelites' contrasting positive experiences were intended to show them that parallel things were beneficial for God's peo-

Contrasts between the Israelites and Egyptians	
Israelites	Egyptians
1. Water from a rock in the desert	1. The Nile turns to blood
2. Quail in the desert	2. Plagues of animals
3. Saved from fiery serpents	3. Plagues of locusts and flies
4. Manna from heaven	4. Hail, storms, and fire from heaven
5. A pillar of fire	5. The plague of darkness
6. Protected during the first Passover	6. Death of the firstborn
7. Israel passes through the Red Sea	7. The Egyptians drown in the Red Sea

ple. Thus, in the fourth contrast the Egyptians were hit with hail, storms, and fire from heaven, while the Israelites received manna from the same source, and the idea from Wisdom 5:17–23 that creation punishes the wicked appears again in 16:24. Fifth, the plague of darkness in Egypt is contrasted with the pillar of fire that protected the Israelites in the wilderness, and the Egyptians' terror is also contrasted with the anticipation of the light of the Torah (18:4). Sixth, the death of the Egyptian firstborn is compared with the first Passover; and seventh, the Egyptians drown in the Red Sea, but Israel passes through it.

Wisdom 19:10–22 summarizes and comments on the preceding. The Israelites remember both the plagues that led to their deliverance and the miraculous quail they ate in the wilderness. The Egyptians deserve their punishment, because their treatment of the Israelites was worse than the evil done by the people of Sodom and Gomorrah (19:13–17). The latter refused strangers or treated them with hostility, but the Egyptians added deception to mistreatment—they invited the Israelites to Egypt with promises that they would share the richness of the land with them (Gen. 45:17–20) and then enslaved them. As punishment, the Egyptians were unable to see due to the plague of darkness, just as those in Sodom and Gomorrah were struck blind. Wisdom 19:18–21 reflects the Stoic idea that just as musical notes can change without destroying the melody, so too an alternation in the elements will not destroy the cosmos. Similarly, God's miraculous interventions on behalf of the Israelites transformed things without undermining creation: the Israelites became sea creatures when they passed through the Red Sea, frogs moved from water to land, and lightning burned the Egyptians despite the accompanying rain (cf. Wis. 16:16–17) but its fire did not affect the Israelites or the manna (Wis. 16:18, 22). The book ends with a one-verse doxology affirming God's constant exaltation and protection of the Israelites.

Summary

The central concern in the Wisdom of Solomon is theodicy. The first part deals with the contrasting fates of the righteous and the wicked, with immortality of the soul presented as a reward for righteousness whereas the souls of the wicked will cease to exist. This motivates rulers to establish justice in their realms. The second section focuses on Wisdom as the means to immortality. She is distinct from God yet acts like a god, functioning as a savior and creator. But at the beginning of the third section she is functionally equated with God, such that obedience to her is the same as obedience to God and therefore the guarantee of salvation. Finally, the general principles of reward for the righteous and punishment for the wicked in Wisdom 1–5 are illustrated in particular terms through the contrasting experiences of the Israelites and Egyptians during the exodus and wilderness periods.

FURTHER READING

Commentaries

Clarke, Ernest G. *The Wisdom of Solomon*. CBC. Cambridge: Cambridge University Press, 1973.

Clifford, Richard J. *Wisdom*. New Collegeville Bible Commentary 20. Collegeville, MN: Liturgical Press, 2013.

Geyer, J. B. *The Wisdom of Solomon: Introduction and Commentary*. Torch Bible Commentaries (Apocrypha). London: SCM, 1963.

Larcher, Charles. *Le Livre de la Sagesse ou la Sagesse de Salomon*. EBib 1, 3, 5. Paris: Gabalda, 1983–85.

Reider, Joseph. *The Book of Wisdom: An English Translation with Introduction and Commentary*. JAL. New York: Harper & Brothers, 1957.

Reese, James M. *The Book of Wisdom, Song of Songs*. OTM 20. Wilmington, DE: Glazier, 1983.

Winston, David. *The Wisdom of Solomon: A New Translation with Introduction and Commentary*. AB 43. Garden City: Doubleday, 1979.

Other Works

Kolarcik, Michael. *The Ambiguity of Death in the Book of Wisdom 1–6: A Study of Literary Structure and Interpretation*. AnBib 127. Rome: Biblical Institute Press, 1991.

Larcher, Charles. *Études sur le Livre de la Sagesse*. EBib. Paris: Gabalda, 1969.

McGlynn, Moyna. *Divine Judgement and Divine Benevolence in the Book of Wisdom*. WUNT/2 139. Tübingen: Mohr Siebeck, 2001.

Reese, James M. *Hellenistic Influences on the Book of Wisdom and Its Consequences*. AnBib 41. Rome: Biblical Institute Press, 1970.

Xeravits, Géza G., and József Zsengellér, eds. *Studies in the Book of Wisdom*. JSJSup 142. Leiden: Brill, 2010.

CHAPTER 8

Wisdom Influence
in the First Testament

Israel's wisdom traditions were not restricted to the five wisdom books discussed in the preceding chapters. Since the sages did not exist in isolation within ancient Israel, one would expect to find indications of wisdom influence in some other First Testament books. So it is not surprising that scholars have detected wisdom influence in the Pentateuch, the Deuteronomistic History, numerous prophets and psalms, as well as other biblical books. In fact, the proposed wisdom influence is so widespread that wisdom risks losing its distinctiveness in comparison to the rest of the First Testament.[1] Therefore it is necessary to have criteria for determining wisdom influence outside the traditional wisdom books.[2]

First, demonstrating the influence of the wisdom tradition requires evidence of wisdom elements, namely wisdom terminology, forms, or content.

---

1. This is the conclusion of Mark Sneed, "Is the 'Wisdom Tradition' a Tradition?" *CBQ* 73 (2011): 50–71; note especially his references in p. 64 n. 39. See also Mark R. Sneed, *The Social World of the Sages: An Introduction to Israelite and Jewish Wisdom Literature* (Minneapolis: Fortress, 2015), and compare the essays in Mark Sneed, ed., *Was There a Wisdom Tradition? New Prospects in Israelite Wisdom Studies*, AIL 23 (Atlanta: Society of Biblical Literature, 2015).

2. Compare the methodological discussions in James L. Crenshaw, "Method in Determining Wisdom Influence Upon 'Historical' Literature," *JBL* 88 (1969): 129–42; R. N. Whybray, *The Intellectual Tradition in the Old Testament*, BZAW 135 (Berlin: de Gruyter, 1974), 71–76; Donn F. Morgan, *Wisdom in the Old Testament Traditions* (Atlanta: John Knox, 1981), 13–29; Roland E. Murphy, *The Tree of Life: An Exploration of Biblical Wisdom Literature*, 3rd ed. (Grand Rapids: Eerdmans, 2002), 98–102; Lindsay Wilson, *Joseph, Wise and Otherwise: The Intersection of Wisdom and Covenant in Genesis 37–50*, Paternoster Biblical Monographs (Carlisle, UK: Paternoster, 2004), 28–37; Simon Chi-Chung Cheung, *Wisdom Intoned: A Reappraisal of the Genre 'Wisdom Psalms,'* LHBOTS 613 (London: Bloomsbury T&T Clark, 2015), 28–50.

But because wisdom writers were part of a shared Israelite culture, this means more than just finding parallels between the wisdom books and other biblical literature. Wisdom derives its insights by reflection on common human experience, and individuals outside wisdom circles could reach similar conclusions based on that shared experience. Therefore it is important to consider whether or not a wisdom element is actually characteristic of the wisdom tradition, appearing primarily if not exclusively in wisdom books apart from the proposed non-wisdom text. Second, even if a distinctive wisdom element appears outside the wisdom books, by itself this could be coincidental. It is necessary to consider whether that element is being used in the same way as in the wisdom literature. For example, someone could have a passing familiarity with a wisdom form in itself but not use it the same way that the sages did. Moreover, a speaker could consciously adapt a wisdom element to a different purpose, including to critique the originators of that element, without being part of the original group.[3] Third, one can make a stronger case for wisdom influence when there are multiple instances of a wisdom element in a single book or passage, even more so when these include more than one type of wisdom element, and best when these elements play a greater role in the overall text than non-wisdom elements. So rather than simply counting individual wisdom elements, one needs to consider the combined weight of multiple lines of evidence. Based on these criteria, one can find (1) parallels that could be derived either from the wisdom traditions or a shared culture, (2) items that indicate points of contact with the wisdom literature but not wisdom usage, and (3) clear evidence of wisdom influence, where distinctive wisdom elements are used in a manner that is consistent with a didactic wisdom approach. Moreover, an individual passage or book could display more than one of these levels of connection with the wisdom tradition.

> **Criteria for Determining Wisdom Influence**
>
> 1. Distinctively wisdom elements (terminology, forms, or content)
> 2. Consistent with wisdom usage
> 3. Multiple elements together, especially different ones

---

3. William McKane, *Prophets and Wise Men*, SBT 44 (London: SCM, 1965), 65–112; Joseph Jensen, *The Use of tôrâ by Isaiah: His Debate with the Wisdom Tradition*, CBQMS 3 (Washington, DC: Catholic Biblical Association, 1973).

The Pentateuch

We begin by noting some isolated echoes of the wisdom tradition in the book of Genesis. In Genesis 10:9, "Like Nimrod, a mighty hunter before the LORD" is introduced as a popular proverb ("therefore it is said"). The role of creation theology in the wisdom tradition is discussed in chapter 9 below, but for now it is enough to note that there are no specific contacts between Genesis 1 and Proverbs 8:22–31; their common interest in creation is expressed through different genres and vocabulary, and so they derive from independent creation traditions.[4] Walter Brueggemann suggests a series of motifs scattered throughout Genesis 6–11 that parallel sayings from Proverbs, including Cain's anger and hatred plus his wandering as a result of his folly (Gen. 4:5, 16; cf. Prov. 10:12; 15:18; 10:30; etc.), the evil inclination of the heart (Gen. 6:5; cf. Prov. 10:8; 12:20; etc.), Noah finding favor with Yahweh because of his righteousness (Gen. 6:8; 7:1; cf. Prov. 10:2, 6; 12:2, 28; etc.), and Ham dishonoring his father (Gen. 9:22; cf. Prov. 15:20; 17:21). Brueggemann notes that the Tower of Babel story (Gen. 11:1–9) combines the concern for a name (cf. Prov. 10:7) with arrogance (Prov. 11:2; 18:12; 21:4), shows God destroying the building in which the people take pride (cf. Prov. 12:12; 14:11; 15:25), and uses the same verb "propose" (Gen. 11:6) that is used of bad intentions in Proverbs 12:1; 21:27; 24:8–9.[5] In addition, Whybray considers the Babel story a "kind of parable" with a "theological moral" concerning "the possibilities of human achievement," which he identifies as *ḥokmâ* ("wisdom"), even though the word itself is not used.[6] As noted, with the exception of the final cluster, all these wisdom echoes are isolated instances and do not constitute evidence of a concerted wisdom intention.

> **Possible Wisdom Influence in the Pentateuch**
>
> - Genesis
> - Exodus
> - Deuteronomy

In contrast, Luis Alonso Schökel identifies four "sapiential themes" in Genesis 2–3: the knowledge of good and evil, the shrewdness of the snake, the first human as a sage (in light of Ezek. 28; Job 15:7) classifying the animals

---

4. Cf. George M. Landes, "Creation Traditions in Proverbs 8:22–31 and Genesis 1," in *A Light Unto My Path: Old Testament Studies in Honor of Jacob M. Myers*, ed. Howard N. Bream, Ralph D. Heim, and Carey A. Moore (Philadelphia: Temple University Press, 1974), 279–93.

5. Walter Brueggemann, *In Man We Trust: The Neglected Side of Biblical Faith* (Atlanta: John Knox, 1972), 57–59.

6. Whybray, *The Intellectual Tradition*, 107–8.

and naming his wife, and the elaborate treatment of the four rivers.[7] To these Joseph Blenkinsopp adds the woman who results in death whereas obeying God's commands leads to life, plus the appearance of a "tree of life" in the garden (Gen. 2:9; 3:22), using the same expression that describes Lady Wisdom in Proverbs 3:18 (cf. Gen. 2:9; 3:22). Walter Brueggemann, meanwhile, notes parallels between the wisdom tradition and the serpent's false advice leading to death, inordinate desire (ḥmd in Gen. 3:6; cf. Job 20:20; Prov. 1:22; 6:25; 12:12; 21:20), and the land cursed with thorns and humans with hard work.[8] Finally, Whybray notes that the tree makes one wise (hiśkîl), employing a common wisdom term, while outside of its use in Genesis 3:1 to describe the serpent, ʿārûm ("shrewd") appears only in Proverbs and Job.[9]

Gerhard von Rad proposed that the Joseph story (Gen. 37–50) was not just influenced by the wisdom tradition but is an instance of wisdom literature itself.[10] He views the chapters as a self-contained novella marked by the absence of concrete historical concerns or interest in the cult and salvation history, while also demonstrating Egyptian parallels. Joseph is the model of an administrator who resists the temptations of a woman, controls his passions, and guards his tongue. He can interpret Pharaoh's dreams when the Egyptian wise men cannot (Gen. 41) and is acknowledged by Pharaoh as "discerning and wise" (Gen. 41:33, 39).[11] While individual aspects of von Rad's proposal have been critiqued, it still "contains definite wisdom influence and as such is an important part of the evidence for the wisdom tradition in early Israel."[12] Based on his book-length examination of the Joseph story, highlighting how Joseph exercises his wisdom in public (Gen. 39–41) and in private (Gen. 42–45), Wilson also concludes that the passage is not a wisdom text but does display significant wisdom influences.[13]

Brevard S. Childs has argued that the story of Moses' birth in Exodus 1:8–2:10 is an "historicized wisdom tale."[14] He notes parallels with the Jo-

7. Luis Alonso Schökel, "Sapiential and Covenant Themes in Genesis 2–3," TD 13 (1965): 5–6.

8. Joseph Blenkinsopp, "Theme and Motif in the Succession History (2 Sam. XI 2ff) and the Yahwist Corpus," in Volume du Congrès: Genève, 1965, ed. G. W. Anderson et al., VTSup 15 (Leiden: Brill, 1966), 51–56; Brueggemann, In Man We Trust, 56–57.

9. Whybray, The Intellectual Tradition, 106–7, 137–38, 148.

10. Gerhard von Rad, "The Joseph Narrative and Ancient Wisdom," in The Problem of the Hexateuch and Other Essays (London: SCM, 1984), 292–300.

11. See also Whybray, The Intellectual Tradition, 87.

12. Morgan, Wisdom in the Old Testament Traditions, 50. See also the review of scholarship, pro and con, in Lindsay Wilson, Joseph, Wise and Otherwise, 7–37.

13. Lindsay Wilson, Joseph, Wise and Otherwise.

14. Brevard S. Childs, "The Birth of Moses," JBL 84 (1965): 119–22.

seph story, the book of Esther, and the extrabiblical Ahiqar story. In terms of vocabulary, the passage employs a form of the verb *ḥkm* ("to be wise") that appears only in Exodus 1:10 and Qoheleth 7:16. More persuasive is a shared perspective with the wisdom tradition, in which divine activity plays a minimal role, as well as a number of wisdom motifs. The latter include a distinction between divine and human plans, exemplified by Pharaoh as the stereotype of a "wicked fool" who does not succeed. The midwives disobey Pharaoh because they "feared God" (Exod. 1:17) and act cleverly, then provide a reasoned response when Pharaoh challenges them. Miriam's words at the proper time reflect the skilled court counselor, while the positive portrayal of Pharaoh's daughter reflects the international openness of the Israelite wisdom tradition. These features are highlighted in the subsequent stories when Moses acts contrary to traditional wisdom advice in killing the Egyptian overlord in anger and intervening in another's quarrel (cf. Prov. 26:17) at the Midianite well.

Contrary to earlier scholars who posited that the book of Deuteronomy had influenced the wisdom books, Moshe Weinfeld has proposed that, while not itself an example of wisdom literature, Deuteronomy was composed and transmitted by scribes associated with the wisdom tradition.[15] He argues this through a complex web of relationships: Shaphan, the scribe, discovers the scroll commonly identified as the core of the book of Deuteronomy during temple renovations (2 Kings 22); Shaphan and his family are associated with Jeremiah (Jer. 29:3; 36:10-12; 39:14); wise scribes and Torah are linked in Jeremiah 8:8; and the book of Jeremiah is edited in line with Deuteronomy. These combine to point to a role of "wise scribes" in Deuteronomy and the biblical books associated with its worldview (that is, the Deuteronomistic History, consisting of Joshua, Judges, 1-2 Samuel, and 1-2 Kings).

More concretely, Weinfeld also points to a number of elements that reflect the wisdom tradition.[16] For instance, Deuteronomy 4:6 equates observing the law with wisdom and characterizes those who do so as "wise and understanding people."[17] In addition, earlier Pentateuchal material is adjusted to

15. Moshe Weinfeld, *Deuteronomy and the Deuteronomic School* (Oxford: Clarendon, 1972; reprinted Winona Lake, IN: Eisenbrauns, 1992), 158-78; Moshe Weinfeld, *Deuteronomy 1-11: A New Translation with Introduction and Commentary*, AB 5 (New York: Doubleday, 1991), 62-65; and more recently James L. Kugel, *How to Read the Bible: A Guide to Scripture Then and Now* (New York: Free Press, 2007), 310-13; Jack R. Lundbom, *Deuteronomy: A Commentary* (Grand Rapids: Eerdmans, 2013), 44-58.

16. Weinfeld, *Deuteronomy and the Deuteronomic School*, 244-306.

17. See also Thomas Krüger, "Law and Wisdom According to Deut 4:5-8," in *Wisdom*

introduce a wisdom concern. In Exodus 18:21–22 Moses appoints "able men
. . . who fear God, are trustworthy, and hate dishonest gain" as officers and
judges, while in Numbers 11:24–25 seventy judges receive a share of Yahweh's
spirit previously given to Moses. But in Deuteronomy 1:13–17, Moses appoints
tribal leaders "who are wise, discerning, and reputable (ḥăkāmîm unĕbōnîm
wîduʿîm)," that is, they possess the characteristics of a sage. Similarly, Exodus
23:8 advises against taking a bribe because "a bribe blinds the officials" but in
Deuteronomy 16:19 it "blinds the eyes of the wise." Similarly, Deuteronomy
contains a number of laws from the so-called book of the covenant (Exod.
20:19–23:33) that have been altered to introduce a more humanistic concern
consistent with the wisdom traditions. Such humanism is reinforced by the
introduction of additional laws that do not appear elsewhere, such as those
dealing with impugning the virginity of a new bride in Deuteronomy 22:13–19.[18]

Moreover, Weinfeld finds seven points of specific content in Deuteronomy
that parallel wisdom texts:

1. Do not add or subtract from God's words (Deut. 4:2; 13:1 // Prov. 30:5–6;
   Qoh. 3:14; Sir. 18:6; 42:21).
2. Do not move landmarks (Deut. 19:14; 27:17 // Prov. 22:28; 23:10).
3. Do not use false weights (Deut. 25:13–16 // Prov. 11:1; 20:10, 23).[19]
4. Fulfill vows to God or do not make them (Deut. 23:22–24 // Qoh. 5:1–5;
   Prov. 20:25; Sir. 18:22).
5. Do not return/slander a slave (Deut. 23:15 // Prov. 30:10).
6. Impartial judgment (Deut. 1:17; 16:19 // Prov. 24:23; 28:21).[20]
7. Justice/righteousness results in life (Deut. 16:20 // Prov. 21:21).

In addition, a number of wisdom parallels, often with identical terminology,
are clustered in Deut. 27:15–19, 24–25. These include secret idol worship (Job

---

and Torah: The Reception of 'Torah' in the Wisdom Literature of the Second Temple Period, ed.
Bernd U. Schipper and D. Andrew Teeter, JSJSup 163 (Leiden: Brill, 2013), 35–54.

18. See also Calum M. Carmichael, The Laws of Deuteronomy (Ithaca: Cornell University
Press, 1974).

19. They are called "an abomination to the LORD" in both places, a phrase found
only in Deuteronomy and Proverbs (Weinfeld, Deuteronomy and the Deuteronomic
School, 267–69).

20. See also Reinhard Müller, "The Blinded Eyes of the Wise: Sapiential Tradition and
Mosaic Commandment in Deut 16:19–20," in Wisdom and Torah: The Reception of 'Torah' in
the Wisdom Literature of the Second Temple Period, ed. Bernd U. Schipper and D. Andrew
Teeter, JSJSup 163 (Leiden: Brill, 2013), 9–33.

31:26–28), dishonoring parents (Prov. 15:20; 23:22; 30:17; etc.), moving a boundary marker (Prov. 22:28; 23:10), misleading a blind person (Prov. 28:10), justice for "the alien, the orphan, and the widow" (Prov. 15:25; 23:10; Job 22:9; 24:3; 31:18; Sir. 35:17), striking a neighbor in secret (Prov. 1:10–19), and shedding innocent blood (Prov. 1:11; 6:17).

Weinfeld also notes motifs in Deuteronomy that have been adapted from the wisdom tradition to suit Deuteronomy's nationalistic concerns. "The fear of the Lord" in Deuteronomy refers to covenant loyalty with respect to Israel itself, but to a general moral stance, as in the wisdom literature, when referring to other nations. The doctrine of reward in Deuteronomy includes "the good life, longevity, large families, prosperity, joy and the 'possession of the land,'" with the latter understood as not only conquest but also the ongoing occupation of property, all of which are reflected in the wisdom literature.[21] The two traditions also share a common theodicy, namely that the suffering of the righteous and prosperity of the wicked are temporary states that will be corrected, which is combined with the educational value of suffering for the righteous. In addition to these, David Daube notes an emphasis on a "shame-cultural bias" in Deuteronomy (Deut. 20:8; 22:1–4, 13–21; 23:1–8, 12; 25:11–12) reflecting the wisdom tradition's emphasis on one's reputation, while Jack Lundbom links the laws on false prophecy in Deuteronomy 13:1–5; 18:20–22 with the wisdom concern for distinguishing what is true and false.[22]

Finally, the didactic rhetoric of Deuteronomy is widely recognized. While this can be attributed in part to the use of the ancient treaty model in Deuteronomy, the book also shares an emphasis on a father's instruction with the Instructions in Proverbs 1–7. Weinfeld notes in particular formal and lexical similarities between Deuteronomy 6:6–9; 11:18–20 and Proverbs 6:20–22; 7:3; 8:34, as well as shared pedagogical terminology distributed throughout Deuteronomy and the wisdom books.[23]

21. The quotation is from Weinfeld, *Deuteronomy and the Deuteronomic School*, 307.

22. David Daube, "The Culture of Deuteronomy," *Orita* 3 (1969): 27–52; David Daube, "Repudium in Deuteronomy," in *Neotestamentica et Semitica: Studies in Honour of Matthew Black*, ed. E. Earle Ellis and Max Wilcox (Edinburgh: T&T Clark, 1969), 236–39; David Daube, "To Be Found Doing Wrong," in *Studi in onore di Edoardo Volterra, Volume Secondo*, Pubblicazioni della Facoltà di giurisprudenza dell'Università di Roma 41 (Milan: Giuffrè, 1971), 1–13; Lundbom, *Deuteronomy*, 58–59.

23. Weinfeld, *Deuteronomy and the Deuteronomic School*, 171–78, 208–306. Lexical connections between Deut. 6:6–8 were also noted by J. W. McKay, "Man's Love for God in Deuteronomy and the Father/Teacher–Son/Pupil Relationship," *VT* 22 (1972): 426–35.

As is usually the case, not every one of the preceding points is equally persuasive, and alternative explanations of individual cases are possible.[24] But the cumulative weight of the evidence is difficult to ignore. Obviously the book of Deuteronomy is a collection of laws focused on and addressed to Israel alone, not a wisdom book, but the preponderance of contacts with the wisdom traditions indicates that the author(s) have used wisdom vocabulary, motifs, and style in formulating their message. In Weinfeld's words, "The book of Deuteronomy is . . . a synthesis of Torah and sapiential thought."[25]

In addition to wisdom influence in Deuteronomy as a whole, some scholars have identified wisdom influence in the Song of Moses (Deut. 32) in particular.[26] They connect the double call to "give ear // hear" with biblical and extrabiblical invocations by a wisdom teacher, note a link between corruption and a lack of understanding (Deut. 32:6, 15, 27, 28), associate the appeal to one's father and elders (Deut. 32:7) and Yahweh's power over Sheol (Deut. 32:22) with wisdom, and identify a number of "linguistic affinities with the wisdom literature."[27] On the other hand, the initial address to the heavens and earth is more characteristic of the prophetic lawsuit, and the extended review of Yahweh's interaction with Israel is decidedly uncharacteristic of early wisdom literature. In balance, the prophetic elements predominate in Deuteronomy 32, with the less frequent wisdom connections subordinated to the former.[28]

24. See, e.g., C. Brekelmans, "Wisdom Influence in Deuteronomy," in *La Sagesse de l'Ancien Testament*, ed. Maurice Gilbert, BETL 51 (Leuven: Leuven University Press, 1979), 28–38. Alexander Rofé accepts wisdom influence in Deuteronomy but places the book in priestly circles; see his *Deuteronomy: Issues and Interpretation*, OTS (London: T&T Clark, 2002), 222–27. Michael V. Fox also acknowledges a connection between Deuteronomy and wisdom, but sees wisdom as subordinated to Torah in Deuteronomy; *Proverbs 10–31: A New Translation with Introduction and Commentary*, AB 18B (New York: Doubleday, 2009), 951–53.

25. Weinfeld, *Deuteronomy and the Deuteronomic School*, 294.

26. James R. Boston, "Wisdom Influence upon the Song of Moses," *JBL* 87 (1968): 198–202; Whybray, *The Intellectual Tradition*, 88–89, 137.

27. The phrase is from Boston, "Wisdom Influence Upon the Song of Moses," 201; he lists seventeen points of contact (201–2). Whybray, *The Intellectual Tradition*, 88–89, 137, adds that the root *ḥkm* ("wise") appears alone in Deut. 32:6 and with *śkl* ("wise, skilled") in v. 29. For arguments against Yahweh's influence over Sheol being a wisdom motif see John L. McLaughlin, "Is Amos (Still) among the Wise?" *JBL* 133 (2014): 295–96.

28. Gerhard von Rad, *Wisdom in Israel*, trans. James D. Martin (London: SCM, 1971; reprinted Nashville: Abingdon, 1988), 295 n. 7.

The Deuteronomistic History

The Deuteronomistic History consists of Joshua, Judges, 1–2 Samuel, and 1–2 Kings. Scholars refer to these books as "deuteronomistic" because there are several key texts that unite these books that also share important themes and language with Deuteronomy; therefore, many believe that the party responsible for composing Deuteronomy also created a grand history of Israel by editing these books together. The Deuteronomistic History contains a number of wisdom forms embedded in narrative contexts, indicating their usage in popular culture rather than direct wisdom influence. Proverbs are found in Judges 8:21; 1 Samuel 10:12; 16:7; 19:24; 24:13; 2 Samuel 5:8; 1 Kings 20:11. The only clear riddle in the First Testament occurs in Judges 14:14, although Crenshaw suggests that the Philistines' answer and Samson's retort in 14:18 also reflect the form.[29] The reference to the Queen of Sheba testing Solomon with riddles (NRSV "hard questions"; 1 Kings 10:1) presumes they were more common. Fables appear in Judges 9:8–15 and 2 Kings

> **Possible Wisdom Influence in the Deuteronomistic History**
>
> - The Succession Narrative (2 Samuel 9–1 Kings 2)
> - Solomon's Reign (1 Kings 3–11)

14:9, although the latter in particular does not serve a didactic function. "Wise women" are mentioned in 2 Samuel 14:2 and 20:16 as an identifiable group.

More comprehensively, Whybray characterizes the Succession Narrative (2 Sam. 9–1 Kings 2) as a political novel with extensive wisdom elements.[30] In addition to similarities of genre with the Joseph story and comparable Egyptian literature, especially the *Instruction of Amenemhet*, Whybray identifies four similarities shared by the Succession Narrative and the book of Proverbs: (1) the importance of "counsel" (*'ēṣâ*) as a concrete expression of "wisdom" (*ḥokmâ*); (2) retribution for sin and wickedness; (3) Yahweh controls human destiny; and (4) reduced attention to cultic activities in comparison to ethics and private piety. He also adduces didactic features in the Succession Narrative, including similes (2 Sam. 14:14, 17, 20; 16:23; 17:3, 7, 10, 12) and comparisons (2 Sam. 13:15;

---

29. James L. Crenshaw, *Samson: A Secret Betrayed, a Vow Ignored* (Macon, GA: Mercer University Press, 1978), 111–20; James L. Crenshaw, "Riddles," in *ABD*, 5.722.

30. Whybray, *The Succession Narrative*, SBT Second Series 9 (London: SCM, 1968), 56–116; Whybray, *The Intellectual Tradition*, 89–91. On whether or not the Succession Narrative is a self-contained story see Serge Frolov, "Succession Narrative: A 'Document' or a Phantom?" *JBL* 121 (2002): 81–104.

14:32),[31] plus "a dramatization of proverbial wisdom" in three main areas. The first area is "wisdom and folly," and includes (1) patience and control of the temper; (2) prudent consideration before taking action; (3) the ability to learn from experience; (4) avoidance of treacherous companions; (5) humility versus pride and ambition; (6) control of sexual passion; and (7) the positive and negative use of speech.[32] The other two areas of proverbial wisdom are "the education of children" and "the ideal king," with the latter comprising the ruler's wisdom, his responsibilities and relation to God, and the courtier's perspective. Lesser themes in the Succession Narrative and Proverbs include ambition, frustration and fulfillment, friendship, loyalty and treachery, and revenge. Together these "illustrate specific proverbial teaching for the benefit of the pupils and ex-pupils of schools."[33]

Whybray's hypothesis has been critiqued on methodological grounds.[34] Most of the correspondences that Whybray makes are not uniquely or even characteristically wisdom elements, but are also found in other parts of the First Testament, including legal and prophetic material. Nor does Whybray account for the extensive non-wisdom features, especially the fact that the story is part of a larger theological history that develops Israel's specific salvation history. In other words, since the wisdom contacts that Whybray notes are neither exclusive to wisdom nor the dominant perspective of the narrative, the Succession Narrative is not wisdom literature, but like the Joseph story does reflect an awareness of the wisdom tradition.

The importance of wisdom in the story of Solomon's reign (1 Kings 3–11) almost goes without saying. The root ḥkm ("wise") occurs eighteen times in these chapters in seven different contexts: his dream during which he asks God for wisdom (3:4–15), his adjudication between two women claiming the same child (3:16–28), two notations concerning the international renown of his encyclopedic knowledge (4:29–34; 10:23–25), his interactions with Hiram of Tyre (5:1–12) and with the Queen of Sheba (10:1–13), and the reference to "all his wisdom" alongside the formulaic "all Solomon's acts" in the concluding summary of his reign (11:41).[35] The historicity of these details is debatable, and it is unlikely that they are the reason for the attribution of Proverbs, Qoheleth, and the book of Wisdom to Solomon. Instead, either the elements in 1 Kings

31. Surprisingly, he does not include the parabolic nature of Nathan's rebuke in 2 Sam. 12:1–15.

32. On the contrast between wisdom and folly see also Carole R. Fontaine, "The Bearing of Wisdom on the Shape of 2 Samuel 11–12 and 1 Kings 3," *JSOT* 34 (1986): 61–77.

33. Whybray, *The Succession Narrative*, 95.

34. Crenshaw, "Method," 137–40; David M. Gunn, *The Story of King David: Genre and Interpretation*, JSOTSup 6 (Sheffield: Sheffield University Press, 1978), 26–30.

35. Whybray, *The Intellectual Tradition*, 91–93.

result from the need for a royal patron for the wisdom books or both are dependent on a common tradition of royal wisdom in Israel (cf. Prov. 14:28, 35; 16:10, 12, 14, 15; 19:10, 12; 20:2, 8, 18, 26, 28).[36]

Psalms

A number of scholars have identified wisdom influence in the Psalms on various grounds.[37] They have noted all the usual identifiers of wisdom terminology, forms, and content, either individually or in conjunction with one another. Whybray identifies five terms that are "exclusive to" or "characteristic of" the wisdom literature that also appear in different psalms: *ba'ar* ("stupid") and *kĕsîl* ("fool") appear only in the wisdom books and Psalms, *lēṣ* ("scoffer") and *petî* ("simple") occur only once outside the wisdom books and Psalms, and in addition to its expected frequent use in the wisdom literature, the root *ḥkm* ("wise," "wisdom," etc.) is found fifteen times in the Psalms and 144 times elsewhere.[38] Significantly, although many consider *'ašrê* ("happy," "blessed") indicative of wisdom influence, Whybray excludes the term due to its more frequent use outside the wisdom literature than within.[39] The proposed wis-

36. Compare R. B. Y. Scott, "Solomon and the Beginnings of Wisdom in Israel," in *Wisdom in Israel and in the Ancient Near East: Essays Presented to Harold Henry Rowley*, ed. Martin Noth and D. Winton Thomas, VTSup 3 (Leiden: Brill, 1955), 262–79; and Ronald E. Clements, "Solomon and the Origins of Wisdom in Israel," *PRSt* 15 (1988): 23–35.

37. See the review of scholarship in Cheung, *Wisdom Intoned*, 2–16. For the debate on whether the placement of the wisdom psalms constitutes an intentional wisdom editing of the Psalter as a whole, contrast the arguments of Kuntz and Oeming with Whybray: J. Kenneth Kuntz, "Wisdom Psalms and the Shaping of the Hebrew Psalter," in *For a Later Generation: The Transformation of Tradition in Israel, Early Judaism, and Early Christianity*, ed. Randal A. Argall, Beverly A. Bow, and Rodney A. Werline (Harrisburg, PA: Trinity Press International, 2000), 144–60; Manfred Oeming, "Wisdom as a Hermeneutical Key to the Book of Psalms," in *Scribes, Sages, and Seers: The Sage in the Eastern Mediterranean World*, ed. Leo G. Perdue, FRLANT 219 (Göttingen: Vandenhoeck & Ruprecht, 2009), 154–62; R. N. Whybray, *Reading the Psalms as a Book*, JSOTSup 222 (Sheffield: Sheffield Academic Press, 1996), 36–87.

38. See Whybray, *The Intellectual Tradition*, 145–46, 136–37, 93–98 respectively. In later works he relied less on terminology and more on wisdom forms and content: R. N. Whybray, "The Wisdom Psalms," in *Wisdom in Ancient Israel: Essays in Honour of J. A. Emerton*, ed. John Day, Robert P. Gordon, and Hugh G. M. Williamson (Cambridge: Cambridge University Press, 1995), 152–60; Whybray, *Reading the Psalms*, 36–87.

39. Whybray, *The Intellectual Tradition*, 125–26; see also Cheung, *Wisdom Intoned*, 131–32. *'ašrê* occurs thirty-five times outside the wisdom books versus only ten times in Proverbs, Job, and Qoheleth; twenty-six of the non-wisdom instances are in the Psalms, which indicates an

dom forms in Psalms include (1) better sayings; (2) x / x + 1 sayings; (3) admonitions; (4) a teacher's address to a son; (5) rhetorical questions; (6) similes; (7) lists; and (8) proverbs.[40] Some, such as rhetorical questions and similes, are evidence of a common cultural context rather than specific wisdom influence, but others are more convincing. Finally, scholars look for wisdom themes and motifs in the Psalms, such as fear of the Lord, contrasts between the righteous and the wicked along with their two ways and the problem of retribution, plus theodicy and Torah. The more instances of each category there are and the more extensively these categories overlap, the greater the probability that a psalm has been influenced by the wisdom tradition. Most recently, Cheung has proposed that a wisdom psalm must have "a ruling wisdom thrust," an "intellectual tone," and a "didactic intention."[41]

There is no consensus on the number of wisdom psalms, with lists ranging from three to thirty-nine psalms.[42] Most scholars who have written on the subject more than once changed their mind over time. For instance, Crenshaw went from nine to none (although he did recognize some "wisdom affinities"), Eissfeldt added nine psalms to his earlier list of seven, Murphy alternated from twelve wisdom psalms to seven, and Whybray began with thirteen, later reduced the number to five, and then increased it to thirteen.[43] In light of this great di-

---

origin in liturgical benedictions. Whybray's discussion of *'ašrê* is part of a larger review of terms that occur frequently in both the earlier wisdom books and the rest of the First Testament that he therefore considers less decisive for establishing wisdom influence (124–34). Compare the list of sixty-four words that Scott considers "useful in assessing wisdom influence in . . . the Psalms"; R. B. Y. Scott, *The Way of Wisdom in the Old Testament* (New York: Collier, 1971), 121–23; the quotation is from p. 121.

40. J. Kenneth Kuntz, "The Canonical Wisdom Psalms of Ancient Israel," in *Rhetorical Criticism: Essays in Honor of James Muilenburg*, ed. Jared J. Jackson and Martin Kessler, PTMS 1 (Pittsburgh: Pickwick, 1974), 191–99; Morgan, *Wisdom in the Old Testament Traditions*, 127–28. Both include "the *'ashre* formula," but see the previous note. For additional discussions of wisdom forms in the Psalms see, e.g., Scott, *The Way of Wisdom*, 192–201; Horst Dietrich Preuss, *Einführung in die alttestamentliche Weisheitsliteratur*, Urban Taschenbücher 383 (Stuttgart: Kohlhammer, 1987), 164–66; Anthony R. Ceresko, *Introduction to Old Testament Wisdom: A Spirituality for Liberation* (Maryknoll, NY: Orbis Books, 1999), 160–64.

41. Cheung, *Wisdom Intoned*, 28–50.

42. See the convenient chart of sixty-one lists from forty-nine scholars between 1851 and 2010 in Cheung, *Wisdom Intoned*, 188–90.

43. James L. Crenshaw, "Wisdom," in *Old Testament Form Criticism*, ed. John Haralson Hayes, Trinity University Monograph Series in Religion 2 (San Antonio: Trinity University Press, 1974), 247–53; James L. Crenshaw, *Old Testament Wisdom: An Introduction*, 3rd ed. (Louisville: Westminster John Knox, 2010), 187–94; Otto Eissfeldt, *Einleitung in das Alte Testament unter Einschluß der Apokryphen und Pseudepigraphen: Entstehungsgeschichte des Alten Tes-*

vergence and shifting opinions it is impossible to review all the arguments for and against all the proposed wisdom psalms. Instead, the following discusses three psalms that are widely but not universally identified as wisdom psalms in order to demonstrate how to evaluate the claims, after which the reader can do the same for other candidates such as Psalms 39, 73, 78, 128, etc.

Psalm 1 contains some important wisdom features. The most obvious is the contrast between the righteous and wicked, which is the focus of the entire psalm. It opens with a blessing (*'ašrê*; but see below) upon those who distinguish themselves from the wicked, with the former explicitly identified as the righteous in 1:6. The characteristic activities of the righteous are developed in 1:2–3: they "delight in the law of the LORD" and "meditate" on it day and night. The verb "meditate" (*hāgâ*) suggests the activity of a sage, but the object of their meditation is not nature or human experience but *tôrâ*, and the verb's usage elsewhere indicates an oral utterance, namely reciting *tôrâ*.

Differing Views on the Extent of Wisdom Psalms		
Eissfeldt, *The Old Testament*	Murphy, *The Tree of Life*	Whybray, *Reading the Psalms*
1, 19, 37, 49, 73, 78, 90, 91, 105, 106, 112, 119, 121, 128, 133, 139	1, 32, 34, 37, 49, 112, 128	8, 14, 25, 34, 39, 49, 53, 73, 90, 112, 127, 131, 139

Three Examples of Wisdom Influence in the Psalms

- Psalm 1
- Psalm 37
- Psalm 49

The parallels between Psalm 1:2 and Joshua 1:7–8 ("meditate day and night" in order to "prosper") link *tôrâ* in the former with the book of laws given by Moses, to which Joshua refers. Thus the psalm contains the link between wisdom and law (see also Pss. 19:8–15; 119) that comes to its fullest expression in Ben Sira's explicit identification of wisdom and Torah.[44] Although the opening *'ašrê* is not a wisdom term, the psalm does distinguish the righteous from "scoffers" (*lēṣîm*), one of Whybray's characteristic wisdom terms. Moreover, the righteous

taments, Neue Theologische Grundrisse (Tübingen: Mohr, 1934), 93; Otto Eissfeldt, *The Old Testament: An Introduction Including the Aprocrypha and Pseudepigrapha, and Also the Works of Similar Type from Qumran: The History of the Formation of the Old Testament*, trans. Peter R. Ackroyd (Oxford: Basil Blackwell, 1965), 124–27; Roland E. Murphy, *Seven Books of Wisdom* (Milwaukee: Bruce, 1960), 29; Murphy, *The Tree of Life*, 103; Whybray, *The Intellectual Tradition*, 154; Whybray, "Wisdom Psalms"; Whybray, *Reading the Psalms*, 36–84.

44. On Ps. 19:8–15 as a wisdom psalm see most recently Cheung, *Wisdom Intoned*, 164–76.

are compared to trees by water, an image also found in Egyptian Instructions such as the *Instruction of Amenemope*. The distinction between the righteous and the wicked includes their contrasting fates, invoking the common wisdom concern with the proper retribution that each should experience. Finally, using Cheung's terminology, the psalm has an intellectual tone and a didactic intent, namely to educate the reader as to the differences between the righteous and the wicked and to persuade the reader to imitate the righteous.

Psalm 37 also incorporates a number of wisdom elements.[45] While acrostics are not exclusive to the wisdom tradition, the successive letters at the beginning of every second verse integrates independent sayings into a larger whole, much like the book of Proverbs. Some lines use clear wisdom forms, including prohibitions (37:1–2, 8b) and admonitions (37:3, 4, 5–6, etc.), most with motive clauses, as well as a better saying (37:16), a proverb (37:21), and insights from personal observations and experience (37:25–26, 35–36), while appeals to revelation are lacking. The cumulative effect is a didactic structure and intent for the poem. Like Psalm 1, the central concern is the sapiential distinction between the wicked and the righteous, here with the added concern about the former oppressing the latter, plus their eventual punishment and reward. The psalm also expresses the relative value of wealth (e.g., 37:16–17, 21–22, 25–26) in ways reminiscent of Proverbs (cf. Prov. 10:2; 11:28; 15:27; 18:10–11; 23:4–5; 30:7–9).[46] Note especially the parallels between the better saying in Psalm 37:16 with Proverbs 16:8.

Psalm 49 is also widely accepted as a wisdom psalm.[47] It opens with a call to "hear" and "give ear" that reflects the initial address in the Instructions found in Proverbs 1–7, except that here it is directed to "all peoples" rather than "my son," and the former are further distinguished in terms of rich and poor, introducing the focus of the poem. The psalm as a whole does not reflect the complete Instruction form, in that it provides no motivation for listening, but the body of the psalm can be categorized as the teaching component of an Instruction. The didactic intent of the poem continues with the notice in 49:3 that the psalmist will express "wisdoms" (plural) and "understanding,"

45. See also the most recent discussion in Cheung, *Wisdom Intoned*, pp. 52–78 and the literature he cites.

46. On wealth and poverty in Proverbs see further R. N. Whybray, *Wealth and Poverty in the Book of Proverbs*, JSOTSup 99 (Sheffield: JSOT Press, 1990); Harold C. Washington, *Wealth and Poverty in the Instruction of Amenemope and the Hebrew Proverbs*, SBLDS 142 (Atlanta: Scholars Press, 1994); Timothy J. Sandoval, *The Discourse of Wealth and Poverty in the Book of Proverbs*, BIS 77 (Leiden: Brill, 2006).

47. Again, cf. Cheung, *Wisdom Intoned*, pp. 79–100.

with the latter characterized as a "meditation" (*hagût*; cf. *hāgâ* in Ps. 1:2). The Instruction form is further developed in 49:4 with the psalmist's intention to "incline my ear," which is the father's directive to the son in Proverbs 4:20; 5:1; cf. 5:13, as well as the opening call in Proverbs 22:17, where it derives from the Egyptian *Instruction of Amenemope*. In addition, the objects of the author's attention are a "proverb" and a "riddle," two of the four wisdom forms that the book of Proverbs will help one understand (Prov. 1:6). Thus, the author indicates in the opening verses that he intends to teach through the use of wisdom forms. Following from this, the comparisons with animals in 49:12, 14, 20 do not prove wisdom influence, especially since they do not directly draw a lesson from observation of nature, but in this context they reflect the wisdom literature's frequent analogies with nature and more particularly Qoheleth's identification of a common fate for humans and animals (Qoh. 3:19–21). The final formal wisdom link is in Psalm 49:13, which adapts the application element found in the "appeal to tradition" form (cf. chapter 2).

The psalm's content also reflects wisdom concerns, primarily the apparent success of the wealthy. Psalm 49:5b indicates that the wealthy persecute the psalmist, but this aspect is not repeated in the rest of the psalm, so the common wisdom motif of the righteous and the wicked is in the background of the psalm but not a central concern. Instead, the subsequent verses expound the relative value of wealth, as does Psalm 37, but add the limiting role that death plays: all must die, after which one's wealth goes to others. The relativization of wealth in Proverbs was noted above, but the combination of these two motifs is especially characteristic of Qoheleth, for whom death is the final end that awaits everyone, and the inability to know when that comes means that many people do not get to enjoy their wealth. In addition to the common fate of animals and humans noted above, Qoheleth's lament that the wise and fools die alike (Qoh. 2:14–16; cf. 9:1–3) is paralleled in Psalm 49:10. The observation is used differently, with this common fate a source of distress for Qoheleth but used for comfort in the psalm. Moreover, unlike Qoheleth, the psalmist hopes that God will "ransom my soul from the power of Sheol" (Ps. 49:15). But while Psalm 49 does not simply duplicate Qoheleth's insistence that death limits the value of wealth but rather adapts it, the issue is very much at home in the wisdom literature.

Each of these three psalms contains multiple features that indicate wisdom influence. These include distinctive wisdom terms, forms, and themes, all used with a didactic intent. Thus, it is clear that they all intentionally reflect Israel's wisdom traditions, which justifies calling them wisdom psalms.

The Prophets

Scholars have detected various amounts of wisdom influence in a number of prophets. Space does not allow a full consideration of each. Instead, Amos and Isaiah will be reviewed in detail, after which the evidence for the remainder will be summarized.

Samuel Terrien first suggested multiple points of contact between Amos and wisdom; Hans Walter Wolff supplemented Terrien's work and concluded that the prophet was a village elder who conveyed clan wisdom.[48] These wisdom connections include geographic ties to areas associated with the wisdom tradition plus supposed wisdom forms, themes, and vocabulary. These proposals do not survive close scrutiny, however.[49] Terrien and Wolff link the sole prophetic references to Beersheba (Amos 5:5; 8:14) with the proximity of Amos's southern home of Tekoa to Edom. They also connect the references to Isaac the father of Esau (= Edom) to the Edomite reputation for wisdom (Jer. 49:7; cf. 1 Kings 4:30-31; Obad. 8). But there is no evidence of contact with Edom in the book of Amos and other names for the nation (Israel, Jacob, and Joseph) are each far more frequent than Isaac. Proposed wisdom forms in Amos include the numerical saying (1:3–2:6), the "woe" saying (5:18–20; 6:1–7), questions (3:3–6, 8; 5:20, 25; 6:2, 12; 9:7), exhortations (4:4–5; 5:4–6, 14–15), and antithetical word pairs. The latter three are far too common in human discourse to be evidence of a specific social background, and Amos's questions are not didactic ones with the answer provided but rhetorical, in that

---

Possible Wisdom Influence in the Prophets

- Amos
- Isaiah of Jerusalem (Isaiah 1–39)
- Hosea
- Micah
- Habakkuk
- Jeremiah
- Ezekiel
- Second Isaiah (Isaiah 40–66)
- Jonah

---

48. Samuel Terrien, "Amos and Wisdom," in *Israel's Prophetic Heritage: Essays in Honor of James Muilenburg*, ed. Bernhard W. Anderson and Walter J. Harrelson (New York: Harper & Brothers, 1962), 108–15; Hans Walter Wolff, *Amos the Prophet: The Man and His Background*, ed. John Reumann, trans. Foster R. McCurley (Philadelphia: Fortress, 1973); Hans Walter Wolff, *Joel and Amos: A Commentary on the Books of the Prophets Joel and Amos*, ed. S. Dean McBride Jr., trans. Waldemar Janzen, S. Dean McBride Jr., and Charles A. Muenchow, Hermeneia (Philadelphia: Fortress, 1977).

49. For a detailed presentation of the following see McLaughlin, "Is Amos (Still) among the Wise?"

the answer is obvious, while his exhortations reflect calls to worship joined to prophetic announcements of judgment. Amos's use of the x / x + 1 formula does resemble that wisdom form, but it functions differently in Amos's oracles against the nations.[50] Rather than enumerate four sins, he names only one, eliminating the didactic function of the wisdom form, while also appealing to divine revelation rather than reflecting on human experience. While the prophet may have been aware of the x / x + 1 form, it is not a true wisdom form in Amos. Finally, Terrien and Wolff propose the "woe" oracle as the counterpart of clan wisdom blessings (*'ašrê*), but in addition to *'ašrê* not being a characteristically wisdom term,[51] the word "woe" (*hôy*) never appears in the wisdom literature. The lone instance of *hôy* outside the prophetic literature (1 Kings 13:30) refers to lamenting the dead, and Jeremiah 22:18; 34:5 have the same context, indicating that the form actually derives from funerals.

The proposed wisdom terms in Amos include *wyṭrp . . . 'pw* ("his anger tore"; 1:11), *swd* ("secret"; 3:7), *nkḥh* ("right"; 3:10), and *mśkyl* ("prudent"; 5:13).[52] Some are not characteristically wisdom terms and none are used the same way they are in wisdom texts. The verb *ṭrp* ("tear") only occurs with *'p* ("anger," literally "nose") elsewhere at Job 16:9; 18:4, but in the former God tears at a human and in the latter a human tears at himself (the infrequency and different nuances hardly justify Terrien's label of the expression as a "sapiential idiom"), whereas in Amos one nation tears at another. The nuance of *swd* as an intimate secret is characteristic of wisdom texts, but it only appears as the object of the verb *glh* ("reveal") in Proverbs 11:13; 20:19; 25:9, where it has the negative nuance of humans betraying secrets. The positive connotation in Amos 3:7 is more consistent with Jeremiah's insistence that a true prophet has entered into the divine council (Jer. 23:18, 22; cf. Job 15:8, also using *swd*). Of the seven instances of *nkḥh* in the First Testament, only two are from wisdom texts (Prov. 8:9; 24:26), where it modifies speech, while Amos 3:10 deals with action. Finally, *mśkyl* is a common wisdom term, but there it means insight into general human experience rather than a "prudent" response to an extreme context as in Amos.

The wisdom themes proposed for Amos are the pervasive concerns for social justice and universalism, and to a lesser extent, knowledge of astronomy, little interest in the cult, and Yahweh's involvement with Sheol (Amos 9:2).

50. See further in chapter 2 above.
51. See n. 39 above.
52. The latter is mentioned by J. Alberto Soggin, "Amos and Wisdom," in *Wisdom in Ancient Israel: Essays in Honour of J. A. Emerton*, ed. John Day, Robert P. Gordon, and Hugh G. M. Williamson (Cambridge: Cambridge University Press, 1995), 123.

Social justice is found in diverse types of biblical literature and is common among the prophets, while the preferential attitude to the orphan, widow, and foreigner links Amos with the legal material related to the exodus, not wisdom. Second, Amos's knowledge of other nations in the oracles against the nations is shared by such oracles (to some extent) in every prophetic book except Hosea. Moreover, in Amos these oracles announce judgment on Israel's enemies, which implies a blessing on Israel. Only Amos 9:7 reflects universalism through Yahweh's interventions for Ethiopians (implied), Philistines, and Arameans alongside Israel, but this does not negate that Israel is "my people" (Amos 7:8; 8:2; 9:10), and that Yahweh is "their/your God" (Amos 2:8; 4:12) and has a unique relationship with them (Amos 3:2). Yahweh's involvement with Sheol is not an exclusive wisdom concern and the absence of idolatry in Amos can be explained by the fact that Israel was not yet monotheistic.[53] As for astronomy, the mention of "the Pleiades and Orion" in Amos 5:8 is probably secondary, but in any case these constellations are not mentioned as wisdom reflection on the nature of the universe but in conjunction with Yahweh, the creator who will punish Israel.

In addition to the proposals by Terrien and Wolff, Crenshaw posits a link between the doxologies in Amos and Job 5:9–16; 9:5–10.[54] Since he considers the former doxologies later additions, this would constitute wisdom editing of the book of Amos. However, most of the proposed parallels are either too general, too different, or weakened by the use of synonyms rather than the same word. Crenshaw also lists three wisdom terms in Amos but none are from the Job theophanies and two are used differently in the two books: in Amos 4:13 God "reveals his thoughts (śēḥô) to mortals" but in Job (and Prov. 23:28) the root śyḥ denotes negative human thoughts (NRSV "complaint"); Yahweh "makes destruction flash out" (hammablîg) in Amos 5:9 but the root is used positively in Job 9:27; 10:20.

In sum, attempts to link Amos to Israel's wisdom traditions are not successful. The proposed geographic links are overstated and the suggested wisdom themes are not distinctively wisdom motifs. Only one of the forms considered is

53. In addition to Prov. 15:11; Job 26:6 (and Ps. 139:7, which Terrien incorrectly considers a wisdom psalm), God engages with Sheol in Deut. 32:22; 1 Sam. 2:6; Pss. 30:3; 49:16; 86:13 (cf. Pss. 18:5, 16; 56:13; 103:4; 116:3, 8); Ezek. 26:20; 31:16; Hos. 13:14; Jon. 2:3, 7. On the development of Israelite religion see John L. McLaughlin, *What Are They Saying about Ancient Israelite Religion?* (New York: Paulist, 2016), and the literature cited there.

54. See James L. Crenshaw, "The Influence of the Wise on Amos: The 'Doxologies of Amos' and Job 5, 9–16; 9, 5–10," *ZAW* 79 (1967): 49–51; and the critique in McLaughlin, "Is Amos (Still) among the Wise?," 301–3.

actually a wisdom form, and even then Amos uses the x / x+1 formula differently than in Proverbs and Ben Sira. Similarly, most of the vocabulary scholars have put forward are not characteristic wisdom terms and the few that are, are not used as in wisdom texts. Thus, the book of Amos does not reflect wisdom influence.

Most scholars accept some degree of contact between the wisdom tradition and Isaiah of Jerusalem.[55] Some instances are considered secondary additions, which could indicate wisdom editing of the book but not influence on the prophet himself.[56] Proposed wisdom terminology includes the roots *ḥkm* ("wise," "wisdom") and *byn* ("insight"), as well as *lēṣ* ("scoffer"), *tûšiyyâ* ("wisdom," "success"), *yāʿaṣ* ("advise," "counsel"), *ʿēṣâ* ("counsel"), *yādaʿ* ("know") and *dāʿâ* ("knowledge"), although Whybray considers only the first four "characteristic of" or "exclusive to" wisdom.[57] Fichtner notes eight instances where wording is similar to passages in Proverbs,[58] but with the exception of the phrase "wise in their own eyes" (*ḥăkāmîm bĕʿênêhem*) in Isa. 5:21, which only occurs elsewhere (in the singular) in Proverbs 3:7; 26:5, 12, 16; 28:11, none of his examples are close enough to require dependence in either direction. Some point to the numerous comparisons and similes, but as

---

55. "Isaiah of Jerusalem," also known as "First Isaiah," refers to chapters 1–39 of the book of Isaiah. The rest of the book, often labeled "Second Isaiah" (chapters 40–55) and "Third Isaiah" (chapters 56–66), likely derives from different, later settings. An early treatment of the connection between Isaiah of Jerusalem and the wisdom tradition is Johannes Fichtner, "Isaiah among the Wise," in *Studies in Ancient Israelite Wisdom*, ed. James L. Crenshaw, Library of Biblical Studies (New York: Ktav, 1976), 429–39; the German original was published in 1949. Subsequent studies include J. William Whedbee, *Isaiah and Wisdom* (Nashville: Abingdon, 1971); Jacques Vermeylen, "Le proto-Isaïe et la sagesse d'Israël," in *La sagesse de l'Ancien Testament*, ed. Maurice Gilbert, BETL 60 (Leuven: Leuven University Press, 1979), 39–58; Hugh G. M. Williamson, "Isaiah and the Wise," in *Wisdom in Ancient Israel: Essays in Honour of J. A. Emerton*, ed. John Day, Robert P. Gordon, and Hugh G. M. Williamson (Cambridge: Cambridge University Press, 1995), 133–41; Hans Wildberger, *Isaiah 28–39*, Continental Commentaries (Minneapolis: Fortress, 2002), 596–615; Lindsay Wilson, "Wisdom in Isaiah," in *Interpreting Isaiah: Issues and Approaches*, ed. David Firth and Hugh G. M. Williamson (Downers Grove, IL: InterVarsity, 2009), 145–67. See also Morgan, *Wisdom in the Old Testament Traditions*, 76–83.

56. For example, Isa. 3:10–11 contrasts the fate of the innocent and the guilty, while 32:1–8 compares fools and villains with the nobles. On their inauthenticity see the commentaries. Vermeylen argues that all the wisdom elements in Isaiah are redactional ("Le Proto-Isaïe," 39–58) and Martin O'Kane does the same for Isaiah 28 in particular; "Wisdom Influence in First Isaiah," *PIBA* 14 (1991): 64–78.

57. Whybray, *The Intellectual Tradition*, 79–80, 142–45, 146, 148–49, 151. Contrast the defense of *yāʿaṣ* and *ʿēṣâ* in Whedbee, *Isaiah and Wisdom*, 114–26.

58. Fichtner, "Isaiah among the Wise," 434–35.

noted above under Amos, such modes of speech may suggest a wisdom origin but are too common to require one.

More convincing is the presence of specific wisdom forms in Isaiah.[59] The most significant of these is the parable. Isaiah 1:2–3 opens with a double call to "hear, O heavens, and listen, O earth," followed by a reference to wayward sons, an analogy from nature (the ox and the donkey), and a contrasting indictment of Israel. As with Deuteronomy 32:1 above, the opening call is consistent with the prophetic lawsuit genre, and that is reinforced by "the LORD has spoken" (Isa. 1:2), while the judgment against Israel in 1:3 presumes a covenantal backdrop. The father-son relationship in 1:2 and Israel's failure to "know" and "understand" in 1:3b are loosely related to wisdom concerns. The nature analogy in 1:3 matches the lessons drawn by comparisons with nature, including the same animals (e.g., Prov. 7:22; 26:3), that are common in the book of Proverbs. Isaiah 1:3 is a didactic parable, albeit one that is used to express prophetic judgment, which makes the other wisdom features of Isaiah 1:2–3 more relevant. The parable form is also adapted to a prophetic function in Isaiah 5:1–7 and 28:23–29. The first parable sings of "my friend's vineyard" and its eventual uprooting for failing to produce good fruit, before announcing the coming destruction of Israel and Judah. The second combines three different wisdom elements: Isaiah 28:23 reflects the teacher's call to listen, 28:24–28 is a parable of a farmer that uses some clear wisdom terms in a number of didactic questions, and 28:29 uses the summary-appraisal form to indicate that the farmer's skill reflects Yahweh's wisdom. The summary-appraisal form is also found in Isaiah 14:26 and 17:14, while Isaiah 2:22; 10:15; 29:16 contain proverbs embedded in larger prophetic discourses. In all these cases, Isaiah uses these forms didactically, as the wise do, but always at the service of his prophetic message.

At the same time, Isaiah attacks the wise in Isaiah 5:21; 19:11–15; 29:14. Fichtner takes this dual attitude to wisdom as evidence that Isaiah was a Jerusalem sage prior to his prophetic call, who then rejected his former compatriots' role in favor of Yahweh's wise plan.[60] However, Whedbee correctly notes that by this reasoning Isaiah's opposition to sacrifice in Isaiah

---

59. See in particular Whedbee, *Isaiah and Wisdom*, 23–79; Morgan, *Wisdom in the Old Testament Traditions*, 77–80; Wildberger, *Isaiah 28–39*, 602–4; Lindsay Wilson, "Wisdom in Isaiah," 153–55. Whedbee devotes an additional chapter to "Woe Oracles and Wisdom" (80–110), but see the discussion of Amos earlier in this chapter.

60. Fichtner, "Isaiah among the Wise," 436–37. Scott suggests that Isaiah was a royal counselor and Anderson that he was a court scribe: R. B. Y. Scott, "Isaiah Chapters 1–39: Introduction and Exegesis," in *IB*, 5.163, 232; Robert T. Anderson, "Was Isaiah a Scribe?" *JBL* 79 (1960): 57–58.

1:10–17 would make him an ex-priest as well.[61] Instead, Whedbee argues that Isaiah simply uses wisdom elements in order to speak to the wise in their own terms.[62] In contrast, McKane claims that Isaiah actively attacks the "old wisdom" of the court advisors in order to demonstrate that true wisdom belongs to Yahweh alone.[63] Related to this is Joseph Jensen's study of *tôrâ* in Isaiah 1:10; 2:3; 5:24b; 8:16, 20; 30:9.[64] Jensen understands *tôrâ* to mean "wisdom instruction," a term Isaiah has taken over in order to argue that the wise are inconsistent with the wisdom tradition's teaching about internal social justice and external politics, and so they have neglected the true wisdom that comes from Yahweh.

It remains to summarize possible influence in other prophetic books. The book of Hosea contains some possible wisdom elements.[65] The final verse of Hosea (14:9) is usually understood as an editorial addition that calls for a wisdom interpretation of the book.[66] However, Seow considers it Hosea's own summary of the "foolish people" motif found in Hosea 4:7; 4:10b–12a, 14; 7:11a; 8:7; 9:7; 12:2; 13:3.[67] The book of Hosea contains a number of proverbs and comparisons that refer to aspects of nature or human affairs (e.g., 4:11, 16; 5:12; 6:4; 7:4, 11, 16; 8:7, 9; 9:10; 10:7; 13:3), and the call to priest, nation, and king in 5:1 has been compared to the start of the Instruction genre. While the references to "knowledge" and the verb "to know" are not exclusive to wisdom, some

---

61. Whedbee, *Isaiah and Wisdom*, 19.

62. Whedbee, *Isaiah and Wisdom*, 152.

63. McKane, *Prophets and Wise Men*, 65–73, 79–81.

64. Jensen, *The Use of* tôrâ *by Isaiah*.

65. For example, Wolff identified wisdom influence in Hos. 2:22–23; 5:1; 8:7; 13:13; 14:9; Hans Walter Wolff, *Hosea: A Commentary on the Book of the Prophet Hosea*, trans. Gary Stansell, Hermeneia (Philadelphia: Fortress, 1974), 53, 97, 142, 228, 239. Cf. the surveys in Morgan, *Wisdom in the Old Testament Traditions*, 72–75; Andrew A. Macintosh, "Hosea and the Wisdom Tradition: Dependence and Independence," in *Wisdom in Ancient Israel: Essays in Honour of J. A. Emerton*, ed. John Day, Robert P. Gordon, and Hugh G. M. Williamson (Cambridge: Cambridge University Press, 1995), 124–32; Katharine J. Dell, "Hosea, Creation and Wisdom: An Alternative Tradition," in *On Stone and Scroll: Essays in Honour of Graham Ivor Davies*, ed. James K. Aitken, Katharine J. Dell, and Brian A. Mastin, BZAW 420 (Berlin: de Gruyter, 2011), 409–24.

66. Gerald T. Sheppard, *Wisdom as a Hermeneutical Construct: A Study in the Sapientializing of the Old Testament*, BZAW 151 (Berlin: de Gruyter, 1980), 129–36; Gerald T. Sheppard, "The Last Words of Hosea," *RevExp* 90 (1993): 191–204. Cf. the survey of other interpretations of the verse in Willem Boshoff, "'Who is wise?' Interpretations of the Postscript of the Book [*sic*] Hosea (14:10 [English 14:9])," *OTE* 18 (2005): 175–76, 180–84.

67. Choon-Leong Seow, "Hosea 14:10 and the Foolish People Motif," *CBQ* 44 (1982): 211–24.

AN INTRODUCTION TO ISRAEL'S WISDOM TRADITIONS

instances may reflect wisdom influence.[68] The roots *ḥkm* ("wise," 13:13) and *byn* ("understand," 4:14) are more clearly indicative of the wisdom traditions. Hosea 2:22–23 and 4:3 correlate order in creation with human affairs, evoking the act-consequence motif, 5:10 echoes the proverbial concern with moving landmarks (Prov. 22:28; 23:10), 13:13 speaks of the proper time (cf. Qoh. 3:1–8), and 14:2 contrasts guilt with what is good (the two ways).

As with Amos, Wolff identifies Micah as a village elder rooted in clan wisdom.[69] He marshals less evidence than for Amos, and much of it is subject to the same critique. In addition to the non-wisdom woe oracle (see above) and a "disputational style" in Micah 2:6–11, he notes a comparison with nature (1:8), concern over good and evil in 3:2 and bribery in 3:11, plus *yāda'* ("to know") and *'ēṣâ* (counsel) in 4:12 and *tûšiyyâ* ("wisdom," "success") in 6:9.

Donald Gowan claims six categories of evidence for wisdom influence in Habakkuk.[70] First, theodicy is a common theme in wisdom and dominates Habakkuk. Second, the dialogical nature of the book parallels some biblical and extrabiblical wisdom works. Third, Habakkuk uses words that are not necessarily exclusive to or characteristic of the wisdom literature but still occur more frequently there than elsewhere in the First Testament. Most significant are the combination of *ra'* ("evil") and *'āmāl* ("wrongdoing") in only Habakkuk 1:13 and Qoheleth 4:8; *rîb* ("strife") and *mādôn* ("contention") appear together only in Habakkuk 1:3; Proverbs 15:18; 17:14; 26:20–21; and Jeremiah 15:10, which is also concerned with theodicy; and the terms *hāmās* ("violence"; Hab. 1:2, 3, 9; 2:8, 17) and *bôgēd* ("treacherous"; Hab. 1:13; 2:5) are combined only in Proverbs 13:2. Fourth, more explicit wisdom usage is indicated by *tôkaḥat*

---

68. E.g., see McKane, *Prophets and Wise Men*, 86–87, concerning Hos. 4:6, 14.

69. Hans Walter Wolff, "Micah the Moreshite—the Prophet and His Background," in *Israelite Wisdom: Theological and Literary Essays in Honor of Samuel Terrien*, ed. John G. Gammie, Walter A. Brueggemann, W. Lee Humphreys, and James M. Ward, Scholars Press Homage Series (Missoula: Scholars Press, 1978), 77–84; Hans Walter Wolff, *Micah, the Prophet*, trans. Ralph D. Gehrke (Philadelphia: Fortress, 1981), especially 17–25. See also Morgan, *Wisdom in the Old Testament Traditions*, 75–76.

70. Donald E. Gowan, "Habakkuk and Wisdom," *Perspective* 9 (1968): 157–66. See also Carl-A. Keller, "Die Eigenart der Prophetie Habakuks," *ZAW* 85 (1973): 156–67; Morgan, *Wisdom in the Old Testament Traditions*, 89; Antonius H. J. Gunneweg, "Habakkuk and the Problem of the Suffering Just," in *Proceedings of the 9th World Congress of Jewish Studies, Jerusalem, Aug 1985: Division A: The Period of the Bible* (Jerusalem: World Union of Jewish Studies, 1986), 85–90; G. T. M. Prinsloo, "Life for the Righteous, Doom for the Wicked: Reading Habakkuk from a Wisdom Perspective," *Skrif En Kerk* 21 (2000): 621–40. Gary A. Tuttle, "Wisdom and Habakkuk," *SBT* 3 (1973): 3–14, critiques Gowan's points but still allows for some wisdom elements in Habakkuk.

("argument"; NRSV "complaint") in Habakkuk 2:1, by *māšāl* ("proverb," but here "taunt") and by *mĕlîṣâ ḥîdôt* ("mocking riddle") together in Habakkuk 2:6, and by the combination of Sheol and the root *śb'* ("be sated, have enough") only in Habakkuk 2:5 and Proverbs 27:20; 30:16. In addition, Janzen notes that in Proverbs 6:19; 12:17; 14:5, 25; 19:5, 9 the nouns *'ēd* and *yapîaḥ* (both "witness" in the NRSV) are paralleled and also modified by adjectives derived from either *kzb* ("lie") or *'mn* ("speak truth"), and all four roots are also present in Habakkuk 2:2–4.[71] As a result, Prinsloo reads Habakkuk 2:1–5b as a wisdom text.[72] Fifth, Gowan notes that Israel, Judah, and Jerusalem, as well as common prophetic themes like election and covenant, are absent from Habakkuk, and other characteristic prophetic elements are rare. Sixth, the book begins with a complaint and ends with a storm theophany, like Job.

Jeremiah employs wisdom themes and forms as well as other influences in shaping his message.[73] He shares an interest in creation, retribution, and social justice with the wisdom tradition, although as we have seen previously they are not exclusive to the latter. However, the prophet shares an interest in the true nature of wisdom and understanding (4:22; 5:21; 8:8–9; 9:23–24; etc.) with the wisdom writers.[74] At the same time, he uses didactic forms such as questions and answers (1:11–12, 13; 24:3), proverbs (e.g., 2:26; 3:20; 6:7; 17:11; 24:5, 8), lists (15:3), rhetorical questions (2:14, 31; 3:5; 8:4; 30:6; 31:20, etc.), and so on. However, he usually goes beyond how the wisdom tradition used such forms. For instance, Jeremiah uses rhetorical questions with obvious answers to establish agreement with his audience by appealing to nature and human

71. J. Gerald Janzen, "Habakkuk 2:2–4 in the Light of Recent Philological Advances," *HTR* 73 (1980): 54–62.

72. Prinsloo, "Life for the Righteous, Doom for the Wicked," 629–34.

73. See the discussions in Morgan, *Wisdom in the Old Testament Traditions*, 83–89; Walter Brueggemann, *The Theology of the Book of Jeremiah*, Old Testament Theology (Cambridge: Cambridge University Press, 2007), 172–76; Katharine J. Dell, "Jeremiah, Creation and Wisdom," in *Perspectives on Israelite Wisdom: Proceedings of the Oxford Old Testament Seminar*, ed. John Jarick (London: Bloomsbury T&T Clark, 2016), 375–90. Günther Wanke proposes a postexilic wisdom interpretation of the Jeremiah tradition in the prophetic book; "Weisheit im Jeremiabuch," in *Weisheit ausserhalb der kanonischen Weisheitschriften*, ed. Bernd Janowski, Veröffentlichungen der Wissenschaftlichen Gesellschaft für Theologie 10 (Gütersloh: Chr. Kaiser Verlag, 1996), 87–108.

74. Brueggemann argues that Jeremiah is in conflict with the sages in Jerusalem over who is truly wise: Walter Brueggemann, "The Epistemological Crisis of Israel's Two Histories (Jer 9:22–23)," in *Israelite Wisdom: Theological and Literary Essays in Honor of Samuel Terrien*, ed. John G. Gammie, Walter Brueggemann, W. Lee Humphreys, and James M. Ward, Scholars Press Homage Series (Missoula: Scholars Press, 1978), 85–105. See also McKane, *Prophets and Wise Men*, 73, 83–84, 88–91, 102–12.

affairs rather than divine revelation. In the wisdom literature that is the end of the pedagogical process, but Jeremiah uses that consensus to argue that Israel's beliefs and actions are inconsistent with that consensus.[75] Similarly, individual sayings in Proverbs simply make observations about human affairs or nature, whereas Jeremiah uses them to establish a basis for his message.[76]

There are very few wisdom elements in Ezekiel.[77] In Ezekiel 17:2 Yahweh orders him to "propound a riddle, and speak an allegory," and the latter form follows in 17:3–8. Additional allegories are found in Ezekiel 16; 19:2–9, 10–14; 23, which justifies the people saying of him, "Is he not a maker of allegories?" (20:49). Ezekiel refers to the people using proverbs in 12:22–23; 16:44; 18:2–3, which indicates their popular usage rather than Ezekiel himself using that form, and he cites them only to dismiss them. The spelling of the name Danel rather than Daniel in Ezekiel 14:14, 20; 28:3 suggests that Ezekiel may be aware of Danel of Ugarit, but apart from the passing reference to Danel's great wisdom in Ezekiel 28:3 to critique the prince of Tyre, Ezekiel does not display any other awareness of the Danel traditions.

Second Isaiah contains a few proverbs reflecting on experience, for example, in Isaiah 45:9 (cf. 29:16); 49:24. Thematically, creation is a significant motif in Second Isaiah, but rather than the focus on order and structure found in wisdom's creation theology, there it is part of the prophet's polemic against the existence of other gods. More specifically, scholars have noted parallels between Second Isaiah and Job. Pfeiffer lists lexical and conceptual parallels, to which Terrien adds the shared motifs of divine transcendence, human existence, and the Servant of God—both assume Second Isaiah's dependence on Job.[78] Ward discusses the Suffering Servant's redemptive knowledge (Isa. 53:11) in terms of knowledge about God as the creator who is wiser than the prophet's human contemporaries.[79] Dijkstra notes wisdom terminology in

75. Walter Brueggemann, "Jeremiah's Use of Rhetorical Questions," *JBL* 92 (1973): 358–74; T. Raymond Hobbs, "Jeremiah 3:1–5 and Deuteronomy 24:1–4," *ZAW* 86 (1974): 23–29.

76. T. Raymond Hobbs, "Some Proverbial Reflections in the Book of Jeremiah," *ZAW* 91 (1979): 62–72.

77. Cf. Morgan, *Wisdom in the Old Testament Traditions*, 109–12; Mark W. Hamilton, "Riddles and Parables, Traditions and Texts: Ezekielian Perspectives on Israelite Wisdom Traditions," in *Was There a Wisdom Tradition? New Prospects in Israelite Wisdom Studies*, ed. Mark Sneed, AIL 23 (Atlanta: Society of Biblical Literature, 2015), 241–62.

78. Robert H. Pfeiffer, "The Dual Origin of Hebrew Monotheism," *JBL* 46 (1927): 193–206; Samuel Terrien, "Quelques remarques sur les affinités de Job avec le Deutéro-Esaïe," in *Volume du Congrès: Genève, 1965*, ed. G. W. Anderson et al., VTSup 15 (Leiden: Brill, 1966), 295–310.

79. James M. Ward, "The Servant's Knowledge in Isaiah 40–55," in *Israelite Wisdom: Theological and Literary Essays in Honor of Samuel Terrien*, ed. John G. Gammie, Walter Brueg-

Isaiah 40:12–31 as well as parallels with the rhetorical questions posed by Elihu and Yahweh (Job 32–37; 38–41). He designates the Isaiah passage a wisdom disputation speech, while Rowold demonstrates parallels between Yahweh's interrogation of the Babylonian gods in Second Isaiah and his interrogation of Job in Job 38–41 to establish a common "challenge to a rival" form, although without establishing either book as the source of the genre.[80] In Third Isaiah, Isaiah 61:11 and 65:8 draw insights from nature, but claims of shared vocabulary between Isaiah 65:1 and Proverbs 1:28–31 and between Isaiah 66:1–2 and Proverbs 9:1–6 are somewhat forced.[81]

Jonah is the final prophetic book for which scholars have identified any significant wisdom contacts. Alongside prophetic and cultic motifs, Phyllis Trible notes similarities between the book of Jonah and wisdom literature: (1) it is not set in a specific historical setting but it does have (2) an international outlook and (3) a didactic interest in nature that culminates with Yahweh drawing a comparison between a bush and the human sphere (4:10–11), (4) its light and even comic tone is used to educate and not just to entertain, and (5) it has an informal style.[82] In addition, Katharine Dell identifies thematic and literary parallels with Job, especially a shared concern with theodicy.[83] More specifically, Robert Dentan argues that the description of Yahweh in Exodus 34:6–7, the first part of which is paralleled in Jonah 4:2, is the product of the wisdom tradition.[84] He notes terminology that, apart from Exodus 34:6–7 and its parallels, occurs either exclusively or predominantly in the wisdom literature, although many of the terms are in Exodus 34:7, which is not duplicated in Jonah 4:2. At the same time, the absence of specific references to Israel and

---

gemann, W. Lee Humphreys, and James M. Ward, Scholars Press Homage Series (Missoula: Scholars Press, 1978), 121–36.

80. Meindert Dijkstra, "Lawsuit, Debate and Wisdom Discourse in Second Isaiah," in *Studies in the Book of Isaiah: Festschrift Willem A. M. Beuken*, ed. J. Van Ruiten and M. Ververnne, BETL 132 (Leuven: Peeters, 1997), 251–71; Henry Rowold, "Yahweh's Challenge to Rival: The Form and Function of the Yahweh-Speech in Job 38–39," *CBQ* 47 (1985): 199–211.

81. See A. Robert, "Les attachés litteraires bibliques de Prov. I–IX," *RB* 43 (1934): 42–68, 172–204, 374–84; 44 (1935): 244–65, 502–25.

82. Phyllis Trible, "Studies in the Book of Jonah," PhD diss. (Columbia University, 1963), 249–57.

83. Katharine J. Dell, "Reinventing the Wheel: The Shaping of the Book of Jonah," in *After the Exile: Essays in Honour of Rex Mason*, ed. John Barton and David J. Reimer (Macon, GA: Mercer University Press, 1995), 85–101.

84. Robert C. Dentan, "Literary Affinities of Exodus XXXIV 6f.," *VT* 13 (1963): 34–51. Trible offers some critique but still accepts the basic thrust of Dentan's proposal ("Studies in the Book of Jonah," 257–59).

its religious history gives the confession a universal outlook, parallel to the basic wisdom perspective. At the same time, motifs such as concern for the fear of the Lord (Jon. 1:9, 16), divine control over creation and nature (1:4, 15, 17; 2:10; 4:6–8), plus opposition to evil (1:2, 3:8, 10; 4:6) and anger (4:1–4, 9) have affinities with the wisdom tradition, although none is unique to it. Thus, George Landes deems the book a didactic example story derived from prophetic circles, albeit with some possible contact with wisdom.[85]

Scholars have proposed wisdom connections for a number of prophetic books, but not all are convincing. Amos and Micah do not contain any distinctively wisdom features, and while Ezekiel and Second Isaiah have a few points of contact with Israel's wisdom traditions, these are not enough to characterize them as wisdom texts. Hosea contains more wisdom features but does not reflect an overall wisdom intent, while Jeremiah uses wisdom themes and forms but goes beyond their original purpose in order to reinforce his message. First Isaiah, Habakkuk, and Jonah have the strongest claims for wisdom influence by virtue of containing larger clusters of wisdom features that also reflect wisdom usage.

Other Books

Shemaryahu Talmon reads the book of Esther as an "historicized wisdom tale" that demonstrates wisdom teaching being lived out in a royal court setting.[86]

---

85. George M. Landes, "Jonah: A Māšāl?" in *Israelite Wisdom: Theological and Literary Essays in Honor of Samuel Terrien*, ed. John G. Gammie, Walter Brueggemann, W. Lee Humphreys, and James M. Ward, Scholars Press Homage Series (Missoula: Scholars Press, 1978), 137–58; so too John Day, "Problems in the Interpretation of the Book of Jonah," in *In Quest of the Past: Studies on Israelite Religion, Literature and Prophetism: Papers Read at the Joint British-Dutch Old Testament Conference, Held at Elspeet, 1988*, ed. A. S. van der Woude, OTS 26 (Leiden: Brill, 1990), 39, 47. Noting as well the fourteen questions in forty-eight verses, James Limburg concurs; *Jonah: A Commentary*, OTL (Louisville: Westminster John Knox, 1993), 22–28.

86. Shemaryahu Talmon, "'Wisdom' in the Book of Esther," *VT* 13 (1963): 419–55. See also Carey A. Moore, *Esther: Introduction, Translation, and Notes*, AB 7B (Garden City, NY: Doubleday, 1971), pp. xxxiii–xxxiv; Robert Gordis, "Religion, Wisdom and History in the Book of Esther—a New Solution to an Ancient Crux," *JBL* 100 (1981): 359–88; Leila L. Bronner, "Reclaiming Esther: From Sex Object to Sage," *JBQ* 26 (1998): 3–11. Kandy Queen-Sutherland reads the book as a parable; "Ruth, Qoheleth, and Esther: Counter Voices from the Megilloth," *PRS* 43 (2016): 233–36. Susan Niditch acknowledges apparent wisdom aspects but links them to folktale motifs; "Esther: Folklore, Wisdom, Feminism and Authority," in *A Feminist Companion to Esther, Judith and Susanna*, ed. Athalya Brenner, FCB 7 (Sheffield: Sheffield Academic Press, 1995), 26–46.

Rather than focusing on specific wisdom forms and vocabulary, Talmon emphasizes general points of comparison. The setting is similar to the stories of Joseph and Daniel as well as the extrabiblical Ahiqar story, Esther's rise parallels those of Joseph and Daniel, and her adoption by a wise man incorporates an element from Ahiqar. The interest in persuasive speech as well as the individualistic outlook reflect wisdom concerns, while the lack of specifically Israelite religious elements, including no reference to salvation history or prayer, the absence of the name Yahweh, and no sense of connection to the larger Jewish community in Judah or the diaspora are all consistent with wisdom's international affinities. Talmon thinks that Mordecai and Haman reflect the stereotypical contrast between the good wise man and the evil schemer, while Ahasuerus represents the foolish king. Talmon compares Esther's role in saving her people to the wise women of Tekoa and Abel (2 Sam. 14:1–24; 20:16–22) and notes that the retribution Haman experiences is not divine punishment but rather his own plan against Mordecai being enacted upon him (cf. Prov. 26:27; Qoh. 10:8; Sir. 27:26).[87] Scholars have criticized Talmon's arguments on multiple grounds, including the fact that many elements noted by Talmon are not exclusive to wisdom, the book has a nationalistic tone rather than an international one, he fails to account for numerous non-wisdom aspects of the book, and Mordecai is not the epitome of wisdom.[88] While McGeough accepts some contacts with wisdom traditions in Esther, he emphasizes that the central character, Esther herself, does not embody wisdom teachings and he interprets the book as going beyond the wisdom elements it contains.[89]

> **Possible Wisdom Influence in Other Books**
>
> - Esther
> - Song of Songs
> - Daniel

87. The last point is also stressed by N. A. van Uchelen, "A Chokmatic Theme in the Book of Esther: A Study in the Structure of the Story," in *Verkenningen in een Stroomgebied: proeven van oudtestamentisch onderzoek: ter gelegenheid van het afscheid van Prof. Dr. M. A. Beek*, ed. M. Boertien, Aleida G. van Daalen, F. J. Hoogewoud, and Elsa H. Plantenga (Amsterdam: Huisdrukkerij Universiteit van Amsterdam, 1974), 132–40.

88. Crenshaw, "Method," 140–42; Michael V. Fox, *Character and Ideology in the Book of Esther*, SPOT (Columbia: University of South Carolina Press, 1991), 142–43; Adele Berlin, *Esther אסתר: The Traditional Hebrew Text with the New JPS Translation*, JPS Bible Commentary (Philadelphia: Jewish Publication Society, 2001), xl–xli.

89. Kevin M. McGeough, "Esther the Hero: Going Beyond 'Wisdom' in Heroic Narratives," *CBQ* 70 (2008): 44–65.

Brevard Childs sees the Song of Songs as wisdom literature.[90] The opening ascription to Solomon (1:1) attributes the book to the supposed author of Proverbs and Qoheleth. This canonical designation has implications for how one reads the book, namely as a wisdom reflection on the nature of married love. This is analogous to the use of erotic language to describe the search for Lady Wisdom (e.g., Prov. 4:6–8; 9:1–5; Sir. 51:13–21; Wis. 7:10; 8:2) and finding her being comparable to finding a wife (compare Prov. 3:13; 8:17, 35 with 18:22; 31:10).[91] Sadgrove proposes a number of riddles in the Song (1:6; 2:7, 15; 3:5; 8:11, 12, 15), an emphasis on nature's annual renewal, and considers 8:6–7 a wisdom reflection on the nature of love.[92] Murphy suggests that the Song's concern for marital faithfulness is compatible with the warnings about adulterous women in Proverbs 1–9 and notes a number of parallels between the Song and Lady Wisdom in Proverbs and Sirach.[93] Both are called "my sister" (Song 4:9, 10, 12; 5:1, 2; Prov. 7:4) and provide food (Song 7:13; 8:2; Prov. 9:5; Sir. 15:3). The woman does not let go of her lover, just as Ben Sira's readers should not let go of Wisdom (Song 3:4; Sir. 6:27) and the woman's lover looks through the window as do those who seek Wisdom (Song 2:9; Sir. 14:23). Most of these correlations are with the later Ben Sira, but they are rooted in the earlier book of Proverbs. Going further, one stream in the history of interpretation identi-

90. Brevard S. Childs, *Introduction to the Old Testament as Scripture* (Philadelphia: Fortress, 1979), 573–79. Most of the following points are reviewed, at times with additional examples or detail, in Katharine J. Dell, "Does the Song of Songs Have Any Connections to Wisdom?" in *Perspectives on the Song of Songs*, ed. Anselm C. Hagedorn, BZAW 346 (Berlin: de Gruyter, 2005), 8–26. See also Edmée Kingsmill, "The Song of Songs: A Wisdom Book," in *Perspectives on Israelite Wisdom: Proceedings of the Oxford Old Testament Seminar*, ed. John Jarick (London: Bloomsbury T&T Clark, 2016), 310–35. Compare the reservations of J. Cheryl Exum, "Unity, Date, Authorship and the 'Wisdom' of the Song of Songs," in *Goochem in Mokum, Wisdom in Amsterdam: Papers on Biblical and Related Wisdom Read at the Fifteenth Joint Meeting of the Society for Old Testament Study and the Oudtestamentisch Werkgezelschap, Amsterdam, July 2012*, ed. George J. Brooke and Pierre van Hecke (Leiden: Brill, 2016), 64–68.

91. See also von Rad, *Wisdom in Israel*, 166–69; Roland E. Murphy, "Wisdom and Eros in Proverbs 1–9," *CBQ* 50 (1988): 600–603; Edmée Kingsmill, *The Song of Songs and the Eros of God: A Study in Biblical Intertextuality*, OTM (Oxford: Oxford University Press, 2009), 46–74.

92. Michael Sadgrove, "The Song of Songs as Wisdom Literature," in *Studia Biblica 1978 I: Papers on Old Testament and Related Themes. Sixth International Congress on Biblical Studies, Oxford 3–7 April 1978*, ed. E. A. Livingstone, JSOTSup 11 (Sheffield: JSOT Press, 1979), 245–48; he proposes lexical parallels on 248 n. 4. On Song 8:6 see also Murphy, *The Tree of Life*, 107.

93. Murphy, *The Tree of Life*, 106–7. See also Sheppard, *Wisdom as a Hermeneutical Construct*, 33 n. 42, 53–54.

fies the woman in Song of Songs as Wisdom herself, with her lover either the historical Solomon or a seeker of wisdom.[94]

Most discussions of wisdom in the book of Daniel focus on the relationship of wisdom to apocalyptic, which is considered in chapter 10 below. With respect to Daniel itself, many scholars note parallels with the Joseph story, wherein the central character is a wise man who interprets dreams, rises in the royal court, and advises the pharaoh/king.[95] Daniel himself may be extrapolated from earlier traditions concerning Danel at Ugarit (cf. Ezek. 14:14, 20; 28:3 above). However, there are few instances of specific wisdom parallels in the book, although the "times and seasons" in Daniel 2:21 can be compared with Qoheleth 3:1 and Sirach 39:34. Similarly, there are frequent references to Daniel's wisdom, usually in contrast to the wisdom of the Babylonian courtiers, and he is able to "explain riddles and solve problems" (5:12). But unlike the wisdom tradition, where insight is gained through reflection upon nature and experience, Daniel's wisdom is a divine gift (e.g., 1:17; 2:19, 21, 30, 47; 5:11–12, 14; 9:22). It is especially concerned with the interpretation of dreams, constituting a form of mantic wisdom dependent on the practitioner's specialized knowledge.[96]

Summary

Israel's wisdom traditions are not restricted to the five wisdom books dealt with in chapters 3–7. Despite the distinctive aspects of their literature, Israel's sages did not operate in isolation from the rest of Israelite society, and so we should expect to see wisdom elements in some other First Testament books as well. But scholars have cast too wide a net, to the point that wisdom material

94. Marvin H. Pope, *Song of Songs: A New Translation with Introduction and Commentary*, AB 7C (Garden City: Doubleday, 1977), 110.

95. These and other parallels were surveyed recently by Funlola O. Olojede, "Sapiential Elements in the Joseph and Daniel Narratives *vis-à-vis* Woman Wisdom: Conjunctions and Disjunctions," *OTE* 25 (2012): 357–61; he lists a few differences that usually go unnoted on p. 362. His effort to link the narratives to Lady Wisdom (pp. 365–67) is not persuasive. Niditch and Doran argue that Gen. 41, Dan. 2, and the Syriac Ahiqar 5–7 have a common folktale form, but that Dan. 2 departs significantly from the established form of the tale: Susan Niditch and Robert Doran, "The Success Story of the Wise Courtier: A Formal Approach," *JBL* 96 (1977): 179–93, especially 187–93.

96. Brian A. Mastin, "Wisdom and Daniel," in *Wisdom in Ancient Israel: Essays in Honour of J. A. Emerton*, ed. John Day, Robert P. Gordon, and Hugh G. M. Williamson (Cambridge: Cambridge University Press, 1995), 161–69.

has been proposed in virtually all parts of the First Testament. Therefore, it is necessary to have clear principles for evaluating such proposals. Applying the three criteria outlined at the beginning of this chapter results in a more restricted body of wisdom texts beyond the five wisdom books, but the resulting body of literature rests on firmer grounds.

FURTHER READING

Cheung, Simon Chi-Chung. *Wisdom Intoned: A Reappraisal of the Genre 'Wisdom Psalms.'* LHBOTS 613. London: Bloomsbury T&T Clark, 2015.

Crenshaw, James L. "Method in Determining Wisdom Influence upon 'Historical' Literature." *JBL* 88 (1969): 129–42.

Jensen, Joseph. *The Use of tôrâ by Isaiah: His Debate with the Wisdom Tradition.* CBQMS 3. Washington, DC: Catholic Biblical Association of America, 1973.

Morgan, Donn F. *Wisdom in the Old Testament Traditions.* Atlanta: John Knox, 1981.

Sheppard, Gerald T. *Wisdom as a Hermeneutical Construct: A Study in the Sapientializing of the Old Testament.* BZAW 151. Berlin: de Gruyter, 1980.

Weinfeld, Moshe. *Deuteronomy and the Deuteronomic School.* Oxford: Clarendon, 1972; reprinted Winona Lake, IN: Eisenbrauns, 1992.

Whedbee, J. William. *Isaiah and Wisdom.* Nashville: Abingdon, 1971.

Whybray, R. N. *The Intellectual Tradition in the Old Testament.* BZAW 135. Berlin: de Gruyter, 1974.

———. *The Succession Narrative.* SBT Second Series 9. London: SCM, 1968.

Wilson, Lindsay. *Joseph, Wise and Otherwise: The Intersection of Wisdom and Covenant in Genesis 37–50.* Paternoster Biblical Monographs. Carlisle, UK: Paternoster, 2004.

Wolff, Hans Walter. *Amos the Prophet: The Man and His Background.* Translated by Foster R. McCurley. Philadelphia: Fortress, 1973.

CHAPTER 9

Wisdom Theology

The presence of wisdom literature in the biblical canon is problematic for some readers. The issue is rooted in the biblical theology movement that flourished in the middle of the twentieth century and sought to identify an all-encompassing theology for the First Testament. For many scholars, the dominant element was salvation history, a recital of the "mighty acts of God."[1] Beginning with the matriarchs and patriarchs (Sarah, Rebekah, Leah, Rachel, Abraham, Isaac, and Jacob), biblical theologians traced God's dealings through the sojourn in Egypt, the exodus, the covenant at Mt. Sinai, the monarchy, the exile as God's correction, the return as God's blessing, and so on. The early wisdom books of Proverbs, Job, and Qoheleth in particular do not fit into this pattern, but rather are silent about the great moments between God and Israel. While this changes with the later books of Ben Sira and the Wisdom of Solomon, the international character of the three earlier wisdom books accepted as canonical by Jews, Protestants, and Roman Catholics does not cohere with the presumed uniqueness of Yahwistic faith. Granted, the book of Proverbs prefers the name Yahweh (eighty-seven times, usually translated "the LORD") far more than the generic noun "god" (*'ĕlōhîm*; five times, usually translated "God") when referring to the deity,[2] but the references to Yahweh are not

---

1. The phrase is taken from *Magnalia Dei, the Mighty Acts of God: Essays on the Bible and Archaeology in Memory of G. Ernest Wright*, ed. Frank Moore Cross, Werner E. Lemke, and Patrick D. Miller Jr. (Garden City: Doubleday, 1976). For Wright himself see G. Ernest Wright, *God Who Acts: Biblical Theology as Recital*, SBT 8 (London: SCM, 1952).

2. Lennart Boström, *The God of the Sages: The Portrayal of God in the Book of Proverbs*, ConBOT 29 (Stockholm: Almqvist & Wiksell, 1990), 33–36. William McKane, *Proverbs: A New Approach*, OTL (Philadelphia: Westminster, 1970), 10–22, proposed that the references to

linked to Israel's specific religious traditions. More importantly, references to the deity using either term are found in just over ten percent of the total number of verses in the book, which means that there is little explicitly "religious" about most of the content of Proverbs. Furthermore, Job and his three friends were Edomites, not Israelites, and referred to the deity by various ancient names and titles. The name Yahweh is restricted to the prose prologue and epilogue plus the narrator's identification of Yahweh as the speaker in Job 38:1; 40:1, 6 and as the recipient of Job's responses in 40:3; 42:1, but Job himself does not use the name.[3] Similarly, Qoheleth uses the noun *'ĕlōhîm* exclusively, never the name Yahweh.

In light of the preceding, it is not entirely surprising that in the middle of the last century some scholars rejected the wisdom literature's presence in the canon. Hartmut Gese considered it a "foreign body (*Fremdkörper*) in the Old Testament's world" and Horst Preuss deemed it heathen thinking that should be excluded from First Testament theology.[4] The various First Testament theologies written in this period did not exclude the wisdom literature, but they did marginalize it.[5] Gerhard von Rad is typical in this regard, treating the wisdom literature in the appendix to the first of his two volumes.[6] The scholarly evaluation of the wisdom books has been decidedly more positive in recent decades, as exemplified by the proliferation of articles and monographs dealing with

---

Yahweh are the result of a late Yahwistic editing of the book, but see the response in Boström, *The God of the Sages*, 36–39.

3. It is significant that the common phrase "fear of the Lord" in Job 28:28 uses the common noun "lord" rather than the proper name Yahweh, as is the norm elsewhere (e.g., Prov. 1:7, 29; 2:5; 8:13; 9:10, etc.).

4. Hartmut Gese, *Lehre und Wirklichkeit in der alten Weisheit Studien zu den Spruchen Salomos und zu dem Buche Hiob* (Tübingen: Mohr, 1958), 2; Horst Dietrich Preuss, "Erwägungen zum theologischen Ort alttestamentlicher Weisheitsliteratur," *EvT* 30 (1970): 393–417. See also Horst Dietrich Preuss, *Old Testament Theology*, trans. Leo G. Perdue, OTL (Louisville: Westminster John Knox, 1995–1996); and earlier, G. Ernest Wright, *God Who Acts*, 104. Contrast the response in Franz-Josef Steiert, *Die Weisheit Israels ein Fremdkörper im Alten Testament? Eine Untersuchung zum Buch der Sprüche auf dem Hintergrund der ägyptischen Weisheitslehren*, Freiburger Theologische Studien (Freiburg: Herder, 1990).

5. See the survey, with the low relative percentages of treatment given to wisdom literature, in Charles H. H. Scobie, "The Place of Wisdom in Biblical Theology," *BTB* 14 (1984): 43.

6. Gerhard von Rad, *Old Testament Theology I: The Theology of Israel's Historical Traditions*, trans. D. M. G. Stalker (1962; reprinted Louisville: Westminster John Knox, 2001), 408–53, 455–59. Von Rad's later monograph on wisdom literature itself still treated it separately from the rest of the First Testament, asserting that it was in "theological tension with traditional Yahwism: a harsher one could hardly be imagined" (*Wisdom in Israel*, trans. James D. Martin [London: SCM, 1971; reprinted Nashville: Abingdon, 1988], 314).

the wisdom literature, but it has still received proportionally less treatment in recent theological treatments of the First Testament.[7] Even James Crenshaw, who devoted much of his career to the wisdom literature, called it "an orphan in the biblical household" in 1976 and thirty-four years later still described it as "*a different world of thought.*"[8] There is no question that the content of the wisdom books is very different from much of the rest of the First Testament. But despite the many scholars who radically separated the wisdom literature from the rest of the First Testament, others have attempted to integrate it with Yahweh's interventions in the world.

Creation

The most common approach has been to make a connection between the wisdom literature and a theology of creation.[9] The starting point for this approach is Walther Zimmerli's oft-cited statement, "Wisdom thinks resolutely

7. The most substantial discussion is John Kessler, *Old Testament Theology: Divine Call and Human Response* (Waco: Baylor University Press, 2013), 447–505, with briefer treatments in Walter Brueggemann, *Theology of the Old Testament: Testimony, Dispute, Advocacy* (Minneapolis: Fortress, 1997), 680–94; Bernhard W. Anderson, *Contours of Old Testament Theology* (Minneapolis: Fortress, 1999), 260–85. Moberly deals almost exclusively with Job 1–2; 28: R. W. L. Moberly, *Old Testament Theology: Reading the Hebrew Bible as Christian Scripture* (Grand Rapids: Baker Academic, 2013), 243–77. Rendtorff provides overviews of Job, Proverbs, and Qoheleth, but devotes only two pages to wisdom as one of eighteen themes, each of which is discussed at much greater length: Rolf Rendtorff, *The Canonical Hebrew Bible: A Theology of the Old Testament*, trans. David Orton, Tools for Biblical Study 7 (Leiden: Deo, 2005), 336–57, 357–69, 374–83, 665–66. The wisdom literature is treated mostly in passing in subordination to other topics in Rolf P. Knierim, *The Task of Old Testament Theology: Method and Cases* (Grand Rapids: Eerdmans, 1995); Erhard S. Gerstenberger, *Theologies in the Old Testament* (Minneapolis: Fortress, 2002); Walter Brueggemann, *Old Testament Theology: An Introduction*, Library of Biblical Theology (Nashville: Abingdon, 2008); John W. Rogerson, *A Theology of the Old Testament: Cultural Memory, Communication, and Being Human* (Minneapolis: Fortress, 2010); Mark McEntire, *Portraits of a Mature God: Choices in Old Testament Theology* (Minneapolis: Fortress, 2013).

8. James L. Crenshaw, "Prolegomenon," in *Studies in Ancient Israelite Wisdom*, ed. James L. Crenshaw (New York: Ktav, 1976), 1; James L. Crenshaw, *Old Testament Wisdom: An Introduction*, 3rd ed. (Louisville: Westminster John Knox, 2010), 24–25 (italics in the original).

9. The most consistent recent supporter of this link is Leo G. Perdue, *Wisdom and Creation: The Theology of Wisdom Literature* (Nashville: Abingdon, 1994); Leo G. Perdue, *The Collapse of History: Reconstructing Old Testament Theology*, OBT (Minneapolis: Fortress, 1994); Leo G. Perdue, *Wisdom Literature: A Theological History* (Louisville: Westminster John Knox, 2007). Note especially his review of scholarship in *Wisdom Literature*, 15–36. On creation in Proverbs in particular see Boström, *The God of the Sages*, 47–89.

within the framework of a theology of creation."[10] Zimmerli takes the divine command in Genesis 1:28 to "be fruitful and multiply, and fill the earth and subdue it; and have dominion over the fish of the sea and over the birds of the air and over every living thing that moves upon the earth" as the theological warrant for the sages' efforts to gain mastery over the created world through their reflection on what it contains, drawing insights from nature and human affairs alike. This directive provides the basis for their repeated assertions about the benefits that will flow to those who follow their teaching as well as the negative repercussions if their words are rejected; they are articulating the divine blessing that God has bestowed upon the world. At the same time, they acknowledge that all of creation and those within it are subordinate to God's will: "The human mind plans the way, but the LORD directs the steps" (Prov. 16:9; cf. 16:1; 19:21). Therefore, the task of the wise is to identify and communicate the attitudes and actions that will elicit divine blessing and those that will not.

> **Aspects of Wisdom Theology?**
>
> - Creation
> - Order
> - Supplement salvation history

Building on this, the sages were attentive to God as the creator. Within the proverbial material this amounts to simple acknowledgement of God as the one who has made everything for a reason (Prov. 16:4; Qoh. 3:11), the maker of both the rich and poor (Prov. 17:5; 22:2) as well as the ears and eyes (Prov. 20:12), and the one who brings light to the eyes of the poor and their oppressor alike (Prov. 29:13). Job 28 and 38–39 reflect on creation and God's role in it at much greater length, with the latter in particular itemizing how various elements of the created order are beyond Job's comprehension while at the same time highlighting God's care for and protection of it all. Ben Sira has numerous hymns in praise of God's creation (e.g., 16:24–17:14; 39:15–35; 42:15–43:33), while Wisdom 7:17–21 acknowledges God as the source of insight into the world, in terms of what today is called physics, chemistry, history, astronomy, zoology, psychology, and botany.

At the same time, wisdom literature connects Lady Wisdom to both the act and the object of creation. Proverbs 3:19 records that "the LORD by wisdom founded the earth; by understanding he established the heavens," and the parallel reference to "his knowledge" in the following verse suggests that 3:19 uses the common noun for wisdom. But Proverbs 8:22–31 clearly associates Lady

---

10. Walther Zimmerli, "The Place and Limit of Wisdom in the Framework of the Old Testament Theology," *SJT* 17 (1964): 148.

Wisdom with Yahweh's creative actions. She was with him "at the beginning of his work," and although the passage does not ascribe any direct agency to her, she is more than just a passive observer. If *'āmôn* in Proverbs 8:30 is correctly rendered as "master worker" (NRSV), then she could have provided the design for Yahweh's creation. In addition, she is a bridge between Yahweh and his creation: she is a "delight, rejoicing before him" (Prov. 8:30b), while at the same time she is "rejoicing in his inhabited world and delighting in the human race" (Prov. 8:31). The repetition of "delight" and "rejoicing" in the reverse order across multiple lines creates a mirror pattern that emphasizes her mediating role between heaven and earth, although there is no indication that she actually enters into the world. However, Proverbs 9:1–6 does describe her invitation to "the simple" to dine in her house, echoing her call to the same group in Proverbs 1:20–33.

Ben Sira shares this connection between Lady Wisdom and creation while also going beyond it. Sirach 1:4–10 also dates her origins to before the rest of creation but is more explicit about her being "poured out upon all his works." In Sirach 24:3 Lady Wisdom says, "I came forth from the mouth of the Most High," linking her to God's creative word in Genesis 1, and Sirach 24:9 repeats her primeval origins. She leaves her heavenly throne to live in Zion (24:4–12), and Ben Sira eventually identifies her as God's revelation to Israel in the Torah (24:23). The Wisdom of Solomon goes further. Even though Wisdom 7:17 says that God gave pseudo-Solomon his knowledge of the created world, in 7:22 he says that it was Wisdom who taught him, identifying her with God and calling her "the fashioner (*technitis*) of all things" here and again in 8:6. This identification of Lady Wisdom with God continues in the recitation of history in Wisdom 10, after which God replaces her as the agent of salvation in Wisdom 11–19.

To summarize, the wisdom writers link their efforts to other Israelite traditions through their use of creation theology. God authorizes their quest for insight into, and understanding of, their world, so that creation is simultaneously the context for and object of their reflections. Reflecting on nature and human affairs entailed acknowledging the one who had created both. At the same time, the sages linked Lady Wisdom with creation, starting with a minimal role in Proverbs 8, then equating her with Torah in Sirach 24 and eventually with God in Wisdom 6–10. The end result of this development was to bring Lady Wisdom into the realm of salvation history itself.

Order[11]

A second emphasis in the wisdom tradition is also derived from reflection on creation, namely the attention to order and structure in the created world and its implications for human action. The creation story in Genesis 1 articulates a series of balancing contrasts, between light and darkness, between what is above and what is below, and between the earth and the water. The structure of the story indicates that there is a proper location for different things. On day one God creates light in contrast to darkness and then on day four the things that dominate the light and darkness, namely the sun, moon, and stars, are made. On day two the sky and water are distinguished, after which the birds and fish that live in those two areas are created on the fifth day. Finally, on day three dry land emerges, and the animals and humans that live on that land emerge on day six. On the whole, then, days one through three each have a counterpart in days four through six. In addition, God repeatedly pronounces this balanced order of creation "good!" Thus, the divinely created world is one of order and structure, with everything in its proper place.

Psalm 104, which clearly depends on Genesis 1 for its basic outline of the world's creation, shares this perspective on creation but goes well beyond its predecessor in its hymnic celebration of individual elements. Important here is that Psalm 104 elaborates in greater detail the fact that all aspects of creation, both the physical elements like the waters and the mountains as well as the living things like plants and animals, are ordered toward a harmonious whole, with everything in its appropriate place and integrated with the rest of creation. In the center of the poem is the acclamation that "in wisdom you have made them all" (Ps. 104:24). Proverbs 16:4 echoes this with its affirmation that "the LORD has made everything for its purpose," while Qoheleth 3:11 states that God "has made everything suitable for its time." In short, based on the insight that the created world has a divinely ordained order, which Psalm 104 declares was created "in wisdom," the wise should be able to determine what this order is by their reflection on the world. Hence the frequent observations in Proverbs (see chapter 3 above) about nature in and of itself, as well as analogies drawn between nature and human affairs, seek to demonstrate how the natural world conformed to certain patterns so that humans could cooperate with nature rather than fight against it. Similarly, observations about how the actions of certain animals produce positive results, such as the industrious ant in Proverbs 6:6–8 or the wise ants, badgers, locusts, and lizards in Prov-

---

11. For the book of Proverbs specifically, see Boström, *The God of the Sages*, 90–140.

erbs 30:24–28, also include an explicit (as in Prov. 6:9–11) or implicit moral that humans should act similarly.[12] In contrast, the comparisons between a biting serpent and the effects of alcohol (Prov. 23:32), a wandering sparrow and a roving human (Prov. 27:8), or a dog returning to its vomit and a fool's repeated folly (Prov. 26:11) presume that the reader will recognize the negative consequences in each analogy.

This interest in good over bad outcomes reflects the sages' concern with what led to balance and order in human society itself. Therefore, in addition to analogies with nature, the wise frequently reflect on the normal outcomes of various human attitudes and actions with a view to promoting what results in both individual success and communal harmony. Thus, in keeping with the frequent contrasts in the wisdom literature between the wise and the foolish, the righteous and wicked, or the industrious and the lazy, Proverbs repeatedly notes that the first type in each of these pairs succeeds or is rewarded, while the second type experiences the opposite result.[13] As noted in chapter 3 above, the sages tend to observe rather than command or prohibit, but their desire for ethical action is transparent. Klaus Koch proposes that the sages held to a hard and fast act-consequence theory in which the effect of an action was built into the deed itself.[14] Some sayings seem to support this view, such as "whoever digs a pit will fall into it, and a stone will come back on the one who starts it rolling" (Prov. 26:27; cf. Qoh. 10:8; Sir. 27:26; Ps. 7:16), and Job's friends hold to a view of reward and punishment that is consistent with this perspective. However, the book of Job as a whole protests against such a rigid application of the theory of retribution and Qoheleth also recognizes that the traditional wisdom concerning retribution does not always apply (Qoh. 7:15; 8:14). Moreover, two things about the book of Proverbs suggest that the sages did not hold a purely mechanical theory of an act and its consequences such as Koch proposes. First, frequent statements indicate that ultimately God is in control and determines the outcome of events, conveying divine blessing or punishment (e.g., Prov. 3:33; 10:27, 29; 12:2; 15:25; etc.); this recognition is summarized by Proverbs 19:21: "The human mind may devise many plans, but it is the purpose of the LORD that will be established." Second, the very fact that

12. For the role of animal references in the book of Proverbs see Tova L. Forti, *Animal Imagery in the Book of Proverbs*, VTSup 118 (Leiden: Brill, 2007). She discusses Prov 6:6–8 and 30:24–28 on pp. 101–18.

13. E.g., Prov. 3:35 and 10:14; 10:2, 3, 6, 7, and 12:24, 27; 13:4 respectively. The references for each pair could be greatly multiplied.

14. Klaus Koch, "Is There a Doctrine of Retribution in the Old Testament," in *Theodicy in the Old Testament*, ed. James L. Crenshaw (Philadelphia: Fortress, 1983), 57–87.

the collected sayings make a consistent effort to persuade the hearer or reader to choose attitudes and actions that yield positive results indicates that they thought humans were free to choose how to act in different situations, rather than their deeds and their consequences being predetermined.

Since the sages recognized a divinely established order in the world that had consequences for human life, identifying regular patterns in nature allowed them to present strategies for cooperating with creation's inherent structures in order to facilitate a positive life. At the same time, attending to the normal outcome of various human choices provides the accumulated insight into human affairs that leads to positive relationships, with the goal of achieving a harmonious social order. The preference for the righteous over the wicked gives their sayings an ethical component that is consistent with the social laws in the Pentateuch without directly appealing to them. Human actions contrary to right order must be avoided since they would disrupt the order of the social world that ultimately derives from God. Moreover, because human society is part of the larger created order, sayings that superficially appear to deal only with the regulation of human society and affairs are also connected with the preservation of cosmic order, since a breakdown in one aspect would threaten all of it.

A Complement and Challenge to Salvation History[15]

The two preceding attempts to link the wisdom literature of the First Testament to a core biblical "Yahwism," understood as salvation history, need to be nuanced in the light of three considerations. First, interest in creation was a late development. In the earliest stages of Israelite religion Yahweh was viewed as a warrior god and then a savior god, whereas interest in him as a creator god gained prominence during the Babylonian exile. This is not to say that the Israelites in general and the wisdom writers in particular were unaware of their place within a created world. Rather, creation provided both the context and much of the content for their reflections on human existence.[16] Their presupposition of a created world might even explain their relative silence about it in the wisdom books. Second, the concept of divine creation is not

---

15. Cf. the similar considerations of Roland E. Murphy, *The Tree of Life: An Exploration of Biblical Wisdom Literature*, 3rd ed. (Grand Rapids: Eerdmans, 2002), 121–26, 225–26, 274–77.

16. Von Rad, *Wisdom in Israel*, 153–55; Leslie J. Hoppe, "Biblical Wisdom: A Theology of Creation," *Listening* 14 (1976): 198–99.

unique to Israel but is also reflected in numerous myths from Israel's ancient Near Eastern neighbors.[17] While the Israelite material has different emphases and perspectives than the surrounding literature, creation theology is not a unique element of Israelite religion. Third, not even salvation history is unique to Israelite religion. Their neighbors also viewed their gods as involved in their history, guiding their affairs and even intervening directly at times.[18] Once again, the particular details of how Yahweh was involved in world events differ, but we cannot escape the fact that the biblical interest in salvation history and creation is also international in flavor, just as wisdom literature is. The difference is one of degree.

But if salvation history is not a unique aspect of ancient Israelite belief, this calls into question its centrality for understanding the entire First Testament. In fact, making salvation history, or anything else, the central theology of the First Testament creates a "canon within the canon," requiring that everything fit into that category. But that raises the hermeneutical question whether one part of the Bible should be determinative for all other parts, which risks excluding those parts that do not fit the chosen framework even though they have been judged canonical. Instead, scholars have recently called into question the very idea of a single theological center of the First Testament.[19] Accordingly, rather than judging it in terms of how it accords with, for example, the exodus tradition, we should allow the biblical wisdom literature to stand on its own merits. By virtue of its inclusion in the biblical canon, this material was deemed to express part of the Israelite people's experience of God, and should be granted that status in and of itself, not just on the basis of how it fits with predetermined views of what is or is not central to the First Testament.

How then should we deal with the supposedly secular nature of the wisdom literature, which led to questions about its inclusion in the Bible in the first place? This is really a modern problem rooted in the increasing tendency over the last few centuries for people in the western world (at least) to com-

17. Richard J. Clifford, *Creation Accounts in the Ancient Near East and in the Bible*, CBQMS 26 (Washington, DC: Catholic Biblical Association of America, 1994); Bernard F. Batto, *In the Beginning: Essays on Creation Motifs in the Bible and the Ancient Near East*, Siphrut 9 (Winona Lake, IN: Eisenbrauns, 2013); Silvia Schroer and Othmar Keel, *Creation: Biblical Theologies in the Context of the Ancient Near East*, trans. Peter T. Daniels (Winona Lake, IN: Eisenbrauns, 2015).

18. Bertil Albrektson, *History and the Gods: An Essay on the Idea of Historical Events as Divine Manifestations in the Ancient Near East and in Israel*, ConBOT 1 (Lund: Gleerup, 1967).

19. Note the use of the plural in the title of Gerstenberger, *Theologies*. See also, e.g., the content of Brueggemann, *Theology of the Old Testament*; Kessler, *Old Testament Theology*.

partmentalize their lives into secular versus religious spheres. Ancient Israelites would not have drastically separated these two areas: the notion that some aspects of one's life are religious and others are secular would have been foreign to them. Simple matters like organizing one's household or daily work would have been permeated with an awareness of the divine. By virtue of its emphasis on common human experience, wisdom literature in particular affirmed that humans experienced God in all aspects of life, not just the mighty and miraculous, and that revelation can occur in simple human events every bit as much as in the exodus, the return from the Babylonian exile, or prophets announcing a direct message from Yahweh.[20] But this is not a "natural theology," leading to knowledge of God in the abstract.[21] Instead, the sages' reflection on the world and human activity leads to Yahweh, the God of Israel. In the terminology of systematic theologians, this is a matter of "revelation from below" in addition to "revelation from above." As such, biblical wisdom literature constitutes a complement to salvation history, showing that the deity revealed in "the mighty acts of God" is also revealed in the normal acts of humans. But at the same time it provides an implicit critique of a one-sided emphasis on only the great divine interventions in human affairs reflected in Israel's history. For much of their history, most Israelites did not experience such actions in their lives. But if one's theology holds that God is present only through miraculous interventions, does this mean God is absent or has even abandoned the community of faith at times when miracles are not obviously occurring? The wisdom tradition says no, that Yahweh is present with the Israelite faith community at all times, not only in major interactions.

FURTHER READING

Camp, Claudia V. *Wisdom and the Feminine in the Book of Proverbs.* BLS 11. Sheffield: Almond Press, 1985.

20. Cf. Kathleen M. O'Connor, "Wisdom Literature and Experience of the Divine," in *Biblical Theology: Problems and Perspectives: In Honor of J. Christiaan Beker*, ed. Steven J. Kraftchick, Charles D. Myers Jr., and Ben C. Ollenburger (Nashville: Abingdon, 1995), 185–86. In her words, "experience of God occurs in daily existence, in the quotidian struggles, doubts, and joys of life. It is these that reveal God, not primarily the heroic, miraculous, or broadly political as in the historical and prophetic books" (185).

21. Contra John J. Collins, "The Biblical Precedent for Natural Theology," *JAAR* 45 Supplement B (1977): 35–67; James Barr, *Biblical Faith and Natural Theology: The Gifford Lectures for 1991 Delivered in the University of Edinburgh* (Oxford: Clarendon, 1993), 58–80, 90–94.

Lang, Bernhard. *Wisdom and the Book of Proverbs: An Israelite Goddess Redefined*. New York: Pilgrim, 1986.

Perdue, Leo G. *The Collapse of History: Reconstructing Old Testament Theology*. OBT. Minneapolis: Fortress, 1994.

————. *Reconstructing Old Testament Theology: After the Collapse of History*. OBT. Minneapolis: Fortress, 2005.

————. *Wisdom and Creation: The Theology of Wisdom Literature*. Nashville: Abingdon, 1994.

————. *Wisdom Literature: A Theological History*. Louisville: Westminster John Knox, 2007.

Ringgren, Helmer. *Word and Wisdom: Studies in the Hypostatization of Divine Qualities and Function in the Ancient Near East*. Lund: Hakan Ohlssons Boktryckeri, 1947.

Sandelin, Karl-Gustav. *Wisdom as Nourisher: A Study of an Old Testament Theme, Its Development within Early Judaism, and Its Impact on Early Christianity*. Acta Academiae Aboensis, Series A: Humanaiora 64/3. Åbo: Åbo Akademi, 1986.

Schroer, Sylvia. *Wisdom Has Built Her House: Studies on the Figure of Sophia in the Bible*. Translated by Linda M. Mahoney and William McDonough. Collegeville: Liturgical Press, 2000.

Sinnott, Alice M. *The Personification of Wisdom*. SOTSMS. Burlington, VT: Ashgate, 2005.

CHAPTER 10

The Continuation of Wisdom

The wisdom tradition did not end with the First Testament but continued to develop. This chapter considers the presence of wisdom in four different groups of texts: apocalyptic literature, the Dead Sea Scrolls, the Second Testament, and rabbinic literature.

Apocalyptic Literature

Apocalyptic literature flourished between ca. 200 BCE and 200 CE. Apocalypses were a way for people to resist occupying forces such as the Greeks and the Romans by using bizarre imagery and coded language that their overlords would not understand to assert that God would defeat their enemies. The only biblical apocalypses are Daniel 7–12 and the book of Revelation, but dozens of contemporary extrabiblical Jewish and Christian apocalypses survive.

Scholarly efforts to link wisdom and apocalyptic literature have their roots in Gerhard von Rad's claim that wisdom rather than prophecy was the basis for biblical and extrabiblical apocalyptic literature.[1] He focused on the deterministic view of history found in apocalyptic works in contrast to the historical and prophetic books in which Yahweh controls history but events are not predetermined. Instead, von Rad linked apocalyptic's determinism to the effort to determine the proper time set by God in Qoheleth 3:1–15; 6:10; Sirach 10:4;

1. Gerhard von Rad, *Old Testament Theology II: The Theology of Israel's Prophetic Traditions*, trans. David M. G. Stalker, OTL (1962; reprinted Louisville: Westminster John Knox, 2001), 303–8; Gerhard von Rad, *Wisdom in Israel*, trans. James D. Martin (London: SCM, 1971; reprinted Nashville: Abingdon, 1988), 263–83. See also R. N. Whybray, *The Intellectual Tradition in the Old Testament*, BZAW 135 (Berlin: de Gruyter, 1974), 101–4.

23:20; 33:7–15; 39:25, 33–34; 42:19. He also noted the description of the central characters in some apocalypses as scribes or wise men, especially the learning displayed by Daniel and Enoch, as well as the attention to nature in the Book of the Watchers and the Astronomical Book of Enoch (1 En. 1–5; 72–82). Most scholars reject von Rad's attempt to replace prophecy with wisdom as the basis for apocalyptic, since the latter clearly has prophetic elements.[2] Nevertheless, many contemporary scholars do acknowledge wisdom as one aspect of apocalyptic, along with prophecy.[3]

Some wisdom forms are found in apocalyptic texts. A Christian redactor (ca. 200 CE) inserted sayings from Pseudo-Phocylides, a collection of sayings dating to ca. 100 BCE–100 CE, into a Jewish oracle (Sib. Or. 2:56–144). They are not integrated into the surrounding apocalyptic material, but are notable for the parallels with biblical proverbial material, such as warnings against wealth, excessive wine consumption, and unjust scales, and protection of the poor and widows. The Instruction form plays a more substantive role in 1 Enoch. The "Epistle of Enoch" (in 1 En. 91–104) opens with the typical call from a father to his son

> **Selected Apocalypses**
>
> - 1 Enoch
>   The Book of the Watchers
>   The Similitudes of Enoch
>   The Astronomical Book
>   The Book of Dreams (includes
>   the Animal Apocalypse)
>   The Epistle of Enoch (includes
>   the Apocalypse of Weeks)
> - 2 Enoch
> - 4 Ezra
> - 2 Baruch
> - The Testament of Moses
> - The Testament of Abraham
> - The Sibylline Oracles
> - The Apocalypse of Peter
> - The Apocalypse of James
> - The Shepherd of Hermas

2. Paul D. Hanson, *The Dawn of Apocalyptic: The Historical and Sociological Roots of Jewish Apocalyptic Eschatology*, rev. ed. (Philadelphia: Fortress, 1975). For a rare defense of wisdom as the predecessor to apocalyptic see Armin Lange, *Weisheit und Prädestination: Weisheitliche Urordnung und Prädestination in den Textfunden von Qumran*, STDJ 18 (Leiden: Brill, 1995).

3. Compare the discussions in John J. Collins, "Wisdom, Apocalypticism, and Generic Compatibility," in *In Search of Wisdom: Essays in Memory of John G. Gammie*, ed. Leo G. Perdue, Bernard Brandon Scott, and William Johnston Wiseman (Louisville: Westminster John Knox, 1993), 165–85; G. W. E. Nickelsburg, "Wisdom and Apocalypticism in Early Judaism: Some Points for Discussion," in *Conflicted Boundaries in Wisdom and Apocalypticism*, ed. Benjamin G. Wright III and Lawrence M. Wills, SymS 35 (Atlanta: Society of Biblical Literature, 2005), 17–37; Leo G. Perdue, *The Sword and the Stylus: An Introduction to Wisdom in the Age of Empire* (Grand Rapids: Eerdmans, 2008), 356–71; Matthew J. Goff, "Wisdom and Apocalypticism," in *The Oxford Handbook of Apocalyptic Literature*, ed. John J. Collins (Oxford: Oxford University Press, 2014), 52–68.

to pay attention to his words, and the section includes a number of rhetorical questions and exhortations to distinguish between the wise and the foolish and against the rich exploiting the poor. But despite these sapiential contacts, the material is presented as divine revelation to Enoch and is motivated by eschatological judgment rather than reward and punishment in this life, as in the wisdom literature. Similarly, in 2 Enoch 39–66 Enoch conveys the revelation he has received to his children through the Instruction genre. The opening call for his children to pay attention to his admonition is followed by multiple blessings and curses that echo material from the book of Proverbs, including concern for orphans and widows (2 En. 42:8–9), the two paths (2 En. 42:10), and respect for the traditions of the ancestors (2 En. 52:9–10). The Similitudes (1 En. 37–71) contain three parables that are labeled "a vision of wisdom" (1 En. 37:1), while the Animal Apocalypse (1 En. 83–90) is an allegory.

Apocalyptic literature also echoes some wisdom concerns. First Enoch often calls its content "wisdom" (1 En. 5:6; 37:1; 92:1; 93:10). John Gammie notes both similarities and differences between the dualism found in wisdom and apocalyptic, and Michael Stone draws parallels between the questions asked in Job 38–41 and Sirach 1 and the "lists of revealed things" that appear either at the central point of the revelation in an apocalypse or as a concluding summary.[4] In addition, the wise Daniel of Daniel 1–6 who uses mantic wisdom to interpret dreams provides the context for the apocalyptic revelations in Daniel 7–12. More specifically, Gammie's dualism includes the two paths of the wise/righteous and foolish/wicked in 1 and 2 Enoch noted above, and 4 Ezra and 2 Baruch are concerned with theodicy. The former in particular employs didactic dialogue, but both offer an eschatological rather than a contemporary solution to the issue. Perhaps the most interesting parallel is 1 Enoch 42:1–2, in which Wisdom returned to heaven after being unable to find a home on earth:

> Wisdom found no place where she might dwell;
> Then a dwelling-place was assigned her in the heavens.
> Wisdom went forth to make her dwelling among the children of men,
> And found no dwelling-place:
> Wisdom returned to her place,
> And took her seat among the angels.

4. John G. Gammie, "Spatial and Ethical Dualism in Jewish Wisdom and Apocalyptic Literature," *JBL* 93 (1974): 356–85; Michael E. Stone, "Lists of Revealed Things in the Apocalyptic Literature," in *Magnalia Dei, The Mighty Acts of God: Essays on the Bible and Archaeology in Memory of G. E. Wright,* ed. Frank M. Cross, Werner E. Lemke, and Patrick D. Miller Jr. (Garden City, NY: Doubleday, 1976), 414–51.

This runs counter to Ben Sira's claim that Wisdom settled in Jerusalem (Sir. 24:7–8, 10–12) but does reflect the hiddenness of wisdom in Job 28 (see also 2 Esd. 5:9–10). In contrast, Unrighteousness easily found a home among humans (1 En. 42:3), to which we can compare the contrast between Wisdom and Folly in Proverbs 9. At the same time, there is some influence in the opposite direction in the Wisdom of Solomon, where the solution to innocent suffering is projected into the future in terms of an immortal soul, just as apocalyptic literature holds out eschatological salvation for the righteous. In addition, the fate of the righteous one in Wisdom 4:10–15 parallels Enoch's assumption into heaven, the argument in Wisdom 2–5 echoes 1 Enoch 102:4–104:8, and the judgment scene in Wisdom 5 has parallels with 1 Enoch 62–63.[5]

In sum, Israel's wisdom tradition continued into apocalyptic literature in a modified form, with traditional wisdom forms and concerns subordinated to the esoteric knowledge in apocalypses. Ultimately the experiential wisdom of the biblical wisdom tradition combined with divine revelation to constitute a new worldview that drew on wisdom, prophecy, and other influences.[6]

Dead Sea Scrolls

There are significant indications that the wisdom traditions carried on into the Dead Sea Scrolls.[7] The Scrolls include fragments of Proverbs, Job, Qoheleth, and Ben Sira, as well as targums of Job (targums were expansions of biblical texts written in Aramaic), indicating that these texts held some authority for the Qumran community. In addition to fragments of Ben Sira elsewhere,

---

5. Charles Larcher, *Études sur le Livre de la Sagesse*, EBib (Paris: Gabalda, 1969), 106–12; G. W. E. Nickelsburg, *Resurrection, Immortality, and Eternal Life in Intertestamental Judaism*, HTS 26 (Cambridge: Harvard University Press, 1972), 70–78, 128–29.

6. John J. Collins, *The Apocalyptic Imagination: An Introduction to Jewish Apocalyptic Literature*, 3rd ed. (Grand Rapids: Eerdmans, 2016), 24–26.

7. The following is indebted to Daniel J. Harrington, *Wisdom Texts from Qumran*, The Literature of the Dead Sea Scrolls (London: Routledge, 1996); Matthew J. Goff, *Discerning Wisdom: The Sapiential Literature of the Dead Sea Scrolls*, VTSup 116 (Leiden: Brill, 2007); John Kampen, *Wisdom Literature*, Eerdmans Commentaries on the Dead Sea Scrolls (Grand Rapids: Eerdmans, 2011). For briefer surveys see John J. Collins, *Jewish Wisdom in the Hellenistic Age*, OTL (Louisville: Westminster John Knox, 1997), 112–31; Perdue, *The Sword and the Stylus*, 372–87; Armin Lange, "Wisdom Literature and Thought in the Dead Sea Scrolls," in *The Oxford Handbook of the Dead Sea Scrolls*, ed. John J. Collins and Timothy H. Lim (Oxford: Oxford University Press, 2010), 455–78. The translations of the Dead Sea Scrolls texts are from Harrington.

Sirach 51:13–19, 30 appears in one Psalms scroll (11Q5), along with two non-canonical poems that reflect on God's wisdom evident in creation and a text describing David as "wise . . . a scribe, intelligent," who wrote under divine inspiration, while attributing 4,050 liturgical compositions to the famous king.

Two texts expand on material from the book of Proverbs. The *Wiles of the Wicked Woman* (4Q184) builds on the motif of the strange/adulterous woman and Lady Folly ("she utters folly"; 4Q184 i 1) from Proverbs 2:16–19; 5:1–23; 6:20–35; 7:1–27; 9:13–18. Like those women, the Wicked Woman is a source of sexual temptation who seeks to lead men into sin and ultimately into death, but the Qumran text provides a much longer description of each aspect than any of the texts from Proverbs, dwelling on the allure of her body parts and at-tire, her home, her attempts at seduction, and their result if successful. Related to this is 4Q*Sapiential Work* (4Q185), a wisdom instruction addressed to "my sons" and directing the reader to follow God's ways in order to avoid judgment; the transitory nature of human existence in the text echoes Qoheleth. The latter part of the scroll discusses "she" who has been given to Israel. "She" could refer to either Wisdom or Torah, both feminine words in Hebrew,[8] but a number of phrases suggest that Lady Wisdom is more likely. God will "slay those who hate his *wisdom*" (4Q185 ii 11; emphasis added), the exhortations to "hold her" (4Q185 ii 12, 14) echo Proverbs 3:18; 4:13; Sirach 6:27, and she provides a long life (4Q184 ii 12; cf. Prov. 3:16, 18; 8:35). In addition, 4Q525 also contains lexical and thematic contacts with the biblical Lady Wisdom texts. But in both cases she is not the central focus, nor is she explicitly contrasted with Lady Folly, although the phrase "she is the beginning of all the ways of iniquity" (1Q184 i 8) may implicitly contrast with Wisdom as the beginning of God's ways in Proverbs 8:22.

A number of texts combine traditional experiential wisdom with es-chatological expectations. The longest wisdom text in the Dead Sea Scrolls, although fragmentary, is 4Q*Instruction* (1Q26; 4Q415–418, 423). It offers ad-

---

Major Qumran Wisdom Texts

- *Wiles of the Wicked Woman* (4Q184)
- *4QSapiential Work* (4Q185)
- *4QInstruction* (1Q26; 4Q415–418, 423)
- *Book of Mysteries* (1Q27; 4Q299–301)

---

8. Harrington, *Wisdom Texts from Qumran*, 38. Cf. Sidnie White Crawford, "Lady Wis-dom and Dame Folly at Qumran," *DSD* 5 (1998): 355–66; Matthew J. Goff, *Discerning Wis-dom*, 132–39, 214–23.

vice on different topics with material comparable to what is found in the book of Proverbs. This includes admonitions addressed to a student (*mēbîn*; "understanding one") who is sometimes addressed as "son." These admonitions discuss business dealings such as loans, accepting deposits, dealing with one's superiors and inferiors, and not dealing with strangers. The text also deals with family matters such as honoring one's parents and having a good relationship with one's wife, as well as advising moderation with respect to food and clothes. It refers frequently to the *rāz nihyeh* ("the mystery that is to be"), which is divine instruction revealed to the elect about the righteous life, the nature of the cosmos, and a deterministic understanding of history from start to finish. Through constant study "the simple" (4Q418 221 2–3; cf. Prov. 1:4, 22; 8:5; 9:4; etc.) will gain insight into matters as diverse as human nature, family relations, farming, the final judgment, and reward and punishment in the afterlife.

The *rāz nihyeh* also appears in the *Book of Mysteries* (1Q27; 4Q299–301), alongside the more frequent *rāz* ("mystery") alone. Wisdom was given so that humans might distinguish good and evil, but since they do not know "the mystery that is to be" they will face an apocalyptic judgment, but "righteousness will be revealed as the sun" (1Q27 1 i 6). The "magicians who teach transgression" (4Q300 ii 1) are singled out for their false wisdom and challenged to speak a parable and riddle before it is uttered. Just as the Babylonian magicians could not tell Nebuchadnezzar his dream and its interpretation (about the end days) because it had not been revealed to them by God (Dan. 2; note *rāz* in vv. 18, 19, 27, 29, 30, 47), so too the "eternal mysteries" have been hidden from these magicians. The text is clearly didactic, seeking to teach about proper wisdom and its role in the final judgment, but it also uses rhetorical questions to convey practical advice concerning wealth, grudges, relationships, and fools.

> **Shorter Qumran Wisdom Texts**
>
> - *Words of the* Maśkîl *to All Sons of Dawn* (4Q298)
> - *Ways of Righteousness* (4Q420–421)
> - *An Instruction* (4Q424)
> - *4QBeatitudes* (4Q525)

There are a number of shorter, often fragmentary, wisdom texts from Qumran. The *Words of the* Maśkîl *to All Sons of Dawn* (4Q298) is an instruction that calls the "men of heart" (cf. Job 34:10, 34; NRSV: "you who have sense") and others to listen to the *maśkîl*'s advice concerning various wisdom virtues, comparable to Lady Wisdom's calls in Proverbs 1–9. At Qumran the term *maśkîl* ("one who causes understanding") designated the office of an important community teacher while "sons of the dawn" is synonymous with "the sons of light" as a designation of the group's members; the latter's frequent contrast with the "sons of darkness" reflects the ethical dualism between the good and evil common to biblical wisdom literature. This text combines wisdom terminology ("wise ones," "knowers," "understanding," "learning," "truth") with an interest in "the end." The *Ways of Righteousness* (4Q420–21) describes a "prudent sage" who "walk[s] in God's ways" according to righteousness and is characterized by reflection and deliberation. "Wisdom's yoke" (4Q421 1 i 1–ii 10) also occurs in Sirach 6:30; 51:26. The Instruction in 4Q424 contrasts a series of individuals who either can or cannot accomplish a desired outcome. The first group includes the intelligent and upright as well as those who have compassion for the poor or do not move a boundary, while the latter comprises liars, fools, complainers, the devious and greedy, and those who incline toward anger. All these individuals are labeled with terms that appear in biblical wisdom texts. The fragmentary opening to 4Q*Beatitudes* (4Q525) identifies its purpose in terms similar to Proverbs 1:1–6, followed by positive statements ("happy") that are consistent with earlier wisdom sentiments. The text subsequently specifies an address from a teacher to his "son" concerning the rewards of acquiring Wisdom, who is connected with Torah, plus the punishments of folly and the importance of controlling one's speech.

> **Lesser Links to Wisdom at Qumran**
>
> - 4Q302, 4Q412, 4Q413, 4Q425, 4Q411, 4Q426, and 4Q528
> - The *Community Rule* (1QS) *Treatise of the Two Spirits* (3:13–4:26)
> - The *Hodayot* (1QH)

There are also some minor Qumran texts with connections to the wisdom traditions. There is a parable in 4Q302, 4Q412 has fragments of an instruction, 4Q413 is labeled a psalm but consists of direct instruction about teaching knowledge and wisdom concerning divinely determined fates, 4Q425 has fragmentary references to speech and fools with parallels to 4Q424 (see above), and 4Q411, 4Q426, and 4Q528 have been classified as wisdom hymns based on their vocabulary and concerns. In addition, while not strictly a wisdom text, the *Community Rule* (1QS) may be an instruction manual for the *maśkîl*, with wisdom affinities. The *Treatise of the Two Spirits* (1QS 3:13–4:26) is identified as an instruction and elaborates on the two paths of biblical wisdom literature; its division between the sons of light and the sons of darkness is also found in the War Scroll (1QM; 4Q491–97). The *Community Rule*'s concluding hymn celebrates the wisdom that comes from the *rāz nihyeh*, while an appendix

(1QSa) mandates instruction in the "Book of Mediation." Finally, the *Hodayot* ("thanksgiving hymns," 1QH) have various amounts of wisdom vocabulary, forms, and motifs.[9]

The Second Testament

Paul's letters are not themselves wisdom books, but he does display an awareness of the canonical and deuterocanonical First Testament books. He cites Job 5:13 and Qoheleth 7:20 as authoritative ("for it is written") in 1 Corinthians 3:19 and Romans 3:10 respectively, and quotes or alludes to a number of other wisdom texts without using an explicit citation formula.[10] Proverbs 25:21–22 is repeated almost verbatim in Romans 12:20, as is the Greek translation of Proverbs 24:12c in Romans 2:6 and of Job 13:16a in Philippians 1:19. There is less, but still significant, lexical overlap with wisdom texts in Paul's warning against overestimating one's wisdom (Rom. 12:16; Prov. 3:7), his exhortations to be honest before

Wisdom in the Second Testament?
• Paul
• James
• The Q Source
• The Synoptic Gospels
• The Gospel of John

God and men (2 Cor. 8:21; Prov. 3:4) and to weep with those who weep (Rom. 12:15; Sir. 7:34), his observations that God desires a "cheerful giver" (2 Cor. 9:7; Prov. 22:8) and that a potter makes different types of vessels from the same clay (Rom. 9:21; Wis. 15:7; cf. Sir. 33:13), plus his identification of the body as an "earthly tent" (2 Cor. 5:1–4; Wis. 9:15). In particular, Romans 1–2 shares vocabulary and ideas with the Wisdom of Solomon, especially Wisdom 12–15,

---

9. Hans Bardtke, "Considérations sur les cantiques de Qumrân," *RB* 63 (1956): 220–33; Sarah Jean Tanzer, "The Sages at Qumran: Wisdom in the *Hodayot*," PhD diss. (Boston: Harvard University, 1987); Matthew J. Goff, "Reading Wisdom at Qumran: 4QInstruction and the Hodayot," *DSD* 11 (2004): 263–88.

10. See Richard B. Hays, *Echoes of Scripture in the Letters of Paul* (New Haven: Yale University Press, 1989); Richard B. Hays, *The Conversion of the Imagination: Paul as Interpreter of Israel's Scripture* (Grand Rapids: Eerdmans, 2005); and the charts in Lars Kierspel, *Charts on the Life, Letters, and Theology of Paul*, Kregel Charts of the Bible (Grand Rapids: Kregel Academic, 2012), 95–108. Tadashi Ino, "Paul's Use of Canonical and Noncanonical Wisdom Literature in Romans and the Corinthian Letters," PhD diss. (Berrien Springs, MI: Andrews University, 2003), identifies twenty-five points of contact between Paul and the First Testament wisdom literature, although not all his examples are equally convincing. The following presents representative samples of the more secure instances of Pauline use of wisdom texts.

including that people should have recognized God in nature (Rom. 1:18-23; Wis. 13:1-9) and that idolatry is foolish (Rom. 1:21-23, 25; Wis. 13-15) and results in sexual sins (Rom. 1:24-28; Wis. 14:12).[11]

In contrast to Paul's letters, the letter of James constitutes wisdom literature with some prophetic and apocalyptic elements.[12] The dominant tone is one of didactic persuasion through the use of wisdom forms such as proverbs, especially admonitions, comparisons (Jas. 1:6, 23-24), and contrasts (Jas. 1:6). These often cluster around themes found in the First Testament wisdom traditions. James 4:6 cites Proverbs 3:34, and a number of passages in James seem dependent on Ben Sira. For instance, true wisdom comes from God (Jas. 1:5; 3:13-18; cf. Sir. 1:10; Wis. 7:7) and God does not lead us to sin (Jas. 1:13; Sir. 15:11-13). Controlling one's speech (Jas. 1:26; 3:5-12) is a common wisdom motif but in particular it is the subject of an extended reflection in Sirach 23:7-15. The idea that suffering is a test (Jas. 1:2-4, 12) is also considered at length in Sirach 2. James addresses the wisdom concern over the dichotomy between rich and poor more than once, culminating in a denunciation of the rich for their exploitation of the poor (Jas. 1:9-11; 2:1-14; 4:13-5:6). James 1:19 even combines the wisdom motifs of listening more than speaking (e.g., Prov. 18:13; 29:20; Sir. 5:11; 20:7) and not being angry (e.g., Prov. 15:18; 16:32; 19:11; Qoh. 7:9) into a single saying as the basis for his subsequent admonitions.

With respect to the Gospels, wisdom origins have been claimed for the Q Source, a collection of Jesus's sayings that underlies most of the material in Matthew and Luke with no parallel in Mark. John Kloppenborg establishes an initial layer consisting of six wisdom instructions to which eschatological sayings were added later.[13] Moreover, in the Synoptic Gospels, Jesus frequently acts like a wisdom teacher. He utters proverbs (e.g., "it is not what goes into the mouth that defiles a person, but it is what comes out of the mouth that defiles"; Matt 15:11 // Mark 7:20), draws analogies with nature (e.g., "consider the lilies"; Matt. 6:28 // Luke 12:27) and tells parables (e.g., Mark 4:1-34; 12:1-11; etc.). Sometimes these wisdom elements draw directly from earlier wisdom books,

---

11. See Ino, "Paul's Use," 171-76, especially the chart of common vocabulary on pp. 172-73.

12. Richard J. Bauckham, *James: Wisdom of James, Disciple of Jesus the Sage*, New Testament Readings (London: Routledge, 2002); Richard J. Bauckham, "The Wisdom of James and the Wisdom of Jesus," in *The Catholic Epistles and the Tradition*, ed. J. Schlosser, BETL 176 (Leuven: Peeters, 2004), 73-92.

13. John S. Kloppenborg, *The Formation of Q: Trajectories in Ancient Wisdom Collections*, SAC (Philadelphia: Fortress, 1987). See also Ronald A. Piper, *Wisdom in the Q-Tradition: The Aphoristic Teaching of Jesus*, SNTSMS 61 (Cambridge: Cambridge University Press, 1989).

such as Jesus's teachings that God forgives as we do (Matt. 6:12, 14, 15; etc.; Sir. 28:2–5) or that our treasure is not earthly (Matt 6:20; 19:21; Sir. 29:11). More directly, the parable about the rich man who dies suddenly (Luke 12:16–21) builds upon Sirach 11:18–19 (cf. Qoh. 5:13–14a; 6:1–2), while the parable of the tenants (Matt. 21:33–41 // Mark 12:1–9 // Luke 20:9–16) relies upon the parable of the vineyard, a wisdom form in Isaiah 5:1–7.

Some Second Testament texts go beyond presenting Jesus as a wisdom teacher to identify him with Wisdom. Paul calls Jesus "the wisdom of God" in 1 Corinthians 1:24 and the statement "through whom are all things and through whom we exist" (1 Cor. 8:6) echoes Wisdom as "the fashioner of all things" (Wis. 7:22; 8:6). Colossians 1:15–17 combines allusions to Lady Wisdom from Proverbs 8:22 and Wisdom 7:22, 26; 8:6: "He is the image of the invisible God, the firstborn of all creation; for in him all things were created . . . all things were created through him and for him. He is before all things." Hebrews 1:2–3 says, "through whom also [God] created the world. He reflects the glory of God and bears the very stamp of his nature, upholding the universe by his word of power" (cf. Wis. 7:25–27). One text from the Q Source seems to link the two as well, when a statement about the son of man being criticized is followed by "yet Wisdom is justified by her deeds/all her children" (Matt 11:19 // Luke 7:34–35). Elsewhere in Q, according to Luke 11:49 Wisdom sends prophets who are persecuted, but in Matt 23:34 it is Jesus who sends them, effectively equating Jesus with Wisdom. The fullest expression of this wisdom christology is found in the prologue to the Gospel of John, as the following illustrates:

1:1	"In the beginning . . . the word was with God"—cf. "I came from the mouth of the Most High"; Sir. 24:3
1:3	he is the creator of everything—cf. Wis. 7:22; 8:6
1:5	"The light shines in the darkness, and the darkness has not overcome it"—cf. Wis. 7:29–30
1:11	"he came to what was his own"—cf. Sir. 24:8, 10–12
1:14	"The word became flesh and dwelt among us [literally 'pitched his tent'; see Sir. 24:8; the incarnation is a step beyond Ben Sira] and we have beheld his glory, glory as of the only Son from the Father"—cf. Wis. 7:25

Rabbinic Literature

The biblical wisdom traditions continued in rabbinic literature as well.[14] The rabbinic material encompasses *halakah*, which is legal interpretation of the laws in the Torah assembled in the Mishnah, Tosefta, and the Palestinian and Babylonian Talmuds, plus *haggadah*, which is nonlegal interpretation found in the Midrash and the Talmuds. The rabbis understood themselves as sages, calling themselves "wise." They taught in synagogues and schools with groups of disciples; by the end of the first century CE the two main schools of thought were those of Hillel and Shammai. Rabbinic literature contains numerous wisdom forms, including proverbs, numerical sayings, rhetorical questions, riddles, parables, fables, etc. A notable feature of the halakic material is the combination of material into lists, such as thirty-nine cases of work forbidden on the Sabbath, ten degrees of impurity, and ten levels of holiness.

Lists also dominate chapter 5 of the haggadic tractate *'Abot*, ranging from how many times the *Shekinah* (divine presence) appeared on earth and how many times it moved locations, the number of names for a prophet and the number of things created on the Sabbath eve (all ten), as well as the seven characteristics of a sage, the four types of students and their four ways of learning. The first four chapters of *'Abot* comprise sayings from a wide variety of rabbis, including the note that Samuel the Little regularly quoted Proverbs 24:17–18 as well as, much like Qoheleth, criticism of the wise themselves (*'Abot* 1:17; 2:15). Related to this tractate is *'Abot de Rabbi Nathan*, which relates stories and parables about the sages represented in *'Abot*.

Summary

Israel's wisdom traditions did not suddenly stop with the Wisdom of Ben Sira. Wisdom reflection continued on into subsequent Jewish and Christian literature. Wisdom forms and motifs provided the basis for ongoing reflection on human experience in apocalyptic literature, the Dead Sea Scrolls, various parts of the Second Testament, and rabbinic literature. Although full consideration

---

14. See the surveys in Günter Stemberger, "Sages, Scribes, and Seers in Rabbinic Judaism," in *Scribes, Sages, and Seers: The Sage in the Eastern Mediterranean World*, ed. Leo G. Perdue, FRLANT 219 (Göttingen: Vandenhoeck & Ruprecht, 2008), 295–319; Perdue, *The Sword and the Stylus*, 388–411; Ishay Rosen-Zvi, "The Wisdom Tradition in Rabbinic Literature and Mishnah Avot," in *Tracing Sapiential Traditions in Ancient Judaism*, ed. Hindy Najman, Jean-Sebastien Rey, and Eibert J. C. Tigchelaar, JSJSup 174 (Leiden: Brill, 2016), 172–90.

of such literature is well beyond the scope of this book, the survey of those four is evidence of the ongoing importance of wisdom reflection on human experience.

FURTHER READING

Ashton, John, ed. *Revealed Wisdom: Studies in Apocalyptic in Honour of Christopher Rowland.* AJEC 88. Leiden: Brill, 2014.

Bauckham, Richard J. *James: Wisdom of James, Disciple of Jesus the Sage.* New Testament Readings. London: Routledge, 2002.

Goff, Matthew J. *Discerning Wisdom: The Sapiential Literature of the Dead Sea Scrolls.* VTSup 116. Leiden: Brill, 2007.

Harrington, Daniel J. *Wisdom Texts from Qumran.* The Literature of the Dead Sea Scrolls. London: Routledge, 1996.

Kampen, John. *Wisdom Literature.* Eerdmans Commentaries on the Dead Sea Scrolls. Grand Rapids: Eerdmans, 2011.

Kloppenborg, John S. *The Formation of Q: Trajectories in Ancient Wisdom Collections.* SAC. Philadelphia: Fortress, 1987.

Lange, Armin. *Weisheit und Prädestination: Weisheitliche Urordnung und Prädestination in den Textfunden von Qumran.* STDJ 18. Leiden: Brill, 1995.

Piper, Ronald A. *Wisdom in the Q-Tradition: The Aphoristic Teaching of Jesus.* SNTSMS 61. Cambridge: Cambridge University Press, 1989.

Wright, Benjamin G., III, and Lawrence M. Wills, eds. *Conflicted Boundaries in Wisdom and Apocalypticism.* SymS 35. Atlanta: Society of Biblical Literature, 2005.

Index of Authors

Index of Subjects

Index of Ancient Texts

A. Biblical Texts

B. Extrabiblical Texts